praise for

LOVE AND WAR IN AFGHANISTAN

"Fascinating . . . [a] unique insider account of today's Afghanistan."
Library Journal

"[W]hat makes this collection ingenious, is the way that the 23-year-long civil war emerges indirectly from every tale of love—requited, unrequited, passionate, chaste, familial, extra-familial, arranged, delayed, tragic, random—and the parallel psychic burdens love and war place on the tellers. . . . It's difficult to imagine a more welcoming entry into northern Afghan culture, or a more touching set of relationships formed, and maintained, under horrific circumstances."
Publishers Weekly

"We tend to think of Afghanistan only as the land of ugly factional fights, the Taliban, warlords, narcotics, the destroyed Giant Buddhas of Bamian and the war on terror. We should be very grateful to Gulchin Gulmamadova-Klaits and Alex Klaits for bringing us in this book the lives of real people—Afghan men and women, old and young, highly educated and illiterate, rich and poor, speaking in their own words. There is drama here, and much suffering, persistence and hope as well as moments of humor. However exotic the external circumstances may seem, every reader will recognize their common humanity, even while wondering how people can preserve their dignity, even survive, under such impossible conditions. Their determination and humanity inspire us to do all we can to prevent them, their children, or anyone else from undergoing such pain again."
LAKHDAR BRAHIMI, Under Secretary-General of the UN and former Special Representative of the Secretary-General for Afghanistan

". . . the last days of winter 2005 . . . in cold Virginia . . . leaning back on a cozy divan . . . in front of a fireplace . . . with a cup of green tea . . . in the presence of silence and peace . . . reading *Love and War in Afghanistan* . . . mourning deep inside, ashamed of this life of comfort . . ."
FARHAD DARYA, renowned poet and musician, originally from Kunduz

"Both rich and disturbing, the closest many readers will come to living and loving others in the midst of an earthly inferno."

SHANNON HENDRICKSON, *Booknews*

"Instead of regurgitating American pundits and politicians, *Love and War in Afghanistan* lets Afghans call it as they see it. Dramatic autobiographies unfold in dozen-page chunks, challenging preconceptions about Afghanistan and the nature of humanitarianism. . . . True to their book's title, the authors prove the possibilities for love in a region of relentless war."

BEN BUSH, *Portland Mercury*

"A highly readable volume on the human cost of 25-plus years of war. . . . [The] stories tend to be roller-coaster rides of euphoric highs—weddings, births, business successes—and devastating lows—murdered spouses, drowned children, destroyed villages. . . . This is a book-length lament on the cost of war in all its forms."

Baltimore Citypaper

"Largely avoiding the tangled political web involved with foreign affairs, the authors focus on the people, finding humanity in a country riddled with inhumanity. . . . [I]lluminating . . . [M]arvelous."

MEYER REECE, *Livingston Weekly*

LOVE AND WAR IN AFGHANISTAN

Alex Klaits and
Gulchin Gulmamadova-Klaits

New York
Toronto
London
SEVEN STORIES PRESS Melbourne

Seven Stories Press
140 Watts Street
New York, NY 10013
www.sevenstories.com

In Canada
Publishers Group Canada, 250A Carlton Street, Toronto, ON M5A 2L1

In the UK
Turnaround Publisher Services Ltd., Unit 3, Olympia Trading Estate,
Coburg Road, Wood Green, London N22 6TZ

In Australia
Palgrave Macmillan, 627 Chapel Street, South Yarra, VIC 3141

College professors may order examination copies of
Seven Stories Press titles for a free six-month trial period.
To order, visit http://www.sevenstories.com/textbook/
or send a fax on school letterhead to 212.226.1411.

Designed by Jon Gilbert

Library of Congress Cataloging-in-Publication Data
Klaits, Alex.
Love and war in Afghanistan / Alex Klaits and Gulchin Gulmamadova-Klaits.—1st ed.
    p. cm.
  ISBN-13: 978-1-58322-675-9 (hardcover : alk. paper) / ISBN-10: 1-58322-675-3 (hardcover :
alk. paper)
  ISBN-13: 978-1-58322-727-5 (hardcover : alk. paper) / ISBN-10: 1-58322-727-X (paperback :
alk. paper)
  1. Afghanistan—History—Soviet occupation, 1979–1989—Personal narratives. 2. Afghanistan—
History—1989–2001—Biography. 3. Afghanistan—Social life and customs. I. Gulmamadova-
Klaits, Gulchin. II. Title.
DS371.2.K577 2005
958.104'5'0922—dc22

                                                    2005003151

Printed in Canada

9 8 7 6 5 4 3 2 1

To our son, Adrian Ali.

Contents

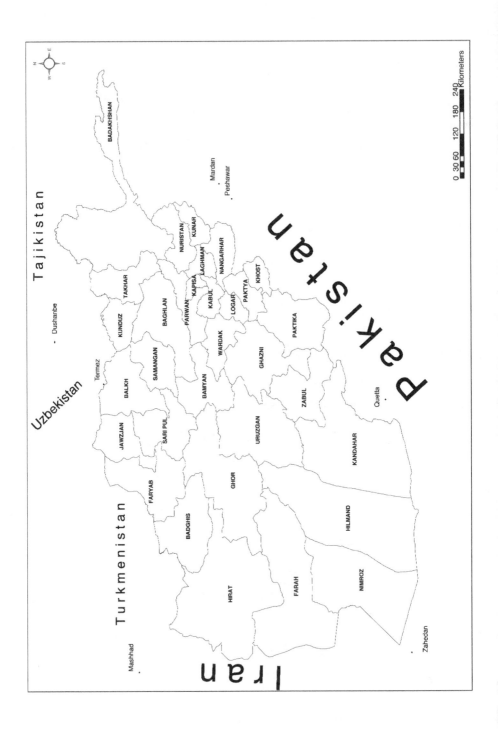

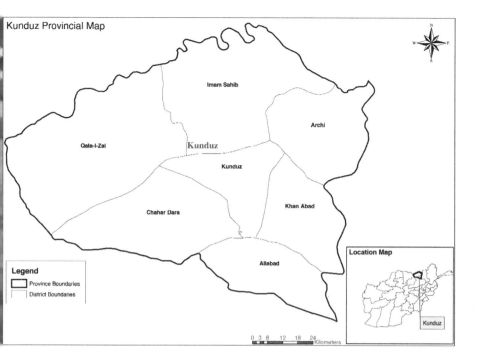

Kunduz Provincial Map

Imam Sahib

Archi

Qala-I-Zal

Kunduz

Kunduz

Khan Abad

Chahar Dara

Allabad

Legend
Province Boundaries
District Boundaries

Location Map

Kunduz

0 3 6   12   18   24
Kilometers

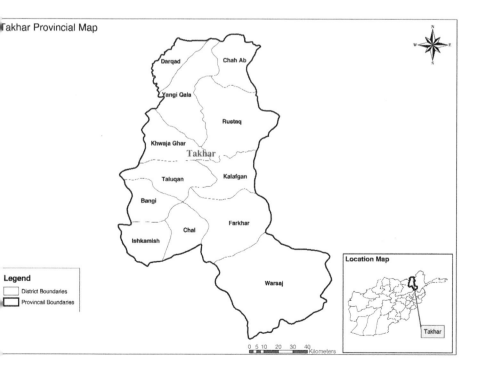

Takhar Provincial Map

Darqad   Chah Ab

Yangi Qala

Rustaq

Khwaja Ghar

Takhar

Taluqan   Kalafgan

Bangi

Chal   Farkhar

Ishkamish

Legend
District Boundaries
Provincail Boundaries

Location Map

Warsaj

Takhar

0 5 10   20   30   40
Kilometers

Introduction

Afghanistan has been torn apart by one of the longest-running civil wars in modern history. Twenty-three years of conflict destroyed most of the country's infrastructure, including schools, hospitals, roads, houses, and irrigation systems. Bombed-out tanks and active land mines remain strewn throughout the countryside, dangerous reminders of Afghanistan's tragic past. More than a million Afghans have died from the fighting directly or from diseases or hunger related to the conflict. And millions more have left the country and never returned.

The accounts from the women and men in this collection are the stories of people who now live in Afghanistan's northeastern provinces of Takhar and Kunduz. Their stories illustrate the profound impact of war and displacement on the lives of Afghans. Even when the stories' principal actors were not directly affected by the fighting through illness and death in their immediate families, the accounts show that the civil war and the accompanying displacement has had an immeasurable impact on the ways in which Afghans interact with neighbors, friends, and relatives. As the Afghan people—with the assistance of the international community—begin to rebuild their lives, it is important to understand the tumultuous history that so many of them have endured. We hope the narratives will help readers gain an understanding of how Afghan culture continues to sustain the universal human search for love and a better life, even during a time of vast social upheaval.

✦ ✦ ✦ ✦

In April 2004, we traveled around Kunduz and Takhar provinces collecting life histories from women and men in the provincial capitals of Taloqan and Kunduz but mostly in the surrounding villages. Alex, an American who had served in the Peace Corps in Kyrgyzstan during the 1990s, returned to Central Asia following the events of September 11, 2001. In January 2002, shortly after the fall of the Taliban, he began working for an international nongovernmental organization in northeastern Afghanistan. He stayed there for nearly two years undertaking humanitarian relief and development projects. Gulchin is from the neighboring country of Tajikistan and worked for several years with international aid organizations that have sought to improve conditions in her own impoverished country. She took a strong liking to Afghan culture and music from an early age—when most of her friends and family told her that there was nothing there but war and destruction. Her interest in Afghanistan only intensified when her grandparents recounted stories from their childhood of growing up inside Afghanistan just across the Amu Darya* in the province of Badakhshan. During the civil war, which raged in her native land from 1992–97, many of her relatives were forced to flee via northern Afghanistan to safer parts of Tajikistan. Gulchin herself also escaped from the capital of Dushanbe during the civil war and, while living in the Pamir Mountains of Tajikistan, heard repeatedly of the kindness and generosity of the Afghan people from her relatives. "The Afghans would share their last crust of bread with us rather than see us go hungry," her uncle had told her one day. "So many of them suffered so much and were the victims of such terrible crimes, but they would never hesitate to open their hearts and their homes to us poor refugees."

We met in Tajikistan in 2001 and were married in Dushanbe in March 2004, and then returned to Afghanistan to conduct research for this book two weeks after our wedding.

---

* River, also known as the Oxus, that runs along the border between Afghanistan and Turkmenistan, Uzbekistan, and Tajikistan.

The process of collecting the accounts is something of a story in and of itself. On our second day back in Afghanistan, we were caught up in a massive sandstorm as we drove in the desert district of Qal-i-Zal in northwestern Kunduz province. The fifty-mile-per-hour wind whirled sand in every direction, and our dirt road quickly dissolved before our eyes. Shortly after our driver decided to turn back and search out a better route, our car sank into the middle of a deep sand dune. For half an hour we pushed and pulled and dug until we finally freed our vehicle. Sand was still coming out of our ears several days later. Once we found our way back to the road, it began pouring. The road instantly turned into a mud pit and deep puddles formed everywhere. We turned to each other and said, "Isn't this a great honeymoon spot! We've got sand, we've got water. And it's warm!" But this was a project we had wanted to do for a long time, and we were determined to see it through. A little sand in our ears wasn't going to stop us.

We conducted interviews with more than 150 women and men from every major ethnic group in Kunduz and Takhar provinces: Pashtuns, Tajiks, Uzbeks, Turkmens, and Hazaras. Representing as they do a cross section of the Afghan population, the interviews demonstrate clearly that the suffering of the last twenty-five years was widespread throughout Afghan society and spared no ethnic group.

Most of the stories were told to us in Dari—the lingua franca of northern Afghanistan, in which Gulchin is fluent—although a few were recounted in English and Russian. All of the narratives were tape-recorded. The interviewees include people of different ages—ranging from sixteen to eighty-one—and people with vastly different levels of education. Many of the narrators never attended school, while others attended college and one even has a PhD from a university in Europe. One account is from a former Soviet soldier from Ukraine who was taken hostage in 1983 and has lived in Afghanistan ever since. We spoke with former commanders, teachers, farmers, drivers, mechanics, shopkeepers, traders, housewives, former soldiers, and many unemployed people. The accounts come from those who sided with the Communists, the mujahedin, and the Taliban, but mostly they are from women and men who were apolitical and just prayed for the day when they and their families could live in peace.

Our initial entrée into Afghan society came through Alex's friends and former colleagues, who introduced us to many of our interviewees and vouched for us. They took us to the houses of relatives, friends, and villagers with whom they worked and who they knew were willing to share their most personal stories with us. Alex would sit with the men, while Gulchin would be led to a separate room to meet with the women. As a foreigner, Gulchin also was allowed to join the men's group, where she often sat with former Taliban officials and mujahedin commanders who, until quite recently, had vigorously enforced rules prohibiting women from showing their faces to strangers. These gatherings were almost always accompanied by cups of tea and glass plates full of candies.

But many accounts came in serendipitous encounters with strangers. Taxi drivers met by chance, like their counterparts in other parts of the world, were a source of striking and vividly told life histories. And one of our most interesting interviews came to us when we decided to have lunch on the school grounds of a boys' high school in Khwaja Ghar district in Takhar province. The teachers had all gone home for their lunch break, so rather than go to a restaurant where women rarely if ever gather, we asked the school's guard if it would be possible to sit next to a small pool of water near the guard's house. The guard, an elderly man with a long beard, immediately agreed and brought a couple of plastic mats and mattresses from his house so that we could enjoy the beautiful spring day under a willow tree. He also served us tea, like any host in Afghanistan. When our driver brought shish kebab and rice pilaf back from the bazaar, we invited the school guard to join us. He then regaled us with his and his son's fascinating story of life as refugees in Iran.

Almost all of the people with whom we spoke were very willing to talk about their life stories. But almost all of our interviewees agreed to speak with us only under the condition that we change their names and occasionally even the names of their hometowns and villages. Many of them were fearful of potential repercussions from warlords or other enemies. As one man we interviewed summed it up, "Nothing in Afghanistan surprises us anymore. If the Taliban were to come back to power, and these stories got out, what do you think would happen to me?" Even when our interviewees' accounts had little or nothing to do with politics, many told us that they would be embarrassed if their names were associated in print with their personal stories.

Sometimes we would sit down with people who had suffered some of the most unspeakable horrors, but because the memories were too fresh and painful, or—as many of our interviewees themselves said—because they lacked sufficient education to be able to express what had happened to them in a way that could be readily understood, they were not willing to discuss their experiences. This was true in spite of our best attempts to ask follow-up questions. There is much pain in these accounts, but even more painful experiences remain as yet untold.

Many of the most interesting accounts are told by people who grew up in the days before the Soviet invasion in 1979. In the 1970s, large cities in Afghanistan were similar to many places around the world. Girls and boys studied and partied together, wore Western clothes, and even dated. This was a world that has very little resemblance to present-day Afghanistan. Many of the interviewees who came of age in the 1970s, especially those who lived or studied in Kabul, were more effectively able to contextualize what they had experienced over the past twenty-five years. By contrast, a lot of the younger people with whom we spoke have known only war, displacement, and violence. The stories told by these younger people lack the before-and-after quality of their elders' lives. They have no past to refer to, only the struggles they have known all of their lives.

While many readers may find the episodes recounted in this book almost too horrible to believe, the vast majority of them are not at all exceptional. We would often sit around with our Afghan friends in the evening after we had conducted interviews and tell them about the stories that had deeply affected us. Our friends were invariably unfazed. Often they would say, "Yes, I know, there are many stories like that." And sometimes they would say, "Well, if you're impressed by that, let me tell you what happened to me!"

Many of the interviews were initially conducted in group settings. Because Afghanistan is such a collective society, as soon as we entered a village, we often drew a crowd of people eager to find out what was going on and to hear their neighbors recount their histories. Especially when women were together, the storytellers were often interrupted by others gathered about with words like: "Yes, all of this is true . . ." or "The same thing happened to me . . ." or "I remember that terrible day too . . ." These affirmations, often accompanied by streams of tears, helped to confirm the accuracy of these accounts, which otherwise might seem to the uninformed observer at least embellished, if not completely fabricated. Although we have no way to verify every detail, the accounts in this book are consistent and thus reinforce each other. Furthermore, our own personal knowledge of Afghan history, culture, and tradition helped us filter out any stories that we found to be inconsistent with historical facts. For these reasons we believe that the accounts found in this volume are reliable, though subjective.

We have attempted to maintain as much of the original narrative as possible. In some places, we have added explanatory phrases or sentences to try to illustrate for the readers some of the cultural traditions and broader history of Afghanistan referred to in the accounts—our knowledge of which the narrators took for granted. In some cases, our interviewees provided these explanations themselves, and we did not need to add any further details. Likewise, the spoken narratives, like almost all oral discourse, were sometimes disjointed as the storytellers recalled events that had long since passed. In many of the accounts, we had to rearrange the original descriptions in order to keep the flow of the narrative clear. Similarly, many of the narrators had trouble recalling particular dates in which events in their lives occurred or even the ages of their closest family members. Unlike most of the world, many Afghans don't know their own birthdates. Many interviewees would say something like, "A couple of years after the Soviets invaded Afghanistan and I was studying in eleventh grade, I had my first child." Then we could infer that the child was born in 1981 or 1982 and that the narrator was born around 1965. It should be noted that many of the dates used in this book are not precise, but we thought it important for the reader to be anchored by at least an approximate chronological reference. We hope that the accompanying timeline will assist readers unfamiliar with major events in Afghan history.

Although these accounts mirror much of Afghan society, we understand that many of the stories we heard were not complete. Many middle-aged and older women with whom we spoke were quite open with us about all aspects of their lives—their relationships and marriage in addition to their war experiences. Similarly, we found several younger men who were willing to share the most secret details of their romantic affairs. However, middle-aged and older men were generally reluctant to share these types of intimate descriptions about themselves or their wives and daughters. Many of their stories dealt much more with their roles outside of the home. With a few important exceptions, a couple of which are found in this volume, we also had a very difficult time finding younger women who were willing to share their stories. These women were brought up during a time of such oppression and repression, some of our older Afghan female friends explained to us, that they are unlikely to be able to articulate their experiences in a compelling way. Young women in much of Afghanistan are generally prized for their modesty rather than their gregarious storytelling ability.

We sometimes expressed our concerns to friends that the accounts we had collected might be too depressing for our readers. "What do you mean? These are happy stories," one of our friends told us one evening. We looked at him with puzzled expressions. "Of course they're happy stories. After all, these people survived. I'm sure that many of the millions of people who didn't survive the last twenty-five years would have had much worse stories to tell!" The direct accounts of those victims are lost forever. But the experiences of the living are given voice in this book, teaching us how the human spirit copes with the stresses of violent conflict and its attendant devastation.

CHAPTER ONE

Anisa, Daughter of Isa Muhammad

You might never guess it from looking at me now, but when I was young, I was a very beautiful girl. These wrinkles all around my eyes and the gray hair that now dominate my appearance are a result of my cursed life. Everywhere I've gone, tragedy and destruction seem to have always followed me.

When I was a teenager, I had many suitors. I had long black curly hair, beautiful eyes and eyebrows, and my skin was very soft. Growing up, I thought that I was one of the luckiest girls in the world. My father was very open-minded. Unlike many of my friends, who were forced to wear a burqa and leave school by the time they reached puberty, I was allowed to get an education and show off my beauty. The first time I wore a burqa, I was twenty-three, and I had already been married for several years.

In 1972, when I was in fourth grade, my family moved to Taloqan. My father had been moving around the country for many years as an army commander, but it turned out that his posting in Taloqan was his last. The next year King Zahir Shah was overthrown in a coup by his cousin and brother-in-law, and my father lost his military job shortly thereafter.

My father was a very good man—he never thought that because I was a girl I shouldn't have the same educational opportunities as my brothers. At the time—and as is still the case—most people here in

Afghanistan had a very conservative view of women's education. Many fathers worried that if girls mixed with boys after the sixth grade, they could be led down a path of sin. At the time, in Taloqan, even a quarter century before the Taliban came to power, few women ventured onto the streets without a burqa.

My father never even entertained the notion that I might not complete high school. He always had time to help me, my sister, and my three brothers with our homework. And I actively participated in all school festivities—I read poems, sang songs, and even acted in school plays. I loved reading books, and as a teenager, I even wrote a few poems myself.

When I was in eighth grade, one of my classmates, Shah Mu'min, fell in love with me. There were many boys in my class who were obviously fond of me. But Shah Mu'min was definitely the most persistent. He pursued me for three long years. His mother and other relatives would come to our house repeatedly to request my hand in marriage. He was a really nice, handsome boy, and he treated me with great respect. My parents told me that he was from a good family. But I felt that I was too young to be married, and I didn't agree to the match. It was, by the way, out of the ordinary that I would have veto power over the selection of my husband, but my parents had made it clear from the beginning that I would have to approve their choice before they married me off. Encouraged by my father's tacit support, I was thinking about my future—I dreamed of continuing my studies in Kabul. At the time, I couldn't even consider the possibility of getting married and then being forced to stay home as a housewife.

Up through the tenth grade, Shah Mu'min's proposals continued unabated. When he began to realize that my rejections were more than just ritualistic posturing, he was devastated. He was always very emotional. And when he'd see me in school, tears would fill his eyes. He even began to miss lessons from our special winter sessions, and rumors swirled that he was at home lying in bed suffering from the disease of "unrequited love."

As she had many times over the past several years, Mu'min's older sister came to our house one day in mid-March 1978. Her brother hadn't been at school for the past three days. As soon as she saw me, she threw her arms around me. "My dear, dear Anisa," she said as she smothered my cheeks with her kisses. "Have you by any chance reconsidered the offer from my little brother?" I again restated my objections. "I'm too young to get married . . . I want to get an advanced education in Kabul . . . and I don't want to turn into a housewife."

The poor girl literally got on her knees and began to beg me. "My dear Anisa, you have to understand, my brother has fallen ill because of your rejections. He loves you so much that we now fear for his life if you do not accept his proposal."

I felt awful that I had become such a source of pain in Mu'min's life, not to mention the lives of the female members of his family who obviously adored him so. I couldn't bring myself to repeat my objections right then and there. Instead, I told her that I'd think about it.

That evening, I thought long and hard about my future. Shah Mu'min wasn't a bad guy. He would probably treat me with respect, and maybe he'd even agree to go to Kabul together so that we could both study. By the time I finally fell asleep, I was leaning toward agreeing to the match.

But as fate would have it I never saw Shah Mu'min alive again. Like many Afghans, Mu'min traveled to Mazar-i-Sharif the next morning to take part in New Year's festivities, which we celebrate on March 21. But along a mountain pass, in the province of Samangan, his car skidded off the road and fell into the valley below. His car was so demolished, I was told, that it was only through the heroic efforts of emergency rescue personnel that they were able to disentangle his body from the wreckage and return it to his family. This was my first, but by no means last, painful experience connected to love and romance.

I heard about Mu'min's passing the day after the accident. Along with many of the teachers and students from our school, I went to his house to mourn. Everyone knew that Mu'min had been in love with me, so all eyes were fixed upon me as I entered the house. When Mu'min's mother saw me, she hugged me tightly and wailed so loudly that it seemed that the house's walls were shaking. Choking back tears, she finally gasped, "You know what, my daughter? Mu'min jaan* took all of his love and all of his dreams with him to his grave." As she continued crying and holding me in her arms, she lost consciousness and her limp body fell on top of me. We both collapsed to the ground.

---

* Jaan is a term of endearment afixed to the end of a person's name.

Two months later, Shah Mu'min's mother came to my house again, just as she had so many times in the past during happier times. She was still visibly shaken by her son's death. As my mother and I spoke with her, tears would well up in her eyes every couple of minutes, and she would begin weeping. We quickly ran out of conversation topics, and my mother and I shot one another nervous glances. Finally, Mu'min's mother began collecting some of her things, which suggested to us that she would leave soon. I breathed a sigh of relief. But instead, in the tone of voice one might use if one were to say, "Oh yes, and one more thing, . . ." she turned to my mother and asked for her permission to speak with me alone.

Honestly, I dreaded being alone with her. I had never breathed a word to anyone about my last minute change of heart regarding Mu'min's proposal, and I certainly wasn't about to bring it up now. When my mother reluctantly left us alone, Mu'min's mother turned to me. "Anisa, I saw Mu'min jaan in a dream last night . . ." She cut herself off with her sobbing, which might have lasted about five minutes. When she finally managed to more or less compose herself again, she continued. "So in the dream, Mu'min jaan said to me, 'Since I wasn't able to marry my one and only love, it is my last wish on this earth that Anisa marry my brother instead.'" She looked at me very seriously. "It is of course up to you to decide if you would like to honor his request. But I thought that I should at least tell you about my dream."

In Afghanistan, some widows marry their deceased husband's brother, but I hadn't even agreed to be engaged to Mu'min, much less marry him. So although I pitied Mu'min's mother and knew that she must be experiencing horrible pain, I just couldn't agree to marry his brother—a man who I had never even met. I didn't need any time to consider my decision. When I told the poor grieving woman how I felt, tears just streamed down her face. She was inconsolable. I felt like the most self-centered, evil person on the face of the planet. But what could I do?

➔   ➔   ᛜ   ᛜ

I completed school at the age of sixteen, and enrolled at the pedagogical university in Kabul, where I specialized in physical education. In my sophomore year, a young man named Ismail fell in love with me. I liked him—this time from the beginning. He was a tall, handsome man with dark shiny hair who was one of the most attractive men in our university. For six months, his parents came frequently from the district of Farkhar—three hours from Taloqan—to my house to propose marriage on behalf of their son. But my parents were opposed because he wasn't a relative. They didn't want to give up their daughter to a "stranger." They didn't know about his background, who his relatives were, or what kind of family he came from.

But Ismail jaan was determined to marry me—and I certainly didn't do anything to dissuade him. After having studied for a couple of years in Kabul, I felt as though I had attained as much education as I needed. I was ready to settle down and live a quiet life, raise some children, and allow my husband to support me. Ismail jaan would regularly update me about his progress in convincing my father. At the risk of compromising my humility, I secretly offered him whatever ideas came to mind. The best solution, we decided, was to search out some sort of connection between his father and my own. Eventually he discovered that they had some mutual acquaintances in the army who were willing to vouch for him and his family. So after an extended lobbying effort, my father finally relented and we were married.

I was thrilled that our plotting had brought about the marriage. Ismail jaan treated me very well. And he provided me with everything I needed for the family. Furthermore, he would always give me little presents of clothes or gold jewelry. After the wedding, we moved back from Kabul to Taloqan and started a family. Over the course of seven years, we had three boys—Andaleb, Firuz, and Nasim—and one girl, Yagona. But it proved impossible to enjoy a peaceful life together because the war between the government and the mujahedin fighters was already in full swing.

Shortly after we got married, my husband joined the government army. Thanks to his tactical thinking, social skills, and no doubt his familial connections, he quickly moved up in rank. After a few years in the army he became infamous among the mujahedin for his tough approach to quelling insurrection. There were jealous people who would circulate rumors about my husband, saying that he had committed terrible acts of cruelty, but I never believed them. How could it be, I used to think at the time, that a man who treated his wife and children with such warmth could be such a cruel man outside the home?

Ismail jaan became a high-level target among mujahedin fighters, and he began to spend more and more nights at the military base for his and our own protection. Before then, mujahedin fighters would occasionally come looking for him at our house in the middle of the night. We had a secret escape route over our compound's surrounding mud-brick wall and into our neighbor's yard. Far too many times we had to run out into the dark with out hearts pounding and scamper across the wall to our neighbor's sanctuary.

But the attacks and threats weren't only physical. They were also psychological—designed to make us live in an atmosphere of fear. I heard that some of the mujahedin began asking the neighbors about me. "Where is Ismail jaan's wife? Where is that communist's wife?" I heard rumors that they would joke about me. "We know that those communists are making everything 'the people's property.' Land is the people's property, apartment houses are the people's property. We want to see Ismail jaan's wife—she should become part of the people's property, too."

By the mid-1980s, it had grown unsafe for us to remain at our house in Taloqan. The fighting between the mujahedin and government factions was growing fiercer by the day, and no one could be at all certain about our security. So one night, with only a few possessions, my two small boys, Andaleb and Firuz, and I set out toward my husband's family's house in the Farkhar district of Takhar province. We locked up the front gate and door of the house with a couple of strong padlocks and hoped against hope that it wouldn't be robbed.

I didn't enjoy living in Farkhar at all. I had never lived outside of the city, and I was always exhausted from serving my husband's family hand and foot. And I missed my husband terribly. My only respite came on rare strolls with my children, when we'd sit along the banks of the wide, rushing river that ran by my father-in-law's house. One day I received a letter from my husband, who had been involved in a protracted battle with some mujahedin insurgents. In the letter, he instructed me to leave Farkhar as quickly as possible because he had received a report that it might soon come under attack. He suggested that we travel with his uncle Rashid to Kabul. But I categorically refused to travel to a whole different part of Afghanistan without even so much as laying eyes on my husband. As it turned out, in a way I could have never anticipated, the decision to see my husband at that time indirectly saved my life many years later.

Uncle Rashid and I resolved to go to my husband's military base located on the other end of Takhar province. In order to travel there, we had to cross the front lines of mujahedin-held territories into those controlled by the government. I wore a burqa, as it was the best way to guarantee my security and maintain my anonymity. It was the first time in my life that I had worn this terrible clothing. It took me many years to become entirely accustomed to a public life beneath a burqa.

I met my husband and we had the chance to spend one evening together. As so many times before, I urged him to quit his work in the army. "It's such a terribly dangerous job, and it's really just a matter of time before your luck runs out. And then what will happen to me and the children?"

As usual, he offered some vague promises and quickly changed the subject. He asked me about our children and reserved a lot of questions for our oldest son, Andaleb, who always had been my husband's favorite and even looked a lot like him. He assured me that we would be much safer in Kabul. "Don't worry about me," he said. "I'm confident this terrible war will be over soon. You need to take care of yourself. Whatever you do, don't allow those mujahedin to capture you. They are horrible. You have to go to Kabul. It's a big city and nobody will know who you are there." On the one night that we had together, we conceived our youngest son, Nasim.

The next morning, I left the military base alone in my burqa so as not to endanger any male escorts who could later be identified by the mujahedin. I had arranged to rendezvous with Uncle Rashid about a mile away. But only a few minutes after I left the base, a huge battle began to rage. Bombs fell everywhere and a rain of bullets whistled through the air. I tried to duck for cover wherever I could. I saw a shallow ditch a few yards away, and I threw myself down into the muddy water. As the bullets continued to fly above, I tried to crawl and squirm away from the front lines. My body paid a heavy price for my escape. My knees and elbows were torn apart, and I still bear the scars from that terrible morning.

However, the tragedy of that day was by no means finished. As the rockets continued to fall, I came upon a tiny village of no more than twenty houses. When I arrived outside the walls of the first house, I decided to try to seek refuge. So I pounded on the front door as the rockets and bullets continued unabated. Eventually, a man in his thirties named Iqbol came to the door. Although I was covered in mud and bleeding from several parts of my body, Iqbol quickly invited me inside. He had been hiding in his house with his wife, three daughters and two sons. They were very surprised to receive an unexpected guest in the middle of the fierce battle, but they welcomed me into their simple home.

Iqbol's wife, Bonafsha, brought me a change of clothes and began tending to my wounds. Their oldest daughter, Ruqiya, who was about sixteen, poured some tea for me. "You really should try to be calm," Bonafsha tried to reassure me. "We often have these kinds of battles here. I'm sure it will be over soon." We attempted to make conversation as the fighting continued, but mostly we just sat there curled up on the floor, huddled close to one another. As the bombs fell closer and closer, I started to grow hysterical. I heard loud voices of children, which rose to a crescendo. "You have to run! You have to run! Run! Run!"

"Let's get out of here!" I shouted to my hosts. I leapt to my feet and expected the rest of the family to follow. But they just looked up at me as though I'd gone completely insane. "Can't you hear what the kids are saying? Let's run!" I begged them. It was then that I realized that the voices were only in my head. But the chorus was too loud to ignore.

When I realized that the family wouldn't heed my warnings, I bolted out of the house like I was possessed. Iqbol got up and shouted after me, "Have you completely lost your mind, woman? Come back here!" But I began to sprint as fast as I did during my days in university gym classes. Iqbol was so concerned about his guest that he started to chase after me. "It's not safe out here! Come back to my house, you crazy woman!" I heard him pursuing me for about thirty seconds, and then he must have given up. I glanced over my shoulder and saw that he was just staring at me in disbelief. The voices in my head began to grow very faint.

Only a few seconds after I'd seen Iqbol stop running, we both turned around as a deafening explosion struck from behind. Two rockets had fallen right in the middle of Iqbol's house. I saw a huge dust cloud form where the house had once stood and items from the home were strewn everywhere. Parts of mattresses, glass, pillows, tin trunks, and many other things went flying through the air in all directions. The poor man must have been in shock. He didn't move for about one whole minute. Then he raced back to his house—"Jalil jaan, Bonafsha jaan, Parawana jaan, Ruqiya jaan, Zahro jaan, Islam jaan . . ."—he was calling out the names of all his children and his wife. I was terribly afraid that another rocket might follow the first two to the same spot, but I felt so horrible for Iqbol that I ran back to assist him.

We were able to immediately locate the bodies of two of his girls and their mother, Bonafsha, but as much as we pored through the wreckage, we just couldn't find the remaining two boys and one girl. "Where's the rest of my family? Where are they?!?" Iqbol crouched on his knees with his arms over his head and started crying. Within an hour, there was a lull in the fighting and some of the neighbors came out of their houses to assess the damage. Iqbol's family was the only casualty in the village that day. Another bomb had landed on a villager's barn and killed all their livestock, but Iqbol was alone in his unbearable grief.

When the neighbors heard that a few of his children were still missing, they brought over their shovels and pickaxes to more effectively rummage through the ruins. But however much they searched, they couldn't find the bodies. I knew that I should have continued on my way. My family, after all, was waiting for me back in Farkhar, and Uncle Rashid must have been worried sick about me. These people who died weren't my neighbors or relatives, and only a few hours earlier, I didn't even know their names. But Iqbol and his family had shown me very kind hospitality, and I couldn't just walk away in this time of mourning.

I spent the night in the village at Iqbol's brother's house, and in the morning I attended the funeral ceremonies for those whose bodies had been found. All night, I heard that Iqbol had continued searching for his three children by kerosene lamp. The next day, when I saw Iqbol, he said to me with a glimmer of hope in his bloodshot eyes, "Who knows? Maybe my children just ran off somewhere or they were transported by Allah straight to heaven." As he and the neighbors continued searching everywhere, someone happened to notice a bee that had been circling repeatedly over a patch of ground for many hours. "Maybe the bee wants to show us where my children have been buried? Let's dig here!" Iqbol urged his fellow villagers.

And precisely in the place where the bee had been buzzing, they found the man's oldest daughter, Ruqiya. She had lost her head and one arm. It was assumed that the missing parts of her body had been blown to pieces. So they buried the girl a few hours later as the search continued for the others.

After the burial, while I was sitting together with the other women from the village, an exhausted Iqbol came in with a bag of what looked like pieces of meat. "What's in the bag?" one of Iqbol's cousins asked. Iqbol just sat down in the middle of the room and burst out crying. "It's my son, Jalil jaan . . . he has no legs or arms or head. He's just a pile of flesh."

As Iqbol cried in front of all of us women, his brother told us the story about how the unfortunate boy had been located. There was a curious little boy from the village who happened to be climbing in a tree near the destroyed house. As all the men were working below, the kid yelled out, "Look, there's Jalil's shirt on the branch." There were a few pieces of fabric from his shirt entangled with what was left of his mangled body in the tree.

When Iqbol was finally able to contain his tears, he suddenly turned toward me. "Who sent you here?" he asked, his voice full of anger. "Are you a witch? I should have died with the rest of my family yesterday. But because of you, I didn't." I didn't know how to respond. But one of Iqbol's sisters quickly came to my defense. "It was Allah who decided that it was time for your family to leave this earth. It was not yet your turn. Anisa jaan here was just the vehicle Allah used to carry out His divine plans. If she hadn't been there, I'm sure you would have left the house for some other reason."

Everyone was in tears. As much as I wanted to stay, I realized that my presence was only upsetting people. So at the first opportunity, I excused myself. "Where are you going, my daughter? It's late," one of the older women from the village asked me as I stood up to leave. I told them about my long trip ahead and everyone understood. Iqbol's brother volunteered to escort me to where I was supposed to meet Uncle Rashid. I walked out of the village still wearing Bonafsha's clothes.

I was completely overwhelmed by what I had experienced over the last two days. Now I finally understood what war was—and what my husband confronted almost all the time.

At the time I left the village, they still hadn't found the remaining child's body. The boy's name was Islam.

❖ ❖ ❖ ❖

By the time I returned to my children in Farkhar, everyone was terribly worried about me. Uncle Rashid had sent word that I had failed to show up at the prearranged meeting place, but he had advised everyone to stay calm. I'll never forget the hugs and kisses that my children smothered me with when I walked through the door. It was one of the happiest moments in my life.

As instructed by my husband, we fled to Kabul the next day with almost no possessions. I once again donned the burqa for our trip. After a couple of weeks in the capital, I managed to find work for myself in an orphanage. For eight months, my two children and I lived in the orphanage in a tiny windowless room that had been built originally as a storage area. We were able to borrow a few mats so that we wouldn't have to sleep on the floor.

After eight months in Kabul, the government forces had apparently brought a certain measure of stability to much of Kunduz province, and my husband sent a letter urging us to move back up north—this time to the city of Kunduz. For four years, my husband continued to fight while we lived in Kunduz. He would come to visit us occasionally, but he was most often directing forces on the front lines in Khwaja Ghar, in the northern part of Takhar province.

When I was finally given the chance to see the condition of our house in Taloqan, I fell on the ground in tears. Thieves had taken absolutely everything—the television, the carpets. They even took the wooden roof beams and window panes. All that remained was the mud frame of our house. When I next saw my husband, I cried again. "We've lost everything. Where will we live in the future? What will we do?" Again my husband comforted me. "You have to stay calm. We will rebuild everything. As soon as the war ends, I promise to build a bigger house for us with all new, modern things. Don't make yourself crazy over what we've lost. The most important thing is that we and our children have our health and our lives."

A couple of years after we had moved to Kunduz, I went back to

Taloqan to attend my niece's wedding. While we were participating in the week-long wedding party with my relatives, my husband sent me a letter saying how much he missed us. He hadn't had a chance to visit for many months as a result of the ongoing fighting in Khwaja Ghar, so he asked me to come with the children to see him.

The road to Khwaja Ghar was notoriously dangerous, so my cousin located a guide who knew the terrain well. He took us by foot through back roads in order to avoid detection. We were in Khwaja Ghar ten days in total, throughout which time there were continuous battles nearby. We lived in my husband's small house, which was located near his headquarters. The fighting was so fierce that he didn't allow the children to come up from the basement the entire time we were there. A couple of days after we arrived, my husband brought over a few toy cars to help our kids pass the time. He would usually come to the house once or twice each day to check on us and try to lift our spirits. But I was so exhausted from worrying that I spent most days sleeping feverishly after he left for work.

One day I had a terrible nightmare. I dreamed I was sitting in my house in Taloqan when suddenly a bomb exploded in it. My house was consumed by fire while I stood in the middle, completely unharmed. I was frozen in place for a few moments and then I began to run from the house. As I ran, the flames flew from the house as though in pursuit.

I woke up screaming at around noon, and I was covered in sweat and shaking with fear. It was a dream reminiscent of my terrible experience in the village a few years earlier, but for some reason I had the feeling that it presaged more tragedy.

I rushed to the cook with a handful of afghanis and asked him to distribute the money to poor people out on the street. I hoped that this generosity would somehow help to ward off evil spirits. I also asked him to buy me some food from the market. I felt as though I was suffering from heartburn, and I wanted to prepare some of my favorite dishes to help ease the pain. Every day we were served rice pilaf, and I was longing for something new. So I asked the cook to bring me a milklike sauce, *chaka*, and some basic ingredients to make a soup called *oshi burida,* which is made with noodles.

About an hour later, I had already cut up the noodles, onions, and tomatoes and was awaiting the cook, who had gone out for the remaining ingredients. I listened attentively for his arrival, as I needed his assistance to move the preparation forward. But instead of the cook coming through the door, I heard a car stop near the front gate of the house. After several quick and loud knocks, I opened the front door of the courtyard. It was one of my husband's soldiers. When I saw him and the look on his face, I practically screamed. "What's wrong? What happened? What happened?" The soldiers said with deep gravity, "Let's go to the hospital. The commander has been wounded."

I felt as though someone had just punched me in the stomach, as all of my strength rushed out of my body. I knew that I had to go back to the house to gather a couple of items, but I had no energy to move. The soldier saw the effect that his news had had on me, so he quickly tried to reassure me. "You shouldn't be so concerned, his injury isn't serious. After you see him, you'll feel much better."

We rushed to the hospital. My first impression of my husband was that his face had lost all its color. His black hair looked even darker in contrast to his pale face. He had been wounded in an area around his stomach. I was full of sadness and anger and wanted to blame someone or something. I grabbed his arm and cried out, "What happened to you? How did you manage to injure yourself like this? You had wanted us to come here to spend some time with you. But you had to go off to the war while we waited for you at home. What am I supposed to do here now? I have no friends or relatives here. What do you think will happen to us?" I broke down crying.

After crying for several minutes, I started into him again. "You see, I warned you again and again to quit your work in the army. You could have gotten a normal job and we could have lived like a normal family. Why didn't you listen to me?"

"You're right, Anisa jaan," he said slowly, with all the strength he could muster. "And you've been right all along. You always wanted me to quit the army and now look what's happened to me."

One of the doctors who must have heard my screeching rushed over. "You have to calm down," he whispered to me. "Your husband needs to relax and not to worry. If you make him excited, it will only worsen his condition. You really shouldn't be so worked up. Everything will be fine— so long as he is given the opportunity to recuperate."

My husband's commander knew that he needed better medical attention than was available in Khwaja Ghar. So he organized a helicopter to transport my husband—along with me and the kids—to a hospital in Mazar-i-Sharif. On the helicopter trip, they placed him on a folding bed near the seats where we surrounded him. I could tell that our three boys were excited to be riding a big helicopter for the first time, although their enthusiasm was obviously tempered by the sight of their father. There were also two doctors aboard. One repeatedly dipped some gauze into cold water and placed it on my husband's forehead while the other measured his pulse and blood pressure from time to time.

My husband calmly looked around at all of us—his family that loved him and couldn't imagine life without him. But most of all his gaze remained fixed on our youngest son, Nasim, who was two years old at the time. As my husband lay on the bed, he gently caressed Nasim's face over and over. My husband didn't utter a word. His voice wasn't strong enough to compete with the maddening whir of the helicopter engine. But it was clear from the look in his eyes that he was thinking about all of us.

In Mazar, my husband was examined by a well-known doctor. He ordered a blood transfusion and then conducted a close examination of my husband's wound. After a couple of hours, the doctor announced that there was no choice but to send him to the Soviet Union for better medical attention. They chose the city of Termez, now in independent Uzbekistan located just across the border, only about forty miles from Mazar. A bullet had apparently been lodged in such a way that it was impossible for them to do anything about it anywhere in Afghanistan. "We just don't have the medical expertise here," the doctor told me, shaking his head in resignation.

The helicopter that had brought us from Khwaja Ghar carried him on to Termez. Ismail jaan was accompanied from the hospital to the helicopter by his brother, Abdullah, who happened to be living in Mazar at that time. When my brother-in-law returned to meet us, he brought with him my husband's gold ring. "Here, he wanted you to have this," Abdullah said to me simply. The tears flowed from my eyes like a torrential rainfall.

The children and I remained behind in Mazar with Abdullah's family. In total, we were in Mazar seventeen days awaiting word about my husband's condition. It was the longest seventeen days of my life. In spite of our frequent inquiries, there was no word from the army about his operation and recovery.

On the seventeenth night after he had left Afghanistan, I had another nightmare. I saw my husband traveling back home to me in an ambulance. He was crouching on the cold, dirty floor of the ambulance with his legs folded and his head ducked down between his knees. Hundreds of people had gathered out in front of the house where we were staying. I also saw a helicopter surrounded by men in military uniforms.

I woke up in a cold sweat. It was about three o'clock in the morning and I couldn't get back to sleep. About an hour later, I heard a loud and ominous knock at the door to my bedroom. It was Abdullah. I expected the worst but instead he said to me, "Gather your things and let's go to the airport. You're heading back home to Kunduz with your husband by helicopter. He came back from Termez and is waiting for you at the airport." But the tone of his voice was not one of joy or excitement.

I had clearly heard my brother-in-law's words but the expression on his face betrayed the truth. "You're lying to me. He's dead, isn't he? I saw it in my dream!" I yelled. My dreams and visions had always been so frighteningly prophetic in the past that I was certain that my husband was dead. I began to beat myself, tear at my face, and cry in pain. I was trying to suppress the emotion of the moment with physical suffering. I had imagined this day many times in the past, but for some reason I never thought that it would actually happen . . . or at least that it would happen so quickly.

Abdullah tried to calm me. "You have to relax. It was just a bad dream. He's all right and he's even here in Mazar. If you gather your things together, you will see him soon."

But I was unable to control myself. "Why are you lying to me? I know the truth. I saw everything in the dream." I wasn't able to listen to reason. So my brother-in-law allowed me to go on shrieking as he gathered up all our family's belongings from around the house. He didn't have to worry about waking up the children—my crying had already taken care of that.

We were told that an ambulance had taken my husband from the Soviet border to Mazar. But by the time we arrived at the airport, the authorities told us that my husband had already been flown to Kunduz in a separate helicopter. This seemed to confirm my worst suspicions. It was then that I became entirely certain that I had lost my husband. So we boarded a different helicopter and headed to Kunduz. When we arrived, some military officials took us home without answering any of my questions.

As we approached our house, we saw that it was surrounded by hundreds of people in army uniforms as well as neighbors and friends. My husband's body, resting inside a zinc coffin, followed us home in an ambulance later. Several men carried his coffin on their shoulders to our house. His military compatriots rushed over, and began banging their heads and their fists against his coffin and against the ambulance. They cried out for the fallen martyr. It looked as though the entire city of Kunduz had come to our house to mourn my poor husband's death.

My husband's family wanted to bury him in his hometown of Farkhar. But the mujahedin were then in control of the district, and they were dead set against his burial taking place in their lands. They didn't want a communist commander honored under their watch, nor allow free passage to many of their most bitter rivals. We were just renting a house in Kunduz at the time and didn't have any long-term connections to the area. But we had no choice but to bury him there. We placed his body in the Davra graveyard.

Two months after my husband's death, I gave birth to my fourth and last child—a baby girl. I named her Yagona, which means "the only one."

→ → ← ←

After my husband's death, I got a job at a girls' school as a Dari language teacher. Two or three years later we moved back to Taloqan and, shortly thereafter, my life became very difficult. After the mujahedin came to power in Kabul, they stopped doling out pensions to the widows and families of martyrs. My teacher's salary was so miserably small, it wasn't sufficient to support my family's needs.

It seemed that every day was worse than the previous one. Eventually, I declined to such a condition that I was hardly able to afford bread to feed my children. The only items that I had of any value were the jewelry that my husband had given me. I had twelve golden rings, including my husband's ring, several bracelets, necklaces, and four pairs of earrings. I wanted to do everything in my power to hold on to these things—they had so much sentimental value to me. And they seemed to be all that symbolically separated me and my family from abject poverty. But in the end, piece by piece, I sold off my gold—except my husband's ring—so I could afford food for my children.

I managed to make an arrangement with an auto mechanic who agreed to take on my oldest son, Andaleb, who was only twelve at the time, as an apprentice. He continued to study at school in the morning, and in the afternoon he worked with the mechanic. But when my son returned home in the evenings, he was totally exhausted from working and studying all day long. After about a month, he came home and said to me, "Mom, I have to choose either school or my work as an apprentice. I just don't have the physical strength to do both."

I still harbored dreams that Andaleb would become a highly educated man one day. Both my husband and I had received a higher-level education, and I wanted even better opportunities for my children. If he dropped out of school, I feared that all he would achieve in life was this vocational skill. I always had hoped that he would be able to support himself one day with his mind, not his hands. But I saw very clearly that he was much more interested in remaining as an apprentice than he was in continuing his formal education. So I reluctantly agreed for him to drop out of school.

One morning, after I had sold off all of my valuables and had completely run out of money, I had to wash my children's clothes. My father-in-law had moved to Taloqan and ran a very small shop, where he managed to sell a few odds and ends. I sent one of my sons to his shop to ask for a small bar of soap. But he told my son, "I don't lend anything to anyone. Go and bring me some money for the soap, and then I will give it to you." I knew that my father-in-law was also in difficult financial circumstances, after losing his house in Farkhar, but I couldn't believe that he wouldn't help his own grandchildren with at least a little bar of soap. I was mortally offended. And I never spoke to him again.

So I had no choice but to sell my husband's ring. I've had many terrible experiences in my life, but this was one of the most difficult things I've ever done.

It was then that I realized that nobody would help me—not the government, not my relatives, and not my husband's relatives. I had been working as a teacher, but we hadn't received our salaries for such a long time that most of us had given up hope that we'd ever be compensated for our work. I decided I had to swallow whatever shred of pride I had left in order to survive. So I started to ask some of my wealthier friends if they needed help with their housework. I would clean their homes, wash their clothes, and clean up their courtyards. Usually I was paid in food and used clothing for my children. This is how I managed to feed my family for a couple of years.

Although my teacher's salary was practically nonexistent, I continued working in the local girls' high school until the late summer of 1999. Much of the rest of Afghanistan had been involved in a bloody civil war involving the Taliban and many other mujahedin factions. Even neighboring Kunduz province had already been under Taliban rule for more than two years. But aside from some limited fighting, Taloqan had been generally quiet under the conservative rule of the mujahedin. Girls and boys studied separately, and women needed to wear burqas on the street, but at least we were allowed to continue educating females.

I enjoyed working with the girls in the school, and I had many friends among the teachers. One day, after a teachers' meeting, I was sitting around with a bunch of my colleagues. We were complaining about the stifling heat that had gripped Taloqan over the past week.

"Why don't we go somewhere in the mountains or by a river and have a picnic?" one of my friends suggested offhandedly. Many of the teachers immediately agreed. "That's a great idea! Where should we go?" The women tossed out many ideas, but I knew of a quiet spot near the river in Farkhar district, where my husband's family was from, which would be ideal.

So I said, "I want to go to a place where there's a big wide river, where I can enjoy the cool breeze rising from the rapid current."

"And what else do you want?" one of the teachers asked with a broad grin.

"I want to be able to spread out a mattress and relax under the sprawling branches of an old maple tree," I continued on dreamily.

"And what else do you want?" another colleague asked. There were giggles around the room, but everyone was listening to me attentively.

"I want to lean again the large trunk of a tree, put on a cassette, and lose myself in the music of Ahmad Zahir,"* my fairy tale continued.

"And what else do you want?" another teacher repeated. Everyone burst out laughing. "What poetry! We almost felt that we had traveled with you to this wonderful land!"

My simple daydream of a calm picnic was nearly impossible for my friends to imagine. All of us women were so busy working so hard to simply survive that this vision seemed almost as absurd as . . . going off to America.

But I was serious. "Come on, girls! Why don't we collect a little bit of money and buy some food in the market. We'll each take a couple of mattresses from our houses. Anybody who wants to can bring their husbands and children. . . . And I'll be responsible for bringing my cassette player and the Ahmad Zahir tapes!"

A few of the women made excuses to bow out. But most of the women were bubbling with excitement. "I'll prepare some rice pilaf and *qorma*," one woman called out. "I'll take care of the kebab," said another. We even set a date—for the following week, when summer vacation was scheduled to begin.

→　→　←　←

But only two days later we began to hear Taliban helicopters circling above. They were heavily bombing the district of Bangi, only ten miles outside of Taloqan. Ethnic Uzbeks from Bangi began flooding the streets of Taloqan, having left everything behind—everything but horror stories about the ruthlessness of the Taliban.

The mujahedin commanders knew that Taloqan could not be readily defended against the Taliban onslaught, so they advised Taloqan residents to leave immediately. An estimated 75 percent of the population left Taloqan within the next two weeks or so. There was a mad rush to secure a place in a vehicle. Luckily, one of my neighbors, whose son I occasionally tutored, happened to own a truck. So our family, as well as our relatives, packed up all our most valuable possessions and headed off to Warsaj district in the southeastern part of Takhar province. My

---

* Ahmad Zahir, also known as Afghan Elvis because of his popularity and appearance, is the most well-known and widely beloved pop singer from Afghanistan. He died in a car accident in 1979, the circumstances of which continue to be regarded with suspicion.

sister-in-law's husband was from Warsaj, and he knew that the mountainous terrain of Warsaj made it an extremely difficult target for the Taliban.

Along with a couple of other fleeing refugee families, we piled into the back of a large, uncovered truck with all of our possessions. Our group consisted of my children and I, my sister and her family, and my sister-in-law and her husband and their children. There were also many other children, women, and elderly people aboard. I would guess that there were about twenty-five people on the truck in total.

It was ten o'clock at night when we had finished loading the truck and we were ready to leave for Warsaj. The first ten miles outside of Taloqan was a smooth asphalt road. But afterward, we crept along slowly on dirt roads that had been destroyed by floods, mines, and bombing during the past twenty years of fighting. All night long, we slowly rode down the destroyed road. We had to hold on tightly to the side of the truck so that we wouldn't bounce out of the vehicle when we hit particularly rough patches.

I couldn't sleep all night. We were worried about bandits and mines along the road as well as the steep mountain passes where one bad decision by the driver could launch us to all but certain death. At six in the morning the first traces of light began to form behind the mountain ridge. I breathed a great sigh of relief. We had survived the night. And I even recognized the area we were passing through. We were in Farkhar—my husband's homeland and the place my colleagues and I had dreamed about only a few days earlier. I knew that the road to Warsaj took us through Farkhar and was hoping to catch a glimpse of the land I remembered as so stunning.

The beautiful wide river was rushing alongside the road. Although the early morning mountainous air was crisp, and my life was being turned upside down yet again, I couldn't help but smile at the wonderful natural beauty before me. My children had just woken up, and we were huddling together for warmth.

Just as I was enjoying a moment of comfort in the midst of so much turmoil, I noticed that our truck started to go off the road into the river. We had completely missed the bridge which was only a few yards away. The driver must have fallen asleep at the wheel.

I started screaming. My oldest son, Andaleb, who was sixteen at the time, immediately sized up the situation and instinctively jumped over the side of the truck before we even reached the water. My youngest son, Nasim, then thirteen, knew how to swim very well. As soon as the truck entered the river, he swam away easily. But the ice-cold rushing waters that had come straight from the mountains quickly swept me off. Although I didn't know how to swim, I kept moving my legs and arms—I just did whatever I could to try to stay afloat. I had seen people swim before so I knew the general motions.

As I tried to keep my head above the rapidly flowing water, I saw all kinds of items that were aboard the truck floating by: mattresses and pillows, various bags, and even a couple of wooden cradles. I saw the heads of many of my cousins and other passengers trying desperately to stay alive. They were bobbing slightly above and then below the surface of the rapid current, but it was clear that many of them were going to drown. Nevertheless, I'm sure that all of us were thinking only of ourselves.

After a few minutes in the water, my arms and legs were exhausted from perpetual movement. The river's current kept forcing me back to the center, even though I was trying desperately to reach one of the banks. At one point when my head was slightly above water, I caught sight of my two sons rushing alongside the bank, screaming, "Mama! Mama!" They must have been yelling very loudly for me to have heard their shouts above the loud crashing of the water around me. They continued running along the river, trying to keep up with me.

As I was nearing the end of my strength, I saw a large boulder sticking out well above the water level in the middle of the river. I prayed silently: "Please, Allah, please take me in the direction of that rock and give me the strength to grab hold of it."

God heard my prayers and sent me in the direction of the boulder. But the rock was too big and slippery, and I had trouble grabbing hold of it. My head and arms were above water, but try as I might I couldn't scramble my way up onto the rock. I let out a series of yells that succeeded in dispelling some water from my lungs, but I just couldn't muster the strength to lift my legs onto the boulder.

I saw my boys rushing toward me and calling for me. The water had brought me so far downstream, I couldn't see anybody else around. It was only me and my two children—alone in this stark, cruel setting.

Nasim got into the water a little farther down the river, and he screamed out to me. "Mama, let go of the rock and I'll save you. You're too far away right now for me to help you."

I was so frightened at the sight of my youngest son entering the river. I cried out: "Nasim, you have to get out of the water right now! It's too dangerous. Don't worry about me. Leave me here and take care of yourself!" I knew I couldn't possibly bear the sight of the river taking him away. Although I was only thirty-six at the time, I continued, "I've lived a full life, now it's your turn to carry on. You have everything before you."

"Please, Mama," he called out. "Don't be afraid. I know how to swim very well and I can save you. Just push your way from the boulder in my direction, and I promise I'll rescue you."

"How could this little boy possibly save me?" I thought to myself. I was an adult woman and he was just a little baby—at least that's the way I had always thought of him.

But my strength was failing me. And in spite of my objections to my son's pleas, I couldn't hold onto the boulder any longer. So, after reciting my death prayer, I let go. I immediately sank into a small whirlpool that had gathered near the rock. I tried my best to stay afloat, but I knew that I didn't have the power to carry on. My head had been swallowed underwater by the strong whirlpool, but I was still moving my hands and feet as I sank. I was convinced that this was my last minute on earth.

But suddenly, I felt a hand grab me by my arm. I was being pulled slowly but steadily toward the bank of the river. Allah had endowed my thirteen-year-old son with the strength to rescue me from the swirling river currents. Today, Nasim is a tall, sturdy young man. But then he was all skin and bones. My oldest son didn't know how to swim. So he had no choice but to stand on the bank of the river praying for me and Nasim.

When I was dragged all the way to the shore, I was completely exhausted. I was spitting up water from my water-logged lungs. I had water in my ears, nose, mouth, everywhere. I collapsed on the ground. My sons grabbed me by my shoulders and started shaking me. "Are you OK, Mama? Please open your eyes! Please say something!" They were afraid that maybe I'd died. They tried to pick me up from the ground, and I just waved to them to indicate that I didn't want to be moved or disturbed. They were just children, I thought—they couldn't understand that I was just too tired to move.

But my sons pulled my limp body up into a sitting position and bent my head down so that water would escape from my nose and mouth. Over the course of several minutes, I coughed up lots and lots of water. And afterward, I finally began to breathe relatively well again.

My purse, shoes, and burqa had been lost in the river, but most importantly, I lost the poems I had written in my youth and had managed to carry around with me throughout all of my life's adventures. My clothes were of course thoroughly soaked. I began to shiver in the mountain's dawn air. The sun had just risen above the mountains, and my sons helped me walk gingerly over to a sunny spot so that I could warm myself.

When I finally regained full consciousness, I asked my sons, "What happened to your sister and brother—Firuz and Yagona? Where are they? Where are our relatives?" Reassured that I would, in fact, survive, Andaleb decided to venture back up the river to investigate, while Nasim stayed with me. A few minutes later, the driver's son, who I had once tutored, came rushing up to us. "Have you seen my wife?" he panted with a frantic look in his eyes. Only one week before, we had all been dancing at his wedding party, and now he had lost his new bride in the river.

We could only shake our heads, sadly.

The boy was hysterical. He began running around us, clapping together the palms of his hands as in mourning and crying out, "Teacher, the love of my life has been taken away. The river has swallowed her up. She's no more." He repeated these words again and again as he beat himself over the head.

He then continued to run down the river, screaming her name. "Nozanin jaan! Nozanin jaan!" He never saw his beloved wife again—not even her body. The river had indeed swallowed her and taken her to another world.

I was still in shock. I felt as though my teeth were frozen and I was having a terrible nightmare. Nasim helped shake me out of my stupor. "Come on, let's go and look for the others. What's the good of just sitting here?" I nodded my head, and we started walking back in the direction of the truck accident.

By the time we arrived, dozens of people had gathered around the scene of the accident. There were many other trucks traveling on the road that morning, and most were filled with families fleeing the fighting in Taloqan. It turned out that there were five people who had managed to maintain a hold on the truck's back railing after it struck the riverbed, and their heads were slightly above water. I can't express my relief—and also my horror—when I saw Firuz and Yagona among those who were still holding on for dear life in the middle of that freezing cold river. By the time we arrived, they'd already been in the water more than an hour and a half!

Among those who had stopped along the road, there were a few people who knew how to swim well. After a long discussion of how to help the poor survivors in the ice cold river, they had come up with a rescue scheme. First they found a long, strong rope. Then, a few swimmers took one end of the rope with them to the part of the sunken truck still above water. At the same time, several bulky men stood on the bank of the river holding the other end of the rope. As the men in the water reached each of the victims, they tied their end of the rope to their waists. When everything was secure, they gave the signal and the men on land reeled in the survivors.

When we arrived at the scene, this operation had just begun. And I was able to be the first person to hug my daughter and son after their lives were saved. They were shivering so much, I was worried that they would fall terribly ill. Thank God they're resilient kids and were able to pull through just fine.

In total, among the twenty-five passengers, twelve were swept away by the current and nine of them died. Two of the passengers who had survived were in such deep shock that it took a long time to bring them back to their senses. A commander who happened upon the accident site, reported that there were twelve presumed dead to other military officials in Taloqan. These commanders quickly passed along the news to our relatives, who had remained behind in the city. Likewise, the commander contacted others downstream to ask them to assist with search-and-rescue efforts.

Among the dead, five were our relatives: my sister, my brother's wife, and their three children. My brother was beside himself with grief. He had lost his entire family to that frigid, unforgiving river. We found out later that the families of the victims had prepared twelve graves—including one for me. Neighbors, friends, and colleagues all came to our house to mourn for me and my relatives.

We were so shaken by our experience that we could not continue our journey. We decided to abandon our plans and to head back to Taloqan, despite the threat that the Taliban would soon be on our doorsteps. We just wanted to be back home with those we loved.

We waited a few hours for the commanders to recover the bodies, and then we headed back to Taloqan. When we arrived, the mourners were filled with contradictory emotions. They had taken me for dead and were overjoyed to see that me and my children were safe.

Now that a fair amount of time has passed, my fellow teachers like to tease me. "Hey Anisa, don't you want to go have a picnic in Farkhar? I hear it's very beautiful there!" But my bones still shiver when I think about that horrible day.

A few days later, the Taliban entered Taloqan, and we were forced to flee yet again. But this time, I refused to go anywhere near Farkhar or Warsaj. Instead, my children and I traveled to the district of Kishem located in Badakhshan province, near the border with Takhar. There were so many refugees flooding into Kishem at that time that there was hardly a decent space to erect a tent.

We lived in Kishem for three months before we left for Khwaja Bahawuddin in northern Takhar province, where we had heard there was a large camp set up by international organizations for internally displaced people. When we arrived in Khwaja Bahawuddin, I was shocked at the size of the camp. It looked like a town. For miles around, thousands of tents had been erected for people who had fled their homes with little or nothing. Many of the tents were set up in even rows. So this place that was home to such chaos and disorder had at least the outward semblance of structure.

However, many of the newcomers were forced to set up makeshift housing out of their physical possessions. Many people simply dug a hole in the ground and covered it with some plastic sheeting that was planted in the ground with sticks. Then whole families would sleep in these shallow holes.

The camp residents were very poor. Many of them had lost their homes in Taliban arson attacks and had no idea how they would rebuild after the war ended. But a lot of other families arrived from places that had not been directly affected by armed conflict. They were generally from poor mountainous regions in which agricultural livelihoods had been destroyed by the ongoing drought. These people had come to the camp with the hope of finding something decent to eat.

After we managed to register our family, we were issued an identification card and provided with a tent. In addition, every person in my family received a blanket, and we also got a large plastic mat, 70 kilograms of wheat, 35 kilograms of rice, 16 liters of cooking oil, and 14 kilograms of beans. Every month, we received more supplies; sometimes we'd get more wheat or oil, and other times, they'd give us sugar or even clothes. In order to collect our monthly allowances, I had to wake up before dawn and line up with other women from the camp. Invariably, dozens of women were already in line with their children and infants when I would arrive. I thought that they must have slept there to have arrived before me. There was sickness all around. As we stood in line, children and their mothers would cough and sneeze, and many suffered from skin diseases. The smell from diarrhea and from women who hadn't bathed in months was nearly unbearable. I'd try to wait as patiently as possible until nine o'clock when the men in charge of the distribution would arrive. The women who emerged from the warehouse with their humanitarian aid were always so thrilled and proudly marched past the rest of us. But sometimes the people who were handing out the food would run out of supplies before it was my turn in line, and we'd all be told to come back the next day.

The soldiers who were charged with keeping order would sometimes sadistically whip the women who they thought were "getting out of hand." They were especially cruel when they wanted to break up the crowd after the daily food supplies ran out. Women would scream out, "If I don't get food today, my children will die! I need food!" But their only answer came from the guards' whips. And then all of this would start anew the next day. It was a terribly dehumanizing experience.

We survived this way for nine months. But I decided that this was not any way for my family to live. Some people in the camp began discussing the idea of seeking refuge in Iran, and I thought that anywhere had to be better than this terrible camp. I knew that my brother had left for Iran a few years before, and I managed to track down his address.

As my children and I packed up our possessions and prepared to make the long trek across the country, Andaleb, who was then seventeen, announced to me that he wanted to stay behind. He had managed to find a little work for himself as a day laborer, and he said that he couldn't imagine living outside of Afghanistan. I was very reluctant to allow my son to be separated from the rest of us. But he was insistent. "Mother, I'm a grown man and I can take care of myself," he told me. "I'm sure that my brothers will be able to support you from now on." He was right of course—he was no longer my little boy.

It was only a couple of years later that I found out the real reason he didn't want to come with us to Iran. It was love that kept him behind—but it was love for a girl, not his homeland. Andaleb had apparently fallen in love with one of his father's distant relatives, a beautiful young girl named Mehri. Her family had fled Farkhar as refugees. I found out later that Andaleb would often make "dates" with her to meet at the water pump at a certain time each day. He was afraid that he'd never see her again if he left with us to Iran.

✦ ✦ ✦ ✦

In Iran, we were quickly able to find my brother, who had settled outside the city of Zabul located near the Afghan border. He was working as a guard at a greenhouse and large garden. He had a two-room house on the edge of the garden yards, where my children and I also lived. After a few months in Iran, my two sons managed to find work in a large car lot where they bought and sold used cars. Thanks to my sons' income, we were able to live fairly well. Best of all, we didn't have to count the days until our next rations or stand in long lines to collect handouts.

As a result of his work, my son Firuz was able to gather together some money to pay a smuggler to take him to London. He's been there now for over two-and-half years and has acquired official refugee status. For one year, the British government assisted him with his education and housing and even provided him with a stipend. He's currently taking some classes there and is trying to do whatever he can to stay in England permanently.

During our time in Iran, I often wrote to Andaleb, urging him to join us. I had heard that there were a number of opportunities for widows whose husbands had fought and died during the war to leave for the West along with their children. I thought that our whole family might be able to emigrate and begin our lives anew in a peaceful land. I don't speak any foreign languages, and I knew it wouldn't be easy for me abroad. However, I was willing to sacrifice everything for my children's future.

But my stubborn son didn't want to move to Iran or any other place. He actually did come to Iran to visit once during the two years that we lived there. But after a week, he announced that he was terribly homesick and left later that same day for Afghanistan—a country that was still controlled by the Taliban and torn apart by a never-ending civil war.

"If we go to another country, how would we live there?" Andaleb asked in one of his letters a few months later. "We don't know the culture or language. We don't have any friends and relatives abroad who could help us. No one would employ us. How would we survive? I know I can't live outside of my homeland—I would miss it too much. Mother, let's remain here in Afghanistan." By the time he wrote me this letter, he had already moved back to Taloqan from the Khwaja Bahawuddin camp after the Taliban had fallen from power.

My father-in-law—the one who had denied me soap to wash my children's clothes—died in December 2001. His relatives from Farkhar arrived for the funeral and among them was the object of Andaleb's admiration, Mehri. He hadn't seen her for several weeks, after the camps began to empty. And when he laid his eyes on her again, he was completely love struck.

Immediately after the funeral, my son began writing me the nicest letters. "My dearest mother, nothing would make me happier than to have you and the rest of our family rejoin me here in Taloqan. Please come back home. We are all enjoying a peaceful life now that the Taliban have been expelled. Women are now free to go back to work, and everyone says that girls will start attending school again after the New Year. Please return home and we can start all over again."

I received this letter at the same time I found out that our family's refugee asylum documents were ready. We needed to decide as quickly as possible if we were planning to take advantage of an international aid organization's offer to move us to Canada.

But Andaleb's letter convinced me that we needed to return to Afghanistan. After all the wars and the terrible experiences we had survived together, I couldn't bear the thought of leaving my oldest son behind. I didn't want to break up our family. So we came back here to Taloqan.

Shortly after I returned, Andaleb told me about his feelings for Mehri. I didn't remember seeing her at the camp—I was too preoccupied with other things, I guess. I only remembered the girl when she was very small, so I was reluctant to endorse his marriage plans so quickly. "Why don't you marry one of my cousins from Kabul?" I asked him. "I could choose the most beautiful girl among them for you."

But he was very stubborn and remained adamant that Mehri was the right girl for him. After I spent many days hemming and hawing over his request, my son became fed up. He eventually told me, "Either you go and arrange our wedding, or I leave Taloqan forever and you'll never see me again." My son knew very well that if I had passed up a chance to leave for Canada because I wanted to be with him, I would have no choice but to give in to his threat.

So that's how I ended up returning to Farkhar for the first time since the tragic truck accident. I bought some sweets—an obligatory part of the wooing process—and began the negotiations with Mehri's family. The girl's mother told me that she had received many suitors in the past. "Just in the last couple months, the mothers of four boys have come to the house to ask for my daughter's hand," Mehri's mother proudly reported to me. I knew very well that it was a tried-and-true method in Afghanistan to exaggerate the desirability of one's daughter in order to drive up the bride price. So I just smiled and played along.

But the girl's mother had apparently looked up to me for a long time. "I don't really know your son, but do you know how much I love and respect you? I've always admired your courage in the face of so many hardships. I would do anything for you. My daughter is your daughter."

The second time I returned to the girl's house in Farkhar, her mother gave me sweets in return. This meant that she had consulted with her husband, and everyone had agreed to the match. When I brought the sweets back home to my son, he was overjoyed. He knew that he should control himself and show modesty before his mother, but he couldn't control his emotions. He ran out of the house literally jumping for joy.

They've been engaged now for a year and a half, and I don't know how I will ever afford to pay the bride price on my teacher's salary. Afghan brides are very expensive. Because she's a relative and we have a good relationship, her parents agreed to lower the price. Rather than the going rate of $5,000 for a girl, they agreed to give her up for *only* $3,000. She's considered a real bargain at $3,000! So far I've managed to come up with $2,000 by taking loans from friends, but I haven't been able to raise the remaining $1,000. Recently Andaleb was employed as a driver by an international aid organization, and his monthly salary of $160 goes directly to paying off my debts. I was very pleased that one of the main reasons he was chosen for the job was for his skills as a car mechanic.

But now I wonder how in the world I can possibly raise the remainder of the money for the bride price. I just don't know. If my husband were alive, I'm sure he'd find a way. But I'm just a single widow.

I understand very well that our system, which requires an exorbitant bride price, is a terrible tradition. But this is our culture. My beautiful daughter Yagona is now fourteen years old. And when mothers of would-be grooms come to my house to ask for her hand, I also will quote a very high price. I usually start at $6,000 for nonrelatives. What am I supposed to do? If I agreed to give my daughter away for cheaper, everyone would laugh at me.

One time, after all the agreements for my son's marriage had been made, I pulled Mehri aside as she was serving me tea and said, "Why don't you go to your father and convince him to lower the bride price? Then you can get married sooner."

But the little tart looked at me, batted her eyelashes, and said with a knowing smile, "Did you think it would be a piece of cake to marry off your son?"

CHAPTER TWO

Gulbuddin, Son of Mahfat Khan

I was born on the same day that the Soviet army first entered our village. I don't remember my father at all. People say that he was tall and had red hair and blue eyes like me. But I was only eight months old when he died. When I was older, my mother told me that some people had come to our house in the dead of night and murdered him. She thinks that my father's killers were allied with the mujahedin, but they might have just been common thieves. My mother, who was only a teenager at the time, was left to care for me and my sister, Malaliy, who was only two years old.

My home district of Chahardara in Kunduz province was a hotbed of mujahedin resistance to Soviet rule. While fighting the mujahedin in our village, the Soviets bombed many houses, and many innocent people lost their lives in the fighting. When I was four years old, the situation in our village got really bad. There wasn't enough food for us, and all of my father's relatives who had lived in our village were killed. They were gathered together in one house when it was bombed by Soviet helicopters. Among the twenty-three men, women, and children in the house, there wasn't a single survivor.

I lived in a small mud-brick house with my older sister and my mother. Since there were no men in our family, we didn't think that anyone would bother to attack us. What threat could two small children and a young widow possibly pose to anyone? But one day, as I sat on my mother's lap and she fed me, a Soviet tank stopped behind our house and fired on it. The roof nearly collapsed as my mother grabbed my sister and me, and we ran out of the house. Homeless and without relatives, my mother decided to join a group of villagers who were fleeing to Pakistan.

When we got to Afghanistan's southeastern border, we had to fork over the last of our money to smugglers in order to cross into Pakistan. Although I was only four, I have vivid memories of this crossing. The smugglers shuttled us across a wide rushing river in the middle of the night to avoid the border guards. It was late spring, when the melting snows from the mountains swell the river to its highest levels. The smugglers told my mother, "If you agree to send your children across this river, it is your responsibility. If they die on the way, their blood will be on your hands, not ours." They made it clear that pure chance would decide whether we lived or died.

My mother reluctantly agreed—she couldn't think of a better alternative. So the smugglers put the three of us on two small rafts made from cow's skin, tied the small rafts together, and we floated across to the relative safety of Pakistan. I can still hear the roar of the sweeping current and remember how scared I was that we'd fall out and drown.

Shortly after arriving in Pakistan, we made our way to Peshawar. But the city was already flooded with Afghan refugees searching for work, so we decided to move on. In whatever city we could find work for a crust of bread, we would stay. We had no home, so our family would sleep on the street using my mother's legs as a pillow. We had no possessions so we weren't very concerned about being robbed; besides, there were many other Afghan refugees living under similar conditions at that time. After a few weeks in Pakistan, we latched on to a few other families who also traveled from place to place looking for temporary work. My mother would occasionally find jobs like washing clothes and cleaning houses for some Pakistani families. She would usually be paid with their leftover food.

Unfortunately, my sister and I were too young to work. We would spend the entire day begging for money and for food. We would go from street to street targeting well-dressed Pakistanis. We used to reach up, tug their arms, and say, "Please, give us money. We are poor refugees from Afghanistan. We have no place to live and nothing to eat . . . I haven't eaten anything for three days. Please, in the name of Allah, make a contribution." We usually wouldn't get very far in our speech before we'd be elbowed aside. But sometimes we'd keep trying and repeat it again and again.

After a while, we realized that my sister could earn more money because, although we were both always covered in dirt and our clothes were torn, she was a beautiful, blue-eyed girl. When we figured out that she was more successful, I did little more than watch out for her as she begged.

Sometimes along the road, we would sleep in the hills where it would grow icy cold at night. My teeth would chatter and my skin would break out in goose bumps as our family huddled closely together for protection. Usually, some kind Afghan family would allow me and my sister to join them under a blanket so that we wouldn't freeze to death. We would sometimes use stones as pillows during those long nights, and I was always deathly afraid of the snakes that would come slithering around in the middle of the night. Sometimes I would wake up in a sweat as a snake hissed just a couple of feet away.

One time, after a close brush with a snake, I jumped on top of my mother who was fast asleep. "Mama, Mama," I said, poking her so that she'd be sure to wake up. "I don't like it here at all. Can't we go back home? I'm too scared to live here with all these snakes."

Tears welled up in my mother's eyes. "You have to be brave, my son. If you're quiet and don't move, the snakes won't bother you. They're more afraid of you than you are of them. . . . I promise you that as soon as the war is over in our homeland, we will go back. But now it's just too dangerous to go there." She hugged me tightly. "Don't worry, my sweet son, we have each other and we have our health. Allah is kind and merciful. We will get through this. These days will pass. . . . You have to go back to sleep now." She held me in her arms as I drifted back into the sweet world of dreams.

In the morning, the sun rose brightly over the mountains. It always seemed less scary in the sunlight. We gathered together our strength and continued on our endless journey.

➔ ➔ ⬅ ⬅

At one point, we drifted to the city of Mardan located in the Northwest Frontier Territories. Like in other cities in Pakistan, there was a special area near the bazaar where laborers would gather, hoping to get hired by rich Pakistanis. I hadn't bothered to look for this type of work before because I was too young. But in Mardan, I decided to try my luck. So at the age of seven, I lined up with grown men, competing with them for work. And because I usually didn't get much of anything to eat, I probably looked closer to five at the time. When large trucks would come to the market in search of laborers, I would try to wrestle for a spot aboard so I could help feed my family.

Sometimes when the employers came looking for laborers, they would stop and look at me for a couple seconds. "What are you doing here little boy?" one man said with a big grin on his face.

"I'm looking for work, uncle," I said. "I'm a strong boy, and I can easily put in a hard day's work. I'm sure I can work as well as any man here."

The Pakistani man chuckled. "But why would I pay you twenty rupees [a little more than one dollar] for the day when for the same price I could get a man twice your size to do all the work I need?" Everyone laughed at me, but for three weeks I refused to surrender my chance of serving as a day laborer.

When I had just about given up hope of ever being employed, one shopkeeper who worked nearby called me over. He must have seen me all these weeks in the bazaar suffering in the harsh world of the adult day-labor market. "So you want to work, huh?" the shopkeeper asked me. "Well, I'll tell you what—I'll hire you. If you go to my house every day and help my wife with her housework, I'll pay you a daily wage of two rupees [about 15 cents]."

I leapt at the chance. It was by far the best the thing that had ever happened to me. Every morning at six o'clock I would show up at the shopkeeper's house and knock on his gate. Then I would help with all the household chores: I cleaned the house, dragged in water from the well down the street, looked after the garden, and even helped around the kitchen. In return, the kind shopkeeper's wife fed me, and I received a steady, though very small, income.

"Why did your family leave Afghanistan?" the shopkeeper's wife asked me one day.

"My father died, our house was destroyed, and my mother couldn't provide food for us," I told her simply. I said it calmly and coldly. Although I was only seven years old, I had been through enough tragedy and suffering for a lifetime. But it didn't occur to me that this was in any way out of the ordinary—it was just the way life was. The kind woman would cry when I'd tell her some of the stories from my life.

My growth had been more or less stunted since the time I had arrived in Pakistan, but with the regular meals I received from this kind family, I began to gain some weight and grow taller.

After a few months of working all day every day at their house, the shopkeeper, whose name was Hafizullah Khan, asked me to assist him at his store after lunch. For the next six months I would clean the house, serve lunch, wash the dishes, and then go off to my second job. Since I was working both in the shop and at the house, Hafizullah Khan began to pay me five rupees per day. This was a small fortune for an eight year old. Between this money and my mother's income from housekeeping, we were able to rent a small room in an area where many Afghan refugees lived. It was a real boost to our spirits to finally move off the streets.

Although I didn't know how to write or, at first, even to count, I managed to learn how to perform work around the shop very well. One day, I think my boss wanted to test my honesty. So he discreetly placed a one-thousand rupee note on the ground and told me that he'd be back in an hour. It was a huge sum of money. It was more than my salary for half a year. I could have run off with it and used the money to help my family in so many different ways. But when I noticed the bill, I quickly and quietly scooped it up and continued my work. I didn't want to even put it in my pocket for fear that it could fall out. So I just held onto it tightly so that I wouldn't misplace it before the shopkeeper returned.

When he came back, I laid the money on the counter and said, "I found this money on the ground after you left. Maybe you dropped it by mistake."

Hafizullah Khan gave me a sly little smile. "Oh, I don't know. It's not my money."

"Well, it's certainly not mine!" I told him.

He must have been satisfied that I had passed his little test. "Well, actually, now that you mention it, maybe that money is mine," he said as he slipped the bill back into his pocket. "Thank you." It's no exaggeration to say that, after this, he treated me like his adopted son.

Over the course of a couple of years, Hafizullah Khan set up a few other shops around the city, and he turned over the first shop to me to run. He began to show up just a few times a week to make sure that everything was all right, but otherwise left me to take care of the store by myself. During the summertime especially the shop did very good business. My drinks were the biggest hit. I sold ice-cold soft drinks by the glass and by the bottle to passersby. Hafizullah Khan was very pleased with my work, and he paid me fives times the going rate for the adult laborers who camped out only half a block away. Over the course of the eight years I worked in the shop, he steadily raised my wages.

By the time I reached the age of eleven, I was earning a monthly salary of 2,000 rupees [$32]. One day after the end of Ramadan, we were celebrating Eid at our house. I had been able to purchase nice clothes for my mother, my sister, and myself. We had spread out the tablecloth on the floor of our house, filled it with food, and awaited the flood of guests that were certain to arrive. As my sister rushed here and there making sure that the food on our *dastarkhan** was beautifully arranged, I pulled her aside.

I took a large wad of bills from my pocket and placed it in front of my sister. "Malaliy," I said proudly, "I've been saving up this Eid money for you. I've noticed how you often go to our neighbor's house to help her sew clothes. I think that you'd be a very successful tailor—if you have the right training and a good sewing machine. I've noticed that the best sewing machines are the ones with a butterfly on them, and that's what this money is for—to help you become a tailor."

Malaliy had probably never seen such a large sum of money in one place before. Her eyes filled with excitement, and she gave me a big smile. "Thank you very much for this, Gulbuddin, but I can't take this kind of money from you. You worked very hard for it, and I don't want you to waste it on me."

After a long discussion, we agreed that I'd buy her the butterfly

---

* A tablecloth usually laid on the floor where food is served.

sewing machine, and she'd sign up for a tailoring course from a well-known tailor.

Malaliy quickly became a very good tailor. By the time she was fourteen, she herself was earning about 1,000 rupees a month as a tailor. In the process, she had also caught the eye of several clients who were thinking about marrying off their sons.

By this time, she had grown into a beautiful, tall girl with bright blue eyes. She had much lighter skin than most Pakistani or even Afghan women, so it was no surprise that she was approached by many suitors. My mother was flattered by all this attention but also was worried about her only daughter leaving home. "Who will help me around the house if she gets married? Who will help me prepare bread and food for us?" she asked me.

Then one day, she came up with a little scheme. "Gulbuddin jaan, why don't you get engaged at the same time as your sister? That way, I'll still have someone to help me with the housework." I always obeyed my mother and treated her with respect, but I was taken aback. "Are you serious, Mama? Don't you think that I'm too young to get married? It's one thing for girls who are my age to get married, but I've never heard of boys getting married at the age of twelve."

"I know it seems a little strange to you," she said with a reassuring smile spreading across her face. "But you have to understand my position. You're away in the shop all day, and if your sister gets married, I will be all alone. Is that really what you want for me? I promise that we'll find you a beautiful young girl about your age who you will be very happy to take as a bride. It will be a great honor for me to dance at your wedding party!"

I still wasn't sure what to think.

"Gulbuddin," my mother said, now very seriously. "You have had to grow up much faster than most boys. And I've always been very grateful that you've provided for me and your sister from such a young age. So I'm asking you, as the man of the house, to please do this for me."

I thought about it for a couple of minutes. It could be interesting to have a wife and live like a grown-up, I thought. So I finally gave in. "As you wish, Mother."

We agreed that the best solution was for us to find another brother and sister about our age. In this way, neither of our families would have to worry about paying a dowry, and my mother would have a ready-made assistant. This kind of marriage exchange is common among Afghans who have trouble coming up with the steep bride prices.

That is how—at the ripe old age of twelve—I became engaged. My future wife and brother-in-law lived in a run-down shack a few houses down the road from us. They were also refugees from a village near our own back in Kunduz province. Our neighbors all laughed when they heard about our plans. My brother-in-law was eighteen, but I was merely a little boy in their eyes. "How can such a young boy get married? How are you going to raise the money for a wedding party? And how can you possibly perform on your wedding night?" I became the butt of many jokes.

But we tried to ignore their mockery. We invited Hafizullah to the engagement party, and he overheard some of the gossip and jokes circulating among our neighbors and friends. The next day, when I went back to work, he pulled me aside. "You shouldn't be concerned about your wedding expenses. I told you many years ago that you are like my son. And I, like your father, will take responsibility for your wedding and pay for it myself," he told me with a kind smile. He followed through on his promise and paid for a nice wedding, which impressed my wife's family and all of our friends and neighbors.

After the wedding, my good fortune continued. One of my customers at the shop, who had grown to become a friend, was a banker who worked down the street. Sometimes he would drink a Pepsi during his lunch break, and I would refuse to accept money from him. But on other occasions, he would shove a big bill into my pocket and run off before I could say anything. One day, he suggested that he could help me open my very own account in his bank. "My guess is that you could probably get by on about half your salary," he advised me. "So why don't you put the other half in our bank and that way you'll know that it'll be safe? We charge only a small fee for the service of keeping your money."

What he said made sense. So after that, I began to make monthly deposits into my bank account. By the age of fourteen, my savings accounts had grown to nearly $1,000! I took this money and bought a small house for my wife, my mother, and I. One year later, our family got bigger when my son Qudratullah was born.

My life was working out better than I could have possibly dreamed. I could meet all of our family's needs without worrying about what the next day would bring. I was able to buy good food and handsome clothing for my whole family. And I had a beautiful wife who cooked very well.

→ → ← ←

We lived in Pakistan three more years after I got married. During this time, I was able to save up even more money in my bank account. But then I decided that it was time for us to return home to our native village in Afghanistan. The Russians had left our country a few years before, and many Afghan refugees in our area had already left for their homeland. With the profits from selling our house and from my savings, I thought we could build a successful, peaceful life there.

So, along with many other returning Afghan refugees, we loaded up all our possessions into a hired truck and headed home. I'll never forget the farewell we shared with Hafizullah Khan and his wife. They had been so kind to us for so many years. I hugged Hafizullah and cried on his shoulder like a little child. I felt as if I were saying good-bye to my own natural father. Many years later, while I was serving the Taliban back home, Hafizullah actually came to visit us. When he arrived in our village, I invited all our neighbors, and we prepared a great party in his honor.

When we returned to my native village of Qarai Yatim, we saw that it had been almost completely destroyed. There was hardly a single house standing. Almost all of the trees had been chopped down, and there weren't even any birds flying around. The truck stopped in front of the muddy shell of our old house. As far as the eye could see, there was only one tree still standing. And it happened to be located just opposite our destroyed house. We unloaded all of our possessions under the tree's shade and just stared at one another. The sun was unbearably hot, so we settled in under the tree. The only problem was that as the sun kept moving throughout the day, the shady spots would also move. So for nearly three months, we spent our waking hours circling the tree, chasing the shade.

But this was a lawless time in the Chahardara district, as well as in much of the rest of Afghanistan. The defeat of the Soviets did not by any means put an end to the trouble. As we rebuilt our house, we spent our nights in a homemade tent that we had built by sewing different colored fabrics to one another and then fastening it to the ground with a few sticks. One dark, cloudy night, five thieves snuck up on us as we lay sleeping in our tent. As one man began to strangle me from above, another thief accidentally stepped on my son's foot, and he cried out. My wife was jolted awake, and the first thing she saw was a man trying to strangle me. Without thinking she grabbed his leg and tried to pull him off of me.

This was just the distraction I needed to defend my family. At that time, everyone in Afghanistan had their own weapons. Even though I was a simple man who had never fought in a war, I had a Makarov pistol, which I kept under my pillow. I quickly grabbed the gun and shot him right through the heart. Then I turned around and shot at the shadows of his friends who had started to run away from the tent. I managed to hit one of them in the arm.

I took the dead man's Kalashnikov and sat on guard in front of the tent all night. In the morning, we saw that the man I'd killed was probably just a few years older than me. A couple of hours after dawn, a few of the dead man's relatives came to the tent to collect the corpse.

"My brother," one of the cousins said as he greeted me, "I understand that there was an accident here last night."

I was furious. "Yes, the so-called accident is that I'm still alive and your cousin isn't. I'm going to throw his corpse to the dogs so that everyone will know what happens to people who mess with me."

The man knew that I was upset but continued speaking calmly. "Listen, my brother, we are Muslims. This man is dead and will never come back to life. If you knew more about his family, I think you would have a little more sympathy. This poor guy lost both of his parents when he was still in the cradle. He had a wife and two young children, and they recently returned from Pakistan. Like many of us, they are nearly starving to death, and his wife is now very ill with malaria. She may die soon. Please let me take his body so that she can at least see her husband one last time before she too enters the next world."

I still didn't want to hand over the body. I was angry beyond reason. But my mother spoke up. "You know, my dear, if it were not for the

blessings of Allah, you could have easily been faced with the same difficulties as this poor man. He probably would never have done this if he
didn't need to feed his family."

My mother as usual had managed to keep her head even under the
most difficult circumstances. In the end, I gave the man the dead body.

From then on, I invited my sister and her family to join us. And my
brother-in-law and I took turns at night guarding our family's tent.

With the money that I had earned over the course of many years in
Pakistan, I managed to pay for all the materials to rebuild our ruined
house. But I wanted it to be much larger than it had ever been in the past.
So I hired laborers to construct a five-room house. It was much bigger than
almost any of the other villagers or returning refugees could afford. I also
managed to purchase a few acres of land on which I planted some wheat
and rice.

Over the next few years, battles between mujahedin commanders raged
all around us. On two or three different occasions, when the fighting
grew too fierce, we were forced to abandon our house and flee to neighboring villages. Luckily, our house was unharmed in these battles. But we
did lose many of our possessions as soldiers would loot the areas they captured. The Uzbek commander General Abdul Rashid Dostum and his
troops were the worst criminals.

When they weren't stealing outright, the mujahedin commanders
would demand high taxes on all that we made from agriculture or anything else. They set up dozens of checkpoints on all the roads, especially along the path to the bazaar. When I would go to the market to
sell my rice or wheat, I would be lucky if I arrived with half of my harvest. When I would settle on a bribe at one checkpoint, they would
then radio their friends up at the next roadblock to tell them how much
they'd managed to squeeze out of me. Then the men at the next stop
would say, for example, "You gave the other guys four sacks of wheat,
so you need to give us four sacks, too!" Anyone who resisted was executed on the spot.

Many people became so fed up with the problems that the mujahedin
had created for us that they began to look back nostalgically at the period
of Soviet occupation. One of the village leaders once told me during this
time, "More and more, I wonder why we worked so hard to get the

Russians out of our country. Is this the freedom that we were fighting for? When the Soviets would carry out abuses, there were resistance fighters we could appeal to. But when it's Afghans who carry out these abuses against other Afghans, who can possibly come to our defense?"

For this reason, many of us Pashtuns in particular were very happy when the Taliban forces captured Kunduz province in 1997. I know that the rest of the world thought of the Taliban as a cruel, backward group of thugs. But at that time, we were hearing glowing reports about how they had successfully brought peace and security to the southern parts of Afghanistan. We had been told that they believed passionately in Islam, and we thought that they would help cleanse our area of infidels. Plus the Taliban seemed to represent a way for us Pashtuns to end the discrimination that we had suffered under the ethnic Uzbek and Tajik mujahedin commanders.

That's why our village met the Taliban forces with open arms. I was part of the group of men who received the Taliban, and I was overjoyed to meet one of my old friends who had been with me as a refugee in Pakistan. "Gulbuddin, is that you?" he asked when he saw me. It was my friend, Abdul Qadir, who had been studying in a madrassa for many years. At one point while I was living in Pakistan, I had wanted to join him in the madrassa, where students were provided with food and clothing, but I couldn't because I had to support my family.

"I recognized the name of your village. I was hoping that I'd run into you here!" he told me as he hugged me. "But with all the displacement here in Afghanistan, I honestly thought that I'd never see you again." I invited him and a couple of his friends to join me for dinner. The next day he introduced me to his commanders, which included a couple men from Pakistan. I spoke to them in fluent Urdu and told them how much I admired their movement and their devotion to Allah. They were so impressed with me and my experience in Pakistan that they invited me to join their ranks.

My job was to travel across my district and force people to obey the Taliban laws. I would put on a white headband like my colleagues and go from village to village enforcing what I believed to be the Sharia laws enshrined in the Koran. After the Taliban arrived in Kunduz, lawlessness became much less of a problem. We made an example of some thieves by cutting off their hands in public, and after that, few people had to worry about crime. Whenever we would carry out our strict penalties like stoning women for adultery or cutting off limbs, we would first announce our plans on the loudspeakers so that everyone from miles around could come and witness the punishments.

Thanks to the Taliban policies, a much higher standard of discipline was established. When there was a call for prayer, shopkeepers wouldn't even bother to lock up their stores before they left for the mosque. They would just place a chair in front of the door to indicate that they weren't inside and walk away with full confidence that nothing would be disturbed.

Probably my most important task was to make sure that all men took part in their required prayers five times a day. If I saw a man on the street during prayer time, I would order him to the mosque. If I caught anyone violating the prayer rules more than once, I would be sure to give him several whacks on the back with my stick. I'd also ensure that men's beards were kept at the length of at least one clenched fist and that hair was cut short. When I would see men with long hair, I'd take out a pair of scissors from my pocket and cut their hair short on one side of their head so that they'd be forced to go to the barber to have them even up the job. I think that the barbers in our area were the biggest Taliban supporters because we always provided them with steady work.

We also enforced other Taliban edicts: women were required to wear burqas and could only go out on the street with a male relative; no one could listen to music or watch television; no one could possess photographs or have drawings of living things. We would receive tips from local people about who was violating these rules and carry out raids. For example, drivers would sometimes try to hide music cassettes up their sleeves. When we would discover the tapes, we would destroy them by stomping them into the ground. Those who couldn't afford to pay fines for their violations were usually punished with beatings on the palms of their hands.

Also, my colleagues and I rounded up weapons from the local people and fiercely punished those who failed to cooperate with our policies. We knew that almost everyone had kept the weapons that the mujahedin had distributed to the people and were trying to hide them from us. So we spent much of our time rounding up the firearms that helped us in our fight against the Northern Alliance. The worst violators of our weapons collection program were sometimes struck with metal cables.

For the first several months of my service to the Taliban, I was a true believer. Although some of the Taliban prohibitions struck me as a little excessive, I believed that we were enforcing Allah's word on earth.

But in the autumn of 1997, I had an experience that completely shook my belief in the Taliban system. Throughout that year, there had been vicious fighting around Mazar-i-Sharif between Taliban forces and those loyal to Generals Dostum and Malik Pahlawan. The city and the surrounding areas had been taken and retaken many times, and thousands of Taliban lost their lives in these battles. After a humiliating and bloody defeat at the hands of Hazaras and Uzbeks in Mazar earlier in the year, many Taliban were thirsty for revenge.

I think it was October 1997 when a Taliban offensive into Mazar had been turned back again. My friends told me later that while some divisions were getting ready to retreat, others went from house to house, taking whatever men they could find from their homes. Hundreds of blindfolded men were stuffed like animals into trucks with their hands tied behind their backs and taken on the ten-hour trip from Mazar to Kunduz. The trucks, filled with men ranging in age from teenagers to old men, were taken up the high hill where the Kunduz airport is situated. When those trucks were brought to the airport, I was taking part in some training operations there. The Taliban commanders ordered us to help deal with the prisoners once they arrived.

I was ordered to unload one of the trucks and escort the prisoners in a line toward a large field by the runway. As I was overseeing this process, I noticed a boy who couldn't have been more than twelve years old lying on the ground near the truck's giant tire, crying like a little baby. His whole body, including his face, was covered in mud as he squirmed on the ground. There had been a recent rainfall and there was thick mud everywhere.

I knew that I should have grabbed the boy and forced him back into line with the rest of the prisoners, but for some reason I felt sorry for him.

I slogged through the mud over to him and asked, "What's your name?"

"Abdul Jalil," he whimpered.

"Where are you from?"

"I'm from Tash Korghan [a town outside of Mazar-i-Sharif]," he said. "I have two younger sisters and a mother back at home. My father died when I was very young, and I'm the only man in my house. If I die, there'll be no one left to provide for them. . . . They have no one else."

I couldn't help but feel an instant connection with this boy. I was struck by the similarities between his story and my own. What, after all, would have happened to my family in Pakistan if something had happened to me? Deeply moved, I decided to take a big risk.

I noticed that the truck driver had been watching us as we spoke. So I went up to him and said, "I'm going to try to hide this boy. Look at him—he's just a child, and he doesn't have a father. . . . Please don't give me away to Maulavi Habibullah." He was the commander who was overseeing that day's operations.

But the driver was afraid. "Have you gone mad? If Maulavi Habibullah hears about this, he will have both of us beaten and killed!"

Nevertheless, I had made up my mind to save poor defenseless Jalil. Because of the angle at which the truck was parked, nobody else was able to see us. "If you just let him jump inside the cabin of your truck and throw some blankets over him, I'm sure that nobody will find him."

The driver didn't look convinced, so I slid a wad of bills into his pocket and said, "Let's do it. Quickly!" We threw the boy into the back of the truck's cabin, covered him with a couple of small carpets and blankets, and told him to lie perfectly still and quiet.

I then ran back to the other end of the truck and completed my work. I stood by as the rest of the prisoners, about 240 men, were all lined up in a field. Ten at a time, they were led forward with their blindfolds on and shot in the head by the Taliban soldiers. In order to save bullets and minimize the chances of missing their targets, the executioners stood within one yard of their victims, so close that they themselves were soon covered in blood. Their long scraggly beards became red and sticky. I even saw a few who were splattered with the brains of the men they had just shot.

At one point during the executions, a middle-aged Hazara man tried to escape and ran off across the field. The Taliban soldiers started laughing. We were in the middle of a vast field with no place to hide, except perhaps behind some bombed-out old Soviet tanks along the runway. "Where are you running, you stupid man? You think the infidels are going to send in parachutists to save you or something?" they called out, their voices dripping with irony.

After letting the still-blindfolded man run around in circles for a minute or two, a few men got into a pick-up truck and took off after him. When he heard the truck roaring behind him, the man let out a scream, had a heart attack, and died. When the soldiers brought back the man's body, they were joking about how he had helped save them a bullet, which would be reserved to kill General Dostum.

After all the men had been massacred, they ordered the truck drivers to drive their heavy vehicles over the corpses. After many trips over the bodies, they had been pushed down until they were even with the surface of the earth. Jalil was riding in one of the trucks as it ground into the earth the bodies of the men with whom he had been traveling only an hour before. Later, I heard from some of my friends who had returned to the airport a few days after the killings that the bodies of the dead men had all been devoured by wild dogs and vultures. The dogs had become mad because of all the human flesh they had consumed. The next time I was at the airport, there was no sign of the mass murder I had witnessed— somebody must have buried whatever was left of the victims.

It was already dark when we were ready to leave. When I went to the truck to check on Jalil, he let out a muted scream when he saw me. He thought that he'd been discovered. But I quickly reassured him. "Don't worry. It's me." The truck driver gave me a ride, and I asked him to drop me and Jalil off at my house. The boy was shaking from head to toe. He didn't say a word as I led him into our house. I shaved his head and heated up some water so that he could bathe, as my wife prepared some rice pilaf. I gave him clean clothes when he came out of the bath. He stayed quiet the whole evening, until it came time for him to go to bed. I think he was still in shock.

As I was saying good night to Jalil, he whispered to me: "You know, it all happened so quickly. The soldiers came for me in the middle of the night. After they broke down the door, they started kicking my mother. She fell on the ground as they kept on kicking her. I tried to run over the side wall to escape, but they grabbed me as I was scrambling over it. My sisters and mother were shrieking as they dragged me away. . . . A lot of my other neighbors were also beaten up. . . ." Then he paused and looked up at me with his eyes full of tears. "I had no idea that there were actually good Taliban."

I couldn't sleep all night. I couldn't understand why one Muslim would kill another innocent Muslim. I had never had any formal religious training—I had never spent a day of my life in a school or in a madrassa. Perhaps there was some sort of Islamic justification for these killings, I thought, but as a human being, I couldn't understand it.

Early the next morning, after my dawn prayers, I took Jalil to Kunduz city where I found a taxi that was about to leave for Mazar. I ordered one of the passengers to get out of the car to make space for the boy and asked the driver to drop him off along the road in Tash Korghan. The boy told me his address, and without another word, he headed home.

About a year later, Mazar fell once again to the Taliban. When I heard the news, I remembered Jalil, and I thought, "Why don't I go visit him and see how he's doing?" When I found his house, I knocked on the door, and a middle-aged, wrinkled Uzbek woman answered. She immediately slammed the gate shut when she saw me and how I was dressed.

From the other side of the gate, I mentioned Abdul Jalil's name and briefly told her how we had met. When she reopened the door, she was in tears. She started hugging me and kissing me on the cheeks. It must have been quite a sight for the neighbors—a lanky Taliban official being hugged and kissed by a stocky Uzbek woman!

When she finally regained her senses, she said, "Please, please come inside." I was shocked when I saw Jalil's house. They had a beautiful house made from fired bricks, rather than the mud bricks you find almost everywhere else, and they even had two cars inside their compound!

As a sign of the closeness Jalil's mother felt for me, she didn't ask me to sit in the guest room reserved for unfamiliar male guests, which is found in most Afghan compounds. Rather, she invited me inside her house, where she and her daughters had been sewing some clothes. As I sat down on the mattress, Jalil's mother heaped praise on me. "May Allah grant you a long life and success in everything you do. May thorn bushes never stick to your feet. May Allah always protect you . . ."

"You've given my son a second life," she said. "And I will forever be indebted to you for making such a sacrifice. Please look around my house. You are like my son now, and everything that I have is yours. The cars, the house, and even my daughters, they are yours. Please choose one of my daughters to marry—or marry them both if you'd like. You must stay here with us and never leave. You will be my second son!"

For several hours, I sat and talked with Jalil's family. Eventually, Jalil entered, and I don't think he could believe his eyes. He ran over and hugged me. Then he said to his mother, "Mama, this is the man I owe my life to. I love him more than I could love my own brother." I had planned to leave before nightfall, but my hosts wouldn't hear of it. They slaughtered a sheep for me and invited their relatives and neighbors to take part in a party in my honor. It was probably the only party for a Taliban official ever in that Uzbek village. The next morning when I left, they gave me a watch, a new *shalwar kameez*, a turban, and a vest.

✦   ✦   ✦   ✦

After the incident at the airport, I became more and more disillusioned with the Taliban. I had always thought of them as a group of people who represented true Islam, but I came to the conclusion that Allah would never approve such senseless murder on such a large scale.

During the Taliban rule, conditions for people who lived in my district declined dramatically. Their seizure of Kunduz in 1997 coincided with the beginning of a widespread drought. Life became very difficult for many people. As a result, many of our neighbors packed up their belongings yet again and headed to Pakistan, Iran, and safer parts of Afghanistan.

But I was sick and tired of moving around. We had spent so much of our resources rebuilding our house and buying land that I hated the idea of leaving it all behind. Besides, as a Taliban official, I had a prestigious position, and I could collect a good salary, especially as a result of the fines we imposed. Although I wasn't enthusiastic about all parts of my job, it did make it possible for me to stay in Afghanistan, defend my family, and provide for their well-being.

Since I was no longer a fervent believer, my enforcement of Taliban rules became much more relaxed. During this time, there was one very funny thing that happened when I was checking to make sure that men were keeping their hair short and beards long. I met a man on the road whose hair was very long, so I grabbed him and asked, "Why is your hair so long?" He began babbling some sort of excuse, but I wasn't interested. I removed his turban, took out a pair of scissors, and began cutting his long flowing hair.

The man became very upset that I had cut enough of his "beautiful" hair that he would be forced to go directly to the barber. But I was caught completely off guard when the man produced a pair of scissors from his own pocket and began to cut his long beard. "Why are you cutting your beard?" I asked.

"The hair was mine and you cut it," the man responded. "The beard was yours, so I cut it. I thought it was very fashionable to have long hair with a long beard. Without my hair, the beard has lost all of its effect." I knew that I should have beaten him soundly for such disobedience, but I thought it was so funny that I let him go after a couple of obligatory lashes across his hands.

But this was not just a time of funny stories. My frustration with the Taliban grew when some of my colleagues arrested my wife's uncle for some minor offense. He was an old man, with a long gray beard. But like many others who were arrested at that time, he was strapped to a tree and beaten with a metal cable. When I happened upon this all-too-common scene, my wife's uncle was bleeding heavily and begging for mercy.

I went immediately to my superior and begged him to have pity on the old man. "Please, that man outside is a relative of mine. He's a good man. And he's old and sick. Please go easy on him." I was frightened that the poor man would die right there, tied to the tree like a common criminal.

But my new boss wouldn't listen to me. "A violation of Sharia law has been committed, and the perpetrator has to be punished!" I was told. Our new commander was from Kandahar, and he wasn't interested in knowing who was related to whom or what kind of community leader was being punished. As I saw more and more clearly over time, to this Kanadahari and to many other Taliban, the world was divided into black and white with no shades of gray. I went out and hunted down two Kalashnikovs to offer the Taliban in exchange for the freedom of my wife's uncle. To this day, the poor old man still can't walk normally as a result of the sadistic abuse he suffered.

During the Taliban rule, increasing numbers of people suffered from poor harvests and cruel punishments. I grew convinced that Allah was on the side of the Americans and the Northern Alliance. For this reason, shortly before the Taliban were expelled from northern Afghanistan, I defected to the other side.

Even though I was once a Taliban, I think that very few people here in our village hold any grudges against me. They know very well that I was neither cruel nor abusive. If anything, I was always trying to defend them against the Taliban's cruelty, but I was generally unsuccessful because of my low rank. Besides, everyone understands that in order to have survived here over the past twenty-five years, it's been necessary at times to do things that we can't be proud of. That's just a fact of life in Afghanistan.

Niyaz Turdi, Son of Rahmanullah Turdi

I was nineteen years old in 1980 when my father decided that it was time for me to get married. My female relatives assured me that my bride, Amina, was a beautiful young girl. She was from the neighboring village of Chargul Teppa and had already learned the basics of carpet weaving from her mother. Thanks to her skills, she fetched a fairly high bride price. My father had saved up funds for several years from our harvest and carpet sales to afford her. He told me that she was like an investment for the future. "Right now, she doesn't have a great deal of skill in weaving, but if she practices with your mother for a few years, she'll be able to bring in a lot of cash for you later on."

The day before my wedding, dozens of my relatives and neighbors had gathered in our village for the celebration. Our small house was abuzz with activity. The women busily cleaned the house, baked more bread than I'd ever seen before, and cleaned a mountain of rice for the pilaf. My mother and three sisters were also putting the finishing touches on some gifts for Amina's family; they had woven a couple of carpets and sewn beautiful dresses for her and her sisters, which they placed inside ornate metal trunks. Some of the men went to the market to buy all kinds of things for the next day, while a few others rounded up the sheep they were planning to slaughter for the hundreds of guests. I relaxed in the guest room and drank tea with the other men.

That night I thought about what lay in store for the next day. Among us Turkmen, there's a tradition whereby the new bride will be brought straight from her own kitchen to the groom's house by her relatives on horseback. She's not supposed to be wearing any special wedding clothes on this day, just some outfit that she might wear around the house. This symbolizes that the bride is more concerned with hard work and serving her groom's family than in indulging in frivolous things.

As I drifted off to sleep, lots of sweet questions swirled in my head: What will I say to Amina when I first see her? What will she look like? Is she as beautiful as my relatives promise? But my dreams were anything but sweet. As dawn approached, I had a terrible nightmare that Soviet helicopters were circling above our village, laying waste to everything in their path. My fellow villagers were screaming and begging me to run for cover . . .

The dream blended quickly into reality. The next thing I knew I was thrown several feet into the air when a Soviet missile struck the mosque next door. I immediately scrambled to my feet and stumbled out into our courtyard. It had just become light outside. And just as I exited the house, a missile landed right next to our kitchen. The bomb didn't cause much damage, but it burrowed so deeply that water from an underground source was sent spouting into the air.

I looked up and saw that there were three or four helicopters circling above our village. Another bomb struck right behind our house, and a few seconds later a third bomb landed on a house a couple of doors away. There was total chaos as my relatives all ran in different directions. Most of them ran out of the house on to the street, shrieking with terror. But I just stood in place watching the helicopters above. Why would it be any safer out on the street or in another house? I thought. Bombs are exploding all over our village. There had been a few raids on our village over the course of the past year but nothing approaching the ferocity of this attack. Why today? I asked myself. Why on my wedding day? Then it occurred to me that some of the guests at the wedding party were actually mujahedin insurgents. So maybe this isn't a coincidence after all, I thought.

As these disconnected ideas were spinning around in my head, a helicopter swooped down maybe one hundred yards away from our house and hung in the air, as though the pilot was sizing up the wisdom of an attack. Instinctively, I ran back inside the house to hide. It turned out that I was suddenly all alone in one section of the house. Most of our guests had fled, but I knew that some of my family members were probably huddled in a room directly across the courtyard from me. I had often hidden in that room with my family during past bombing raids.

As I dashed into the empty room, I looked out the window, whose glass had been shattered, to see whether the helicopter had finally moved on. But just at that moment, it fired a missile directly at the room where my family was gathered. I was blinded by the light of the explosion. The thing that I remember most vividly was how our strong, wooden roof beams had splintered into tiny pieces. Then I heard the screams from all the people who had sought shelter in that room. Even with the helicopter still circling above, I rushed across our courtyard to see if I could do anything to help the survivors.

The force of the bomb was so great that there was very little left of the room. At first, I couldn't even see my relatives—there was thick dust everywhere. I had to shut my eyes to shield them from the debris in the air. The only way I was able to find my way to the victims was by listening for their cries. "Please, somebody help me!" I heard one of my sisters wailing. When I finally groped my way across the room, I found her with a large gash on her head and a badly injured shoulder. As almost all of the people in the room, she was nearly naked as her clothes had been shredded by the explosion. Then I heard another relative crying for assistance.

It wasn't until the dust settled that I could assess the damage. One of my sisters had somehow completely escaped injury, but the remaining eight people in the room, including my parents, were badly wounded and drenched in blood. A couple of my family members had serious injuries on their legs and feet, while others had large chunks of skin torn away. Almost all them had pieces of the smashed timber roof beams lodged in their bodies. My one and only brother, who was five years younger than I, was the only fatality.

Our possessions were strewn in every direction, and a couple of the metal trunks, which were intended for Amina's family, had been thrown

clear over our house's surrounding wall. I had to run around the house collecting clothing so that my female relatives could cover themselves.

The bombs exploded around our village for another half hour or so. But
it felt like an eternity. When the helicopters finally left us in peace, we took
all of our wounded family members to a neighbor who was a doctor.
When we arrived, a large number of wounded people—including women
and children—were already lying in his courtyard awaiting treatment.
The range of injuries was shocking: some had lost arms and legs, others
had serious head injuries, and still others had pieces of shrapnel buried in
their bodies. The fortunate ones only had light injuries on their hands and
feet. There were, in fact, so many injured people from our village that
young men were sent out to neighboring villages to summon their doctors for assistance. To this day, there are many people in my native village
who still bear the scars from that malicious attack: they walk with limps,
are missing limbs, or have big scars on their bodies. In total, sixteen people from our village, including my brother, lost their lives on that awful
morning.

When my mother saw how many severely injured people were in need
of urgent attention, she turned around and started walking out of the doctor's courtyard. "I just have a small cut on my side," she said to me as we
looked at the horrible scene before us. "Why should I waste the doctor's precious time when he has so many other pressing cases?" As a child, my
mother had survived a couple of bouts of serious illness without much
complaint. My Tajik grandfather nicknamed her Sangina, which means
"made of stone." Her friends used to joke that this was a disservice as Allah
had actually endowed her with the strength of steel. I urged my mother to
stay and have the doctor examine her wound, but she insisted on returning home and mourning her lost son. "Your brother's spirit is still in our
house, and I need to be with him," she told me.

As I sat on the ground of the courtyard trying to comfort my injured
relatives, the tragedy of the events of that morning really struck me.
When I had gone to sleep only a few hours previously, I had been in a
house bursting with merriment and joy. But now, it had been trans-
formed into a place of grief and mourning. My family and Amina's family, after consulting the local mullah, agreed that we would delay the
wedding party indefinitely, and we would just be considered married.

According to our traditions, it's disrespectful to celebrate a wedding party in the year following the death of a close family member. In the two or three weeks after my brother's burial, it hardly even occurred to me that I was in fact a newlywed.

As for my mother, she was completely absorbed in the mourning ceremonies for her youngest son. She didn't mention the pain in her side to a single person until one night she started screaming in agony. In all my life, I'd never heard my mother cry in pain. We had no choice but to to wake the exhausted doctor so that he could examine her. After a quick examination, he told me that we would need to take her to the Spinzar hospital in Kunduz city so that she could get an x-ray. "There appears to be some metal stuck in her body, but I can't make a better diagnosis than that," he told me. "She'll definitely need better treatment than I could possibly offer."

First thing in the morning, my mother, my sister, one of my cousins, and I caught a taxi into the city, about an hour away. My mother was suffering terribly, but she tried her best not to show it. When we arrived at the hospital, the corridors were flooded with injured people and their relatives. The crying and moaning were nearly overwhelming. After a few hours of examining my mother, the doctors emerged looking dejected. "Your mother has suffered a serious injury," one doctor told me. "A small piece of shrapnel is lodged in her large intestine. We can try to operate, but the surgery is very risky, and we can't guarantee that she'll survive. Everything is in the hands of Allah." We decided to go ahead with the surgery, and a few days later my mother died.

✦　✦　✦　✦

Over the next couple of years, conditions in my village became worse and worse as the fighting continued. After the attack on our house, my father grew too ill to work in the fields. Without the combined income from my mother's carpet weaving and my father's labor, we fell on very difficult times. My father agreed to marry off my last remaining unmarried sister as a fourth wife to an old man in our village at a very low price. Ever since the attack, she'd walked with a limp so he was grateful to get even a small sum of money for her.

During these difficult times, the only bright spot in my life was that my wife gave birth to two beautiful twin boys, Adil and Kamil, the year after we were married. These boys became my pride and joy. Sometimes, when they were sleeping, I'd admire their tiny bodies breathing softly in and out. "They have such innocent eyes," I remember whispering one day to Amina. "I hope that as they grow up, they'll live in a world full of peace and prosperity." But my simple wish for my children proved to be impossible to fulfill.

The next several months became harder and harder. When my boys were only a year and a half old, my father died, and I could no longer come up with enough money to feed my family. Our irrigation canals had been destroyed during the fighting, and our once lush fields had become practically worthless.

One day in 1983 I told Amina, "I've decided that we have to leave our village. I've heard that other parts of Afghanistan are much safer. And I'm sure that I can find work on a farm somewhere or other." So the next day, my family and I set out on a couple of donkeys in the direction of Kunduz city.

I wanted to find an area rich in agriculture, so we passed through Kunduz city until we reached Chahardara district. Eventually, here in the village of Qarai Karakhani, my wife came across an elderly woman, Bibi Hojara, who felt sorry for her and our small children and invited us to live under a large tree in her courtyard. Bibi Hojara managed to eke out her existence by baking bread for other families throughout the village who repaid her with flour and other basic supplies. We set up a big tent in her yard, which became our home for the next several years. We were very fortunate because Bibi Hojara would never hesitate to pass along pieces of bread to my children during the times when I wasn't able to raise money to support them. Also, during the coldest winter months, she'd allow us to stay in a tiny room in her house. The room was so cramped, we could barely all lie down at the same time, but at least it was warmer than sleeping outside.

When we first moved to Chahardara, I could usually find work as a day laborer in the fields. As the war intensified, the number of displaced people settling in Chahardara increased, driving down the daily wage. But since I was close to many of my neighbors, I thankfully rarely had trouble finding work. That's how I was able to continue feeding my family. However, "luxuries," such as adequate clothing, were unfortunately well beyond my means. For most of the ten or so years that we spent in exile, my family was dressed in little more than rags, and my children looked like beggars.

Although there were decent economic opportunities in Chahardara, it was by no means a peaceful place. There were periodic bombings, and fighting gripped the district throughout the Soviet occupation. But perhaps the fiercest fighting took place a few months after we had settled into our new lodgings. At one point, the famous mujahedin commander Ahmad Shah Mas'ud's forces were hiding out in the nearby village of Qarai Qeshlaq, and then firing from a ridge on the Soviet troops passing below. As soon as the mujahedin rebels completed their operations, they would quickly blend back into the local population.

One afternoon, about twenty tanks and hundreds of Soviet and Afghan troops swept through our village on their way to Qarai Qeshlaq. Then a couple dozen Soviet helicopters passed over us and started carpet bombing Qarai Qeshlaq. For about an hour, the ground shook as if we were at the heart of an earthquake, even though we were a couple of miles away from the village under attack. The Soviets had much better equipment and arsenals than the mujahedin, who could only carry out their guerilla attacks under the cover of darkness. As a mujahedin friend of mine once told me, "The day belongs to the infidels, but the nights belong to us."

Once it finally began to get dark, we saw the Soviet troops and tanks retreat from Qarai Qeshlaq. We waited another hour or so to make sure that they wouldn't return. Then a group of men from our village decided to venture up the road to find out how we might be able to assist the wounded. But shortly after we'd arrived in Qarai Qeshlaq, we realized that our search and rescue mission would be a short one.

I can't begin to describe the complete and utter destruction we witnessed. It was the silence that struck me first—this was a time in the evening when the men are usually on their way home from the mosque, and their voices fill the air. There was not a single house or even a tree still standing. When we entered people's courtyards and barns, there were animal carcasses lying everywhere. And inside the homes, there was noth-

ing but dead bodies lying in pools of blood amid their scattered possessions.

Our small band was joined by a couple of dozen men from other
nearby settlements. We spread out across the village walking from house
to house with small kerosene lamps looking for survivors. At one point,
my friend and I walked into a house where three women were sitting in
their burqas with their legs covered by blankets. If these women were in
fact alive, we didn't want to compromise their modesty by barging in on
them. So we went back outside and called an older man from our village
to investigate. It turned out that they had been shot, and their dead bodies were left leaning up against the walls.

After discussing what we should do, we decided to dig several long
shallow trenches in the ground at the edge of the village to serve as mass
graves. Then we began to carry the victims one by one across the village
to the mass grave. Within a few minutes, I was completely covered in
blood. It took us the whole night to gather the corpses together in their
final resting place.

But as the first light of dawn shone, a miracle occurred. One of the men
from our village appeared holding the hand of the lone survivor from
Qarai Qeshlaq—a young boy who had been using the bathroom when
the Soviets launched their attack. He had jumped down into the pit,
which was half filled with excrement, thus avoiding detection. The child
was still in shock. He didn't say a word to any of us. He only nodded or
shook his head to answer our questions.

The boy was the only lucky one. Every other living thing in Qarai
Qeshlaq—more than 450 people and all the animals—were shot dead.
The village was soon resettled by new residents who wanted to take
advantage of the rich agriculture in the area. But before the new people
arrived in the village, it was renamed Qatli Om, which means "Murdered
en Masse."

✦ ✦ ✦ ✦

The mujehadin weren't discouraged by the cruelty of the Soviets—quite the
opposite. More and more people from our village began to join their cause,
and the Soviets started carrying out bombing raids in our village, too.

At one point, rumors spread that the Soviets were planning to carry out an attack on us like the one in Qatli Om. As the bombing raids got nearer and more frequent, I sat down with a few of my neighbors to try to decide what to do.

"The main thing is to save our women and children," one man said. "Let's send them off someplace, and we'll stay behind and defend our properties."

"Hmmmm . . . I don't know about your plans," another neighbor countered. "What do you think the Soviets and the government forces will do if they find us here in our village? If they so ruthlessly carried out those attacks against so many innocent women and children up the road, what do you think they would do if they found a group of men hanging around here? They'd just massacre us all without giving it a second thought."

"But we have an obligation to stay close by and defend our houses," someone else said. "If we just run away, our houses will be looted by people from neighboring villages, even if the Soviets don't come here first."

After an extended discussion, we eventually reached a compromise. We knew that there was a small cave located at the edge of the village, where about ten of us could hide. We decided that some men would seek shelter in this cave, and the women and children would travel to a safer area with the remaining men. That way, we reasoned, we could come out of our hiding places at any time, once we determined that it was safe or if ordinary thieves arrived in the village.

Just an hour later, we could hear the rumble of tanks in the distance, and we decided that it was time to put our plan into action. That's how eight of my neighbors and I ended up crouching together in a small cave with a few candles and some drinking water. A couple of the young men from our village pushed a large boulder in front of the cave and filled in almost all the cracks with sand. Our only opening to the outside was a small hole, which let in a few rays of sunlight and a little fresh air. Meanwhile Amina and our children, along with almost all of the other women and children ran off to another village nearby.

We lit our candles and tried to sit as quietly as possible. But after a few hours, the candle wicks were nearly gone, and the air seemed to be running dangerously low. There were too many of us gathered in too small a space, and there just wasn't enough oxygen for all of us. When the candles went out, it became pitch black inside the cave. We eventually concluded that we would have to leave our hiding place, or at least find a way for more air to enter. So the strongest young man in our group went over to the boulder to push it aside. But no matter how much he pushed and pulled, he couldn't get it to budge. It had apparently been wedged into place very tightly. There wasn't enough space at the opening of the cave for another person to help him push the heavy rock. So other men took turns trying to move the boulder but had no success.

We were all panic-stricken as we gasped for breath. After a couple more minutes, we started shouting for help. At that point, we didn't even care if the Soviets discovered us. A slow suffocating death seemed far worse than a quick bullet in the head. We thought that we were definitely going to die one way or another.

So I started praying, "Please Allah, show us the way out of this bind." I was far from the strongest man in the cave, but after my short prayer, I wanted to try to move the rock. As I approached the boulder, I noticed that there was a tiny opening right on the edge of the stone where I could fit a couple of my fingers. I slid my fingers into this space, and with my free hand I pushed the boulder with all my strength. And miracle of miracles, the boulder actually started to move! Allah had decided that this was not the way that we would die.

Air immediately rushed into our hideout, and we were able to breathe normally again. Everyone rushed over to hug me and thank me. "God saved us through your hands!" one of my friends exclaimed. This was one of the happiest moments of my life. I felt like a genuine hero!

We stuck our heads out of the cave to look around and listen for any movement. But it was completely still in our village. There wasn't a single person around. So we each crawled outside and collapsed on the ground. We'd suffered from such a shortage of oxygen—not to mention fear—that it took a long time to get the color back in our faces. The Soviet and government armies must have marched right past our village, no doubt on their way to wreak havoc somewhere else.

✦ ✦ ✦ ✦

A few years later, when my twins were about eight years old, I badly injured my back while moving some heavy equipment at my neighbor's barn. I was more or less useless for the next several months. We had no savings, and I was afraid that my twins as well as their three younger sisters would die of starvation if there was no income. Bibi Hojara's crusts of bread were not nearly enough to sustain our family. So I had no alternative but to force my oldest boys, Adil and Kamil, to leave the house each morning to look for work.

They took whatever jobs they could find—cleaning people's barns; gathering together animal feces, which could be used in place of firewood after being dried in the sun during the wintertime; or performing back-breaking work in the rice fields. Sometimes, they'd earn enough to buy a couple boxes of matches and other times, a pound or two of wheat. But my children would invariably return home absolutely filthy and crying from the pain and humiliation of a long day of slavelike labor.

Several times, I remember them shouting at me through their tears, "Tomorrow we won't go back to our jobs! All of our friends are laughing at us—they have time to play games while we have to work like dogs. We won't go back there ever again!" I used every method imaginable to try to coax them back to work; sometimes I would speak to them nicely, sometimes I would beg them, and sometimes I would beat them to get them to obey me. I wouldn't have wished that fate on my worst enemy. I was stealing my children's childhood from them. But I had no choice—we were able to survive only because of their labor.

When my back had finally healed, I went looking for work in Kunduz city. On my third day in town, I happened to run into an old friend of mine, Ergash Boi, who invited me to his house. "Niyaz Turdi, my brother, everything will work out fine," my friend told me. "So many of us have had problems, but you've had just awful luck—losing your parents and your only brother within a couple of years must have been very difficult to bear. . . . I tell you what, I have a couple of shops around town, and I need someone to help me out. Are you interested?"

It was an incredible opportunity, far better than anything I could have imagined. For a couple of years, I sold wheat, rice, and beans at my friend's shop in Kunduz. And I spent every night after work in Ergash Boi's guestroom. He generously provided me with food, and we would almost always stay up late into the night talking. We became very close friends, and he would ask for my advice regarding business decisions. Only once a week would I find time to go back to our makeshift house in Qarai Karakhani to check on my family and bring them whatever food I had earned.

In 1992, after the mujahedin came to power, I moved my family back to our home village of Tarbuzguzar. It was the first time I had gone back home in nearly nine years. I was horrified to see the condition of the house in which I had grown up. Even the portion of the house that hadn't been destroyed by Soviet missiles had been completely looted; people had stolen the doors, windows, and wooden roof beams. All that remained were the four mud-brick walls. Fortunately, with the money that I'd earned over the course of a few years in Ergash Boi's shop, I was able to reconstruct a couple of rooms in our house to make it at least livable.

One evening Ergash Boi and I sat discussing the future of his business. "You know what I've been thinking?" he said. "This little business could make a much bigger profit if we branched out. Why don't we go back to our home district of Qal-i-Zal and try to buy up the local harvest directly? Then we'll take these products straight to Mazar-i-Sharif and sell them at a large profit." And that's how our new business venture was launched.

Ergash Boi decided to remain in Kunduz city to tend to his shops, while I spent most of my time talking to farmers and buying up their harvested crops, mostly rice, wheat, beans, peas, and fertilizer. Then Ergash Boi and I would head to Mazar together to sell our produce.

Within four years, I was able to build a relatively comfortable life for my family, which now included seven children—three boys and four girls. I possessed a few cows and sheep and had enough land to feed my family and make a reasonable profit. We were even able to rebuild our house better than it was before it fell victim to the Soviet helicopters. Meanwhile, my business partner managed to amass enough to make a pilgrimage to Mecca. From then on, he was known as Hajji Ergash Boi.

One day in 1996, a few of my good friends from a nearby village came by my house. Hajji Ergash Boi and I had just returned from a successful trip to Mazar-i-Sharif, where we had resold a large amount of wheat. I was spending the day with my friends, relaxing in my newly renovated guestroom, listening to Afghan music, drinking tea, and swapping stories. My wife had cooked a wonderful batch of rice pilaf, and my guests had brought some fish from a nearby river, which we devoured. As we lounged on our mattresses, a soldier knocked on my door and informed me that the local commander, Abdul Rahmon, wanted to see me as soon as possible in the mosque.

It was by no means a regular occurrence to be summoned by the local commander. So as my guests looked on with concern, I tried to lighten the mood with a joke of some sort and left the house.

The soldier took me directly to Abdul Rahmon, who was saying his prayers at the mosque. After only a cursory exchange of pleasantries, the commander asked me how much money I had made during my most recent trip to Mazar. I'd made a decent profit, but I told him instead that I'd actually lost some money as a result of low demand. I was afraid that he'd ask for a percentage of my proceeds if I told him the truth. The commander grabbed my arm and roughly pulled me aside. In an angry whisper, he said: "I just talked to your partner. So don't bother lying to me!"

I couldn't imagine that Ergash Boi would have actually told the commander about our proceeds. So I insisted that the commander had been misinformed.

But Abdul Rahmon was not interested in my arguments. "Now that you have become so rich," he said with a wry grin, "you will have to help me. You must buy me forty new turbans, forty pairs of French-made shoes, and forty high-quality *shalwar kameez*. I need these items very badly."

Having issued the order, he started walking out of the mosque toward his truck. I followed and tried to think up anything I could to try to talk him out of such an outrageous demand. "I can't possibly afford to provide what you're asking," I pleaded with him. "Even if I were to sell my wife and children, I couldn't raise the kind of money you're talking about. And I have seven children to support."

The commander remained unmoved.

So I tried to buy some time. "You know, I have a business partner, Hajji Ergash Boi, who is now in Kunduz city. I couldn't make an important decision like this without him," I said earnestly.

"Don't worry," the commander barked. "You will provide me with what I asked of you, and then I will deal with your partner separately. . . . You have three days to give me what I've requested."

When we reached his pick-up truck, with his soldiers all around us, he grabbed me close and muttered, "If you breathe a word about this to anyone, I will kill you." With these words still hanging in the air, he climbed into his truck and sped off on the dusty road, leaving me covered in dirt.

I was panic-stricken. I returned home with a million and one contradictory thoughts. My house was still filled with guests who were nervously awaiting my return. They immediately saw the distress in my pale face.

I, of course, wanted to share the details of the meeting with my friends. But I also knew that if I told them, they might tell other people and word might get back to Abdul Rahmon. I knew that the commander wouldn't hesitate to follow through on his threat.

So I quickly came up with an excuse about an urgent business deal in Kunduz and jumped in a taxi. During the hour-long drive to the city, I racked my brain for a decent solution. But I could think of nothing.

I immediately went to Hajji Ergash Boi's house, and we discussed the problem late into the night. Going over it again and again, neither of us could think of a way out of this bind. In the morning, Hajji Ergash Boi proposed that I run away to Pakistan or Iran. Looking back now, that definitely would have been the best thing to do. But I had been an internally displaced person (IDP) before, and I didn't want to repeat the experience. In any case, it would have been impossible to collect all of my children and my wife and slip quietly out of town, undetected by the commander's men.

So we came up with another solution. We knew we couldn't afford to buy such a large order of expensive items for the commander, but we could buy some items that would, we hoped, appease him. So we resolved to purchase two pairs of shoes and two high-quality *shalwar kameezes* for him. With gifts in hand, we returned to Qal-i-Zal and looked around for Commander Abdul Rahmon. We waited with a group of young soldiers in his freezing cold headquarters—it was an especially cold day in late autumn—for several hours before he arrived. When the Commander did eventually show up, we were shivering from both cold and fear.

As he walked in to greet us, the commander noticed our small packets, and his fake smile quickly disappeared from his face. Instead of extending his whole hand in greeting as is traditional, he offered us only two fingers. We knew we were in trouble.

The Commander didn't bother to sit down and join us for a cup of tea. He just told us to accompany him to the mosque.

Hajji Ergash Boi and I explained to the commander that we were not especially wealthy, that we had large families that depended on us, and that we had made very little money on our recent trip to Mazar. "Nevertheless," we tried to make him understand, "we gathered together whatever resources we could as a sign of our respect for you."

The commander was clearly not impressed. "I thought I gave you very simple instructions the last time we spoke," he said to me angrily. "Where are all of the other things you promised me? I could kill you right now for your insubordination!"

Turning to my partner, he raised a further threat of blackmail. "Some reliable people have told me that you've been engaging in illicit relationships with young women. You wouldn't want the husbands or fathers of these girls to find out, would you?" Hajji Ergash Boi had never been involved in any secret affairs to my knowledge, but he knew that the commander could easily persuade certain individuals, certain armed and dangerous individuals, that their wives or daughters had sinned. If Abdul Rahmon breathed even a word about these alleged transgressions to the wrong men, Ergash Boi's life would be over.

As we huddled on the thin carpets of the ice-cold mosque, Ergash Boi and I looked at each other as though we'd just been handed a death sentence. But then the Commander began to smile at us with a mouth full of rotting teeth. "OK, I'll cut you a break," he started magnanimously. A glimmer of hope arose in our hearts. "Instead of forcing you to run all over Kunduz buying me cloth and shoes and turbans, I'll make it much easier for you—just give me the cash equivalent of these items, and we'll call it a day."

Of course this didn't help us at all. Ergash Boi pleaded at length with the Commander that we were men of modest means and that we really couldn't meet his demands. The Commander was very annoyed by his long-winded speech. He turned to me and said, "Why did you bring your partner? I told you last time that we could solve these problems alone."

The Commander no longer had the patience to carry on a discussion. He abruptly stood up and said: "You will either bring me ninety-five laks afghanis [equivalent at the time to about $3,300] or you will die. The choice is very simple." He then marched away. For over an hour, Ergash Boi and I were too stunned to budge from the floor of the mosque.

We knew that the only way we would be able to raise this kind of money was to sell all of the fertilizer we had in our shop in Kunduz and to pass along the proceeds to the Commander. We had bought the fertilizer with a loan from another rich man in Qal-i-Zal, Ahdam Khan, and if we gave the fertilizer proceeds to Abdul Rahmon, there would be nothing remaining to repay the loan.

When the Commander understood that we would raise the funds he demanded through our fertilizer sales, he ordered that the sales be carried out under his watch in Qal-i-Zal. We knew that we could get a much better price for the fertilizer in Kunduz or Mazar, especially if we sold it over the course of a couple of months, but the Commander wanted his money immediately. So we had to slash the prices to sell to the residents of Qal-i-Zal. Abdul Rahmon sent a couple of trusted soldiers to keep an eye on us and our shop and to make sure that all of our proceeds went directly to him.

Until we had managed to sell off the last of the fertilizer, I was a complete wreck. I couldn't sleep at night, and I eventually had to buy some tranquilizers at the pharmacy so that I could relax. But fortunately, after one week of brisk fertilizer sales—and just when our supplies were about to run out—we were able to meet the commander's demands of ninety-five laks afghanis. This was undoubtedly the worst week of my life.

But once the commander's orders had been fulfilled, we still had large outstanding debts. We owed Ahdam Khan alone 150 laks afghanis, or more than $5,000. Our dilemma was that we couldn't tell him why we weren't able to repay his loan—the Commander had sworn us to secrecy. So we had to make up a story about how we had lost a lot of money when we were in Mazar.

At about this same time, my partner and I had a falling out. He accused me of being irresponsible. "You know, all these difficulties we're facing now are because of you," he told me one day. "How was it that you managed to get on Commander Abdul Rahmon's bad side? It was probably because you were going around flaunting your new wealth. Everyone can see that your new house was rebuilt to luxurious standards. You should have been much more careful. You've dragged me down with your stupid mistakes. . . . And now it should be your responsibility to find a way out of these problems."

From that point on, I realized that I was basically all alone in coming up with a scheme to get out of debt. So I decided to sell both of my cows as a down payment against the loan from Ahdam Khan, and I pledged to return the rest of the money as soon as I could.

"I promise you that I will do anything in my power to repay the debt," I told Ahdam Khan as I handed over the proceeds from the sale of the cows. "I could sell you my house, the remainder of my animals, and my lands if you'd like, or I could go to Pakistan and try to find some relatives who might be able to help me. . . . What would be best for me is if I could be given another year to repay the money. After the next harvest, I'm sure I'll be able to get back on my feet again. But it's really up to you to decide how you'd like me to settle this debt."

Ahdam Khan told me that he wasn't interested in my house or my fields. "I have more lands now than I know what to do with," he said laughing. "I'm going to give you another year to repay the loan."

I was greatly relieved. I had lost my business partner, my two cows, and I was still deeply in debt. But now I had some breathing space.

But then, two days later, Commander Abdul Rahmon called me to his headquarters again. "Just this morning, I was just talking to Ahdam Khan about your debts," he told me. "Why don't you return his money?"

"I've already sold both of my cows in order to begin repaying him," I said to the Commander. "I offered to sell him the rest of my animals, my house, and my lands in order to settle our debts. But he agreed to wait one year until the next harvest for me to finish repaying him. I'm very grateful to him for this grace period."

"Aren't you ashamed to walk around with such large debts around your neck?" he asked me. "You really need to pay him sooner. . . . I'll tell you what I can do for you: I will buy your house and land and then you can immediately repay your debt. In fact, I'll even save you some time; I'll repay your creditors myself instead of giving you the money for your properties."

I knew by then that it was useless to argue with the Commander. In any case, he would do whatever he wanted in the end. So I agreed to sell him my lands and my house at a rate undoubtedly lower than I could have secured if I'd had the time to ask around. I heard later that the Commander gave Ahdam Khan only one hundred laks, and kept fifty laks for himself. Apparently the Commander said to Ahdam Khan as he forked over the money, "That's enough for you."

Penniless and homeless, I decided to return back here to Chahardara district. And this is where we have been living ever since.

→ → ← ←

Less than a year later, after the Taliban captured Kunduz, there were widespread rumors that they were planning to disarm all of the local commanders. This is part of the reason the Taliban gained such widespread support at first; almost everyone in the entire country hated these local warlords. Many of us were hopeful that we'd receive compensation for what we'd suffered in the past.

Then one day I heard an announcement that the Taliban's minister of justice, Nuruddin Turabi, was planning to come to the city to listen and respond to official complaints. I hadn't been in touch with Hajji Ergash Boi for a long time, but I decided to contact him regarding Turabi's visit. "Maybe we can present our story to Minister Turabi," I said to my former partner, "and he could force Abdul Rahmon to return the money he stole from us." Ergash Boi agreed that it was definitely worth a try.

So Ergash Boi and I, along with another friend of mine who had also been robbed by the Commander met in Kunduz in order to submit a formal letter of complaint against Abdul Rahmon. Minister Turabi had set up a temporary office in the Takharistan Madrassa, and literally thousands of Kunduz residents gathered outside the madrassa to pass along their complaints. Each man in the crowd held an official letter in his hands detailing the precise nature of his grievance. Taliban guards had to beat back the throngs in order to keep the madrassa from being overrun. We found out that the only way that we could meet with Turabi was to bribe the local commander in charge of security.

Shortly after the "fee" was paid, we were led inside the classroom where Turabi was sitting. We were struck by his appearance; he had a long white beard and only one eye. After quickly skimming through our letter of complaint, he began to reread it slowly while stroking his long beard.

"So who is this commander?" he asked finally.

"He acts like a pharaoh up in our district of Qal-i-Zal," I told him. "He's a legendarily cruel man."

Turabi looked at the letter again and then wrote a short text addressed to the Kunduz provincial governor: "You should investigate these charges. If they prove to be true, you must demand that Commander Abdul Rahmon return the ninety-five laks to the aggrieved." Turabi then promised us that he would personally follow up on this issue when he next returned to Kunduz.

We walked directly across town to the provincial governor's office, where we hoped to be able to deliver Turabi's letter personally. But we were told by his guards that he was busy. After waiting around for several hours, we decided to return another day. But every time we returned to meet with the governor, he was in a meeting or out of town. Eventually, we were forced to pass along the letter through one of the governor's guards. As far as I know, nobody ever investigated our claims, and this whole affair was just forgotten. More than six years have now gone by since we submitted our letter, and we're still waiting for our ninety-five laks!

Nowadays, my sons and I manage to make a living by doing odd jobs. One of my sons, Adil, is a mason who has managed to earn a decent living over the past couple of years thanks to all the rebuilding that's been going on around the province. Kamil works as a day laborer on other people's farms here in Chahardara. My other son is still studying in school.

After the Taliban were overthrown, my hopes were raised again that Commander Abdul Rahmon would get what he deserved. In 2002, I heard that some American special forces had conducted a raid on the headquarters of Abdul Rahmon's brother and that they spirited him away. Nobody knows where he is; maybe he's in some military base inside Afghanistan, although I'm hoping that he's being tortured some-where in Guantanamo. That would be too good a fate for his miserable brother. I really wish Allah would send American B-52s to blow up Commander Abdul Rahmon. That bastard has ruined my life.

While they're at it, the Americans should also bomb a whole bunch of other cruel commanders who are still in power around Kunduz province. They continue to rob people of their livelihood and create all kinds of trou-ble. Recently, I heard that several commanders in different districts of Kunduz had divided up the fields of those who are still refugees abroad or displaced within Afghanistan and are using some of these fields to plant poppies. The commanders don't even allow the refugees' poor relatives to use this land to plant wheat. These commanders are like parasites that enter the human body and remain there until they have sucked their vic-tims dry.

CHAPTER FOUR

Mino, Daughter of Abdul Qasim and Zakira, Daughter of Abdurahman

MINO

People tell me that my father was murdered by his eldest brother when I was only two years old. My uncle accused my father of somehow being responsible for the death of his nephew, that is, the death of my uncle's son. My mother always told me that my father would swear up and down that he had never killed anyone, but his brother didn't believe him. My brother, Tahir, was the one who found our father's body lying in a ditch near our house. For many years Tahir has threatened to avenge our father's death.

After my father died, we—my mother, my two older sisters, my brother, and I—were left to fend for ourselves. A couple of my uncles had large landholdings, but they refused to share anything with our family. They treated us like we were contaminated with some sort of disease. From that point on, my brother, at the age of ten, had to provide for the rest of us. For a few years, he did some work in the bazaar and later joined the mujahedin, and we'd see him only occasionally. But he'd always find a way to send money or gifts back home from the front.

One evening about five years ago, when Tahir was spending a couple of weeks at home, he invited a group of friends over to our house. For many hours, they sat in the guest room near the entrance to our courtyard. It happened to be the day before one of our relatives' wedding, and I decided to try on my beautiful new Punjabi outfit. The dress was claret colored and decorated with small round reflecting mirrors, and the chiffon scarf was lined with golden lace. I was so proud of my newly tailored dress and wanted to see the full effect, so I started putting on make-up.

My mother walked into my room as I was parading about, looking at my reflection in the window. She smiled at me for a couple of seconds, but then she said, "Mino jaan, you're very beautiful. But there's a huge pile of dishes waiting for you." She stomped off back to the kitchen, probably offended that I was goofing off. Just when I was about to get changed back into my house clothes, I noticed that one of Tahir's friends was standing out in the courtyard looking into my room through the window! I was very embarrassed. I rushed over to the curtain and yanked it shut before he could take another look at me. "Oh my God," I thought to myself. "A stranger saw my face!"

A few days later, Tahir informed me that he had selected a husband for me. "His name's Ibrahim Bek, and he's a few years older than me," he told me. "We've been friends for many years so I can vouch for him and know that he's very trustworthy. You'll be his second wife, but I'm sure that he will treat you very well. He's got a good job as a trader, and he's promised to buy you whatever you like—clothes, jewelry, whatever. He's always told me that he doesn't like his first wife, that she was chosen by his parents, and that she's a close relative of his. . . . In any case, it's a dangerous time for teenage girls now that the Taliban are in power. I've heard stories about how they force young unmarried girls to marry their soldiers."

"As you wish, my brother," I responded. "But . . . do you, do you happen to have his photograph?" I asked meekly. I didn't want to appear too eager to see my future husband, but I was of course very curious. The Taliban were ruling over Kunduz province at the time, but I knew that in spite of the prohibitions, most people managed to hold on to photographs one way or another.

The next day my brother gave me a photograph of Ibrahim Bek. I recognized him immediately. He was the man who had seen me as I was trying on my Punjabi outfit.

The first couple of years of our marriage were wonderful. I moved into his big compound, which I shared with Ibrahim Bek's brother and his family, as well as his first wife, Zakira. Zakira and I each had our own rooms, but Ibrahim Bek would spend almost all of his time with me. She was only a few years older than me, but she had tough, dark skin and was very moody. I think she was always jealous of me.

Ibrahim Bek had a very profitable shop in the town nearby. With some of the money he made, he bought a second house and a few acres of land. And, just as he had promised my brother, he would frequently give me small presents when he'd return from his business trips to Mazar-i-Sharif. "I'm so happy that you've become mine, my beautiful flower, Mino jaan," he used to tell me. "Whenever I'm away, I only think about you, and I count down the days until I can be with you again."

A year after we were married, I gave birth to an adorable baby girl named Nazira, and then the next year I had a son, Azam. Ibrahim Bek was a great father, and he'd always play with the children when he'd come home from work. "Our children are so beautiful, aren't they?" he'd say to me. "But of course they're beautiful. Just look at their mother. Each of them has such perfect round eyes and light skin like you."

But when Azam was only a few months old, our troubles began. Ibrahim Bek had gotten involved in the business of selling gasoline. He would buy gasoline from Baghlan province and bring it up here to Imam Sahib* in tanker trucks and then sell it off to some local businessmen. He thought that since his business partner was an ethnic Pashtun, he wouldn't have problems dealing with the Taliban, even though we're all Uzbeks.

Then one day, only a few months before the fall of the Taliban, my husband came home with bruises all over his body. He usually never told me any details about his business activities, but as I nursed him back to health, he told me the full story about how he was beaten up.

"All this happened when we were bringing back two tanker trailers full of gasoline from Baghlan," he explained. "Along the road, in the district of Ali Abad, some Taliban guards flagged us down. 'We're badly in

---

* A town and district in northern Kunduz province.

need of gasoline here. Can't we buy your fuel?' the guard asked us. 'Why not?' my partner replied. 'What difference does it make if we sell it to you here or back in Imam Sahib?'

"One of the guards jumped into the truck with us and guided us to the governor's office farther up the road in Kunduz city. He explained that it's the provincial governor's responsibility to sign off on any financial transactions that are carried out by the government here in the province. So we settled on a fair price with the Kunduz governor Maulavi Abdurazok and his finance assistant, and they said they'd pay us before too long. Then they sent some of their men to escort our tankers to another part of town, while we went to a restaurant to have some lunch and to drink tea. But only a few minutes after we'd sat down to eat, we heard a loud explosion outside. It turned out that one of our tankers had blown up. The flames spread so fast that it even destroyed a house that was nearby, and all the residents in the area rushed out of their homes. The truck driver had managed to escape with his life, but his only source of income had suddenly gone up in smoke.

"So we hurried back to the governor's office, where some Taliban officials told us what had happened. My partner and I were in total shock. After a couple of minutes, my partner decided to ask the question that was on both our minds: 'How will this affect our payment?' One of the governor's assistants who was sitting nearby put his hand on my partner's shoulder and said, 'You should think of your money as a contribution to the Islamic cause. Allah will compensate you.' My partner didn't know how to respond at first. But then he asked, 'But how are we supposed to cover our earthly expenses?' The Taliban then told him, "OK, just show up here tomorrow, and we'll try to help you however we can.'

"The next morning, at about half past eight, we went back to the governor's office. Maulavi Abdurazok, the assistant we'd talked to the previous day, and about fifteen other men were having their breakfast. Among them, there were several local commanders I recognized. Honey, nuts, bread, eggs, and jam were spread out on the tablecloth on the floor, and they didn't look like they were about to get up and start working any time soon.

"'Who are you again?' the governor's assistant asked us. 'Why are you here?' By this time, I had become very annoyed. So although we had been talking in Pashtu, I started speaking in Dari. 'Yesterday you agreed to buy the gasoline from us, and we shook hands on a certain price,' I said. 'When the gasoline tanker exploded, it was under your watch. It was your responsibility, not ours. So I think it's only fair that we receive the money that we were promised.'

"The governor wrinkled his nose and turned toward his assistant. 'What is that guy talking about?' My partner then started translating what I'd said into Pashtu. By the time the translation was finished, the governor's face had turned bright red. 'You two—get the hell out of here! Now!' he yelled at us.

"We didn't say another word. We just left quietly and walked toward the front gate of the governor's office. My partner and I were about to explode with anger, but there was nothing we could do. When we were almost outside the front gates, a guard summoned us back.

"As soon as the governor noticed that we had returned to his office, he walked over toward us and continued his tirade: 'What right do you have to demand payment from me? Who says that I owe you money for the gasoline that exploded?' My friend could no longer contain his anger and started arguing with him. But I could see that it was useless because the governor refused to listen to reason.

"Then he started kicking both me and my partner in the shins with his army boots. Immediately, the Taliban guards with their Kalashnikovs grabbed me and my partner and began beating us. Five bulky men dragged us out of the governor's office and over toward an empty concrete room to continue their beatings. I tried to cover my head and begged the guards not to hit me there, but of course they didn't listen to me. There was one guy with bright blue eyes who was really out to get us. I swear to God, I'll strangle him if I ever catch him alone on the street. I never knew that I could survive so much pain, but as you can see, my dear Mino jaan, I'm still able to walk. I'm sure that Allah sees everything and that on the Day of Judgment, He will punish those sadistic guards as well as the evil governor.

"When it looked like the guards were finally going to let us go, the governor happened to walk by. 'I don't want to see those two alive ever again,' he said as he spat at us. 'Take them outside, shoot them, and bury their bodies somewhere at the edge of town.' It was then that my partner and I got down on our hands and knees to beg for mercy. 'Please, dear respected mullah, don't do this to us,' my partner cried out. 'We both have small children at home, and our families will die if we can't provide for them. We're so sorry that we even mentioned the gasoline. I promise that you'll never see us anywhere around here again.' The governor stared at us. Then with a quick kick to my friend's side, he ordered the guards to free us. I think he just wanted to see us grovel for our lives."

My husband's eyes teared up as he told me this terrible story. "Now I have no idea how I'll ever be able to pay back the money I owe. . . . But don't worry about all this, Mino jaan. Almighty Allah will provide for us."

➔ ➔ ← ←

The solution that Ibrahim Bek came up with was to borrow $5,000 from my brother, Tahir. My husband promised to repay the loan with interest after three months. Tahir didn't have that kind of money readily available, so he had to ask a couple of his friends for the cash. My husband thought that this would be enough to pay his debts and to get his trading operations going again. But it turned out that the money didn't help. Just after the Taliban were driven out, my husband's business went completely bankrupt.

My brother started coming by our house, demanding his money. When he realized that my husband wasn't planning to pay anytime soon, he tried to come up with different ways of getting the money back. My brother had served as a soldier, so like many people in our community, he was armed. One day, he came to the house with his gun and threatened my husband if he didn't return the loan.

"I don't care if you've gone bankrupt," Tahir screamed at him. "I borrowed the $5,000 I gave you, and I need to find a way to get the money back to my friends." After a long, heated argument, my brother reluctantly agreed to accept only $5,000, without interest. In order to return my brother's money, my husband was forced to sell all of his land as well as the new house he had bought the year before.

As his problems with my brother continued, my husband's attitude toward me began to change dramatically. He started beating our kids whenever they cried, and he spent more and more time sleeping in the other room with his first wife.

The same day he'd finally scraped together the $5,000 and returned the loan to my brother, my husband came into my room while I was breast-feeding Azam. "Your brother has ruined me! I have no choice but to divorce you. . . . *Taloq! Taloq! Taloq!*" he yelled out, which, according to Muslim traditions, means that a husband has officially divorced his wife.

"No, please don't say those dreadful words!" I said as little Azam began crying. "It's not my fault that all of this has happened. I've tried to help you. I even spoke to my brother about it, but he wouldn't listen to me. . . . For the sake of our children, please don't divorce me."

"I've suffered too much as a result of your malicious brother! I had to sell off all my lands and house because of him. I want him to suffer, too. Let him see his sister cast out into the street like an unwanted animal. I know this will bring shame on him!"

"No, Ibrahim Bek, the only people who will suffer from this will be our children. Please, my darling, we love each other. There's no reason for us to break up our happy home."

He just squinted at me through his unforgiving eyes, as though all of what we'd shared was meaningless. "I've already said three *taloqs,* and with Allah as my witness, you need to leave my house right now. Even if I wanted to, I can't take back what I said. You have to go! Now!"

I was humiliated. "What will my friends, neighbors, and relatives say?" I thought. I knew that if a husband divorces his wife, it indicates to every-one that she has failed in some vital way. "It's so shameful. How can I ever show my face among my relatives again?" I wondered.

In spite of my husband's order, I refused to leave our compound. I just moved with my children across the courtyard into a small room that was being used for storage by my brother-in-law.

"I'm sure that Ibrahim Bek will calm down soon," I told my brother-in-law's wife. "I can't imagine that he'll really force me to leave the house. What difference does it make that he repeated a little word a few times? We've had a loving relationship for far too long for him to throw it all away like that. I'm sure the only reason he said that to me was to preserve his pride."

For the next four months, I lived on the opposite side of the compound as my husband's first wife spread all her things into my space. During this time, Zakira would come over to my part of the house to taunt me. "Aren't you ashamed to stay here?" she used to say to me. "Why do you insist on tormenting my poor husband? It's bad enough that your greedy brother bankrupted him. Can't you see that nobody wants you here anymore? Why don't you just leave?" The humiliation was very difficult to bear, but I knew that deep down, my husband still loved me. So I stayed on.

Rumors of our divorce spread quickly throughout our village. I wouldn't doubt it if Zakira was responsible for this. Finally, one evening about two years ago, after my husband had finished his prayers at the mosque, the mullah pulled him aside to ask him about our relationship.

"Ibrahim Bek, there's been some talk that you said three *taloqs* to your wife. Is this really true?"

My husband admitted that this was, in fact, the case.

"So why is she still living in your house?" the mullah asked him. "Don't you know that this is a sin in Islam? If you continue to allow her to stay in your house, it will be as though you are sleeping with an unmarried woman. According to Sharia law, if you want to marry her again, she must first marry someone else, that man must divorce her, and then you can get remarried. Given that you've said three *taloqs*, you have absolutely no choice but to send her out of your house. And don't forget that it is your obligation to give her some money when she leaves. There really is no other solution."

That evening, my husband came home and reported to me what the mullah had said. "So you see, even if I wanted you to stay here, Islam forbids it," he explained to me. "I want you to pack up your things and get ready to leave with the kids tomorrow morning."

"But Ibrahim Bek," I pleaded, "what difference does it make what other people say? I know that you still love me. Why are you doing this to me and our children?"

But he was still too angry with me to have a calm discussion. "I'm sending you back to your brother's house where you belong. If he's such a selfish fool, he should take responsibility for you, too."

The next morning he gave me a little bit of money, loaded up my possessions on a donkey cart, and drove me and the children toward my brother's house. I sat on the back of the cart, weeping quietly under my burqa.

With an overwhelming sense of shame, I walked back into the small house in which I'd grown up. My children and I shared the place with my mother, my brother, his wife, and their three children. I was completely devastated. I had turned into a black sheep in the community and knew that everyone was probably laughing at me. Ever since then, I've refused to attend wedding parties, circumcision celebrations, and even funerals. I was already the subject of so much gossip that I didn't want to answer any more questions or endure the rude stares of my neighbors.

After I moved back in with my family, my brother rarely came home. He wasn't able to hold down a steady job and couldn't clothe and feed his own children, much less my children. In the middle of the summer, only a few months after my husband threw me out of the house, my daughter came down with a severe case of malaria. I didn't have money for medicine, and she was weak from malnourishment. Before I even built up the courage to go back to my husband and beg for money, Nazira died. We buried her in the village graveyard just down the road from here.

→ → ← ←

Night and day, I thought about what I might be able to do to convince my husband to take me back. I longed for the old days when Ibrahim Bek would smother me with his attention and love rather than his hatred and spite.

So one day, a couple of months after my daughter had died and Azam had been finally weaned from my breast milk, I decided to send him to live with his father. I thought that Azam's presence around the house would be a constant reminder to my husband about me and that this would encourage him to rethink his decision. I figured that my husband's first wife would look after him. By this time, I had heard that Ibrahim Bek's brother and his family had moved to a new house down the road. So maybe Zakira would get tired of taking care of the boy all by herself, I thought hopefully, and then she might even lobby her husband for my return. Furthermore, I had a very practical consideration: I was afraid that if Azam stayed with me and he didn't get enough to eat, he would suffer the same fate as his older sister.

But my logic was completely flawed because Zakira wasn't at all interested in caring for my son. Rumors began to spread around the village that she would keep him locked up in the bathroom around the clock. People said that she put a small plastic mat in the bathroom so that he wouldn't bother her when he had to use the toilet and that she wouldn't even change his pants after he wet himself. In addition, several people reported that she wouldn't feed him when he cried for food—that she'd just force him to crawl over to the trough reserved for the barnyard animals and eat and drink with them. By the time my son was two years old, his hair began to fall out and he looked like a child no more than nine months old. I didn't know how much of this talk was true, but a lot of women began to pass along these types of reports, so I started to believe them.

I didn't know what to do. Eventually, I decided to visit the community elders and seek their advice on how to resolve this situation. "Can't you do something to help me?" I pleaded. "Don't you know what happened to my poor daughter as a result of our divorce? And now I hear my son is suffering, too." They spoke for a long time among themselves, but they weren't able to offer me any real assistance. "This is a very complicated problem, my daughter," one of the community elders finally explained to me. "This is all tied up with Sharia law, and we have no power to reverse the principles of Islam. If you'd like to be reunited with Ibrahim Bek, you'll have no choice but to marry another man, then he will need to divorce you. Only after this, if Ibrahim Bek approves, could you be married to him again."

I couldn't possibly consider the idea of sleeping with another man. There seemed to be absolutely no way out of this horrible nightmare.

So I decided that I would try to find a way to check on my son and see for myself whether all the awful rumors I'd been hearing were true. So I walked across our village and snuck up to the tall mud brick wall that borders the house where I once lived. I noticed that one of the neighbor's daughters was playing in front of our house, so I quietly motioned for her to come over toward me. She didn't recognize me at first as I hadn't been in that neighborhood for over a year and a half. So I pulled up my burqa for a second so that she would know who I was.

Then I whispered to her, "Go inside the house and bring me my son for a few minutes so that I can take a look at him."

A short while later, as I stood waiting outside our front gate, I heard a loud argument taking place between Zakira and the girl who lived next door.

"Can you explain this to me again? Why do you want to take the little boy?" I heard Zakira ask incredulously.

"His mother is standing outside and told me that she wants to see him for a few minutes," the girl responded.

When she heard that I'd returned, Zakira's voice became hysterical. "What does she want with him?!?" she screeched. "What business does she have coming around here? My husband divorced her. I heard him with my own ears. I'm sure that if she gets a chance to lay her hands on that boy, she'll probably run off with him."

Just then my husband must have walked into the courtyard because I heard him ask the girl what she wanted. After pausing for a few seconds to consider the situation, my husband said, "It's OK. What's wrong with letting her see her child for a couple minutes? Take the boy to his mother," he instructed the girl. Zakira didn't bother to respond. She knew that it was useless to argue with my husband.

After a couple of minutes, the girl appeared with my little baby Azam in her arms. I was shocked by his appearance—his head was much larger than his body, he had little hair, and he was dressed in little more than rags. I instantly realized that all the horrible rumors must have been true. Tears gushed from my eyes. I kissed my baby and hugged him tightly. I couldn't bear the thought of returning my one and only child to this horrible woman again.

So without even thinking about where I was going, I just started running away with Azam. I ran as fast as I could straight though the nearby fields of rice patties. My feet were covered in mud, and I could hardly see from beneath my burqa as it was tugged in different directions.

After a minute or so, I lifted my veil and turned around to try to see whether anyone was following me. From across the field, I saw my husband standing in front of our gate, but he didn't bother to pursue me. I kept on glancing over my shoulder as I moved as fast as I could. But his figure just grew smaller and smaller as he stood staring at me.

➔   ➔   ❦   ❦

It's now been five months since I rescued Azam from my husband's first wife. My son, who is now about three years old, is in much better health. After I ran off with Azam, my husband began sending me a little bit of money so that I could take care of him properly. I'm so relieved that I'm able to provide him with some good food and that he no longer has to drink the dirty water that Zakira was probably giving him. His hair is now growing normally, and he just recently began to walk and now he's even running. I thank God every day that he's still alive.

Meanwhile, my brother Tahir left our house a few months ago, and nobody knows where he ran off to. There are rumors that he's working in some sort of export company in Pakistan, but nobody seems to know for sure. Maybe he's worried that my husband will try to take further revenge on him. Maybe that's why he took off. But in the meantime, other than the small amount of money that my husband sends me for Azam, our family has no source of income.

My brother's unexplained disappearance, however, has had one very positive result: my husband has finally re-entered my life. Every week or so, Ibrahim Bek comes by our house to see our son. Of course he misses Azam, but I feel that his primary motive in coming here is to see me. Whenever my husband shows up, it immediately improves my son's mood. When Azam hears him at the front gate of our courtyard, he runs as fast as he can to greet him. The only problem is that his coordination is still not very good, and he sometimes trips over himself in his haste to see his father. When he finally reaches Ibrahim Bek, our little boy hugs both of his legs so tightly that my husband can't even walk into the house.

Sometimes my husband will stop by for just a few minutes on his way to town, but on other occasions he'll stay for several hours. Recently, he's begun to show up unexpectedly at all hours of the day and night. Whenever he comes by, I prepare some tea for him and we talk. He treats me the way he always used to—with love and attention. And unlike that terrible time in the past when he was fighting with my brother, my husband is now almost always in a good mood. It's like our love has been rekindled. He's told me that he would really like for me to return to our house, but according to Sharia law, that will be impossible. We're hoping that we can find a way to solve this problem.

ZAKIRA

One day about five years ago my husband came home and announced that he was planning to take a second wife. Like all men here who decide to get married a second time, he came up with some sort of lame excuse. "You know, I have lots of relatives and friends who often come to visit, and that means that there's a lot of work to do around the house. I thought that you would need someone to help you with all of the housework," he told me.

Even back then, our relationship had not been good for quite awhile. The first few months after our wedding, Ibrahim Bek treated me very well. But later, he started yelling and beating me over the tiniest little things. It seems to me that my husband's relationship with his second wife had a similar pattern. At first, he spent a lot of time with Mino, but then he began to dislike us both.

When it turned out that Ibrahim Bek was unable to return his brother-in-law's money, his relationship with Mino completely fell apart. Mino's brother insisted not only on his returning the $5,000 he had lent him, but also on his making a large interest payment as well. I couldn't believe that Mino's brother would treat him so disrespectfully. They were one family after all. He should have understood that my husband didn't purposefully deceive him. Mino's brother ought to have sat down quietly with my husband and resolved this problem calmly. But what can one expect from people of that family?

Instead, he immediately resorted to violence to settle their disagreement. On several occasions, he came by with a gun in the middle of the night to threaten my poor husband. One time, he even beat my husband with the butt of his Kalashnikov. And on another night, he fired his gun several times into the air. One of the bullets landed on me and left a permanent scar on my right arm. Does that sound like any way to treat one's relatives?

My husband realized that it would be impossible to talk with his brother-in-law directly, so he decided to use Mino as a go-between. But

Mino was completely unreasonable. She just blindly sided with her brother. It seems to me that she valued her relationship with her brother more than her relationship with her husband. My husband and Mino were constantly arguing at the top of their lungs about this problem, but Mino was as stubborn as a donkey. She refused to see that her brother was acting totally despicably.

My poor husband didn't know what to do. Eventually, he had to sell almost everything he owned in order to repay Mino's brother. And after this, he fell into a terrible depression—he would hardly talk to his friends and relatives. When he would speak to Mino at all, he would just yell at her. Eventually, he had had enough and decided to get rid of her. I was only surprised that he didn't divorce her earlier.

But for some reason, even after he said the three *taloqs*, she just wouldn't leave the house. She stayed with us in the compound for several more months, driving him absolutely crazy. It was so sad to see Ibrahim Bek suffer when she insisted on disobeying him like that. In addition, she would often threaten me because she claimed that I was responsible for their divorce. One time she told me that she'd tear out all my hair and rip apart my face with her nails to punish me for turning my husband against her.

A few months after Mino left she sent her son back to our house to live with us. I still don't understand why. He was constantly crying for his mother. I tried to do whatever I could to comfort him, but he missed his mother too much. After a while, he refused to eat and began to wither away slowly.

Then one day, Mino came back to the house and stole her child back. I was visiting my neighbor at the time, and when I arrived home, I panicked because I couldn't find the boy anywhere. "What could have possibly happened to him?" I wondered. "Could he have crawled off?" Finally, I found my neighbor's girl who told me that his mother had taken him and that my husband didn't try to stop her.

I've heard that my husband sometimes goes to visit Azam over at Mino's house. The boy misses his father so much that the moment he walks in the door, Azam stands up and runs to see him. I think it's terrible that he's deprived of his father's care and affection on a regular basis.

I'm not sure how it happened, but now both my husband and Mino regret that they were divorced. My husband said that he's going to try to solve this problem and bring her back to live with us. But everything depends on what the mullah says. To be honest, I really don't understand why he wants to bring her back here. What use is a wife who made all of us poor? Who's the source of scandal? If she comes back here, I'm sure that she will continue to bring misfortune on our house.

CHAPTER FIVE

Najib, Son of Abdul Shafiq

My father was a very rich man; he had shops all over Taloqan and was able to afford five wives. My mother was his youngest wife. In fact, many of the children from his other marriages are actually older than her. I was the second youngest of his eighteen children. My mother had three boys and one girl.

My father would never tire of telling us the story of how he managed, by hook and by crook, to work his way up out of dire poverty. His parents died when he was very young, and he was raised by some distant relatives who lived in a small village. As is often the case here when orphans are adopted by relatives, his position was the lowest in the household. He was forced to shepherd their animals, clean their house, and perform other menial tasks.

Nevertheless, he was determined to get an education. There were no government-run schools in his village at the time, so he tried to learn to read and write from the mullah at the local mosque. In order to study, he arranged to have some other shepherds look after his animals for a couple of hours each day. When his adopted family heard that he was shirking his responsibilities and was sneaking off to the mosque, they would punish him severely. One time, when his adopted father wanted to beat him up, he escaped into a *tandoori* oven, closed the cover over himself, and hid for several hours.

My father loved to regale my siblings and I with these kinds of stories, so that we might better appreciate how fortunate we were to have the opportunity to study both in school and at the mosque. He was determined that his children would be just as committed to our studies as he had been to his.

When I was in fifth grade, it was a time of lawlessness across Afghanistan. The communist government headed by Dr. Najibullah had just fallen in Kabul, and a variety of mujahedin factions fought for control. During this time, some mujahedin troops came to our house in the middle of the night looking for money. When my father claimed that he didn't have anything to give them, they took him outside and beat him mercilessly. By the way, these types of criminals are some of the same people who are now running our local government these days.

I can still hear my father's anguished but restrained screams as he tried to maintain his dignity within earshot of his family. When my older brothers retrieved him from the yard outside, he was unconscious and my mother and the other wives were wailing in grief. My father was injured so badly that his arms and legs were paralyzed. He died a few months later.

Forty days after my father's death, many conflicts in the family, which had been simmering for years, came to the surface. My older brothers informed my mother that they couldn't support her young children. They had families of their own and just couldn't afford it, or so they said. My mother was still very beautiful at the time, and they assumed that she'd find another husband to take responsibility for us kids.

I remember one terrible morning when one of my oldest brothers, Naim, came into the room where I sat alone with my mother. He owned a couple of shops in town and was pretty well off. Naim was never a kind person, but he was in a particularly vile mood that morning. "You're going to get married again and leave your children behind, aren't you?" he yelled. "But I'm not prepared to take care of them. You should know this right up front so that you'll be sure to take your children with you when you leave with your new husband . . ." My two other brothers came rushing into the room when they heard the yelling and huddled close to our mother and me.

I'll never forget the anger in my mother's eyes. "Never again use the words 'your new husband' when talking to me!" she screamed back. Then she pointed to my two brothers and me. "You see these boys? This is my first husband, my second husband, and my third husband. They are everything that I want and need in this life. If I were to marry some other man, do you think that he'd help support them and look after them? You are their own brother, and yet you're able to say these kinds of things. Just imagine how some stranger would treat them!"

We had a very large beautiful house and courtyard, and it was impossible for my family to come to a reasonable agreement among themselves about how to divide up my father's estate. So they invited some village elders to come to our house and help us resolve the issue. The next day, some masons came and started building a high, ugly wall right through the center of our compound. My mother and my siblings and I were left with a small, three-room house. The village elders also decided that the profits from one of my father's many shops would go directly to providing for my mother and her children.

But the shop didn't bring in enough to maintain the standard of living we were accustomed to. Sometimes there wasn't even enough food for us. My mother was very concerned about my future, so she pulled me out of school so that I could become an apprentice to an auto mechanic. It's a shame that I wasn't able to get the education my father had wished for me. But I'm very grateful that my mother decided to provide me with these skills, because I've never had trouble finding work. There is always a need for experienced mechanics and drivers.

My mother did everything in her power to help me and my other siblings succeed in life, and I wouldn't ever want to upset her. That is why my current dilemma is so painful for me . . .

→ → ← ←

After my father's death, almost all of the relatives with whom we associated were from my mother's side of the family. Eight years ago, when I was only fifteen years old, I fell in love with one of my mother's distant relatives, Shahnoza. Our families would often visit one another while we were growing up. I could tell that she liked me, too; we would exchange knowing smiles and then look away quickly so that no one would notice. I would sometimes catch her staring at me out of the corner of my eye. I was so excited whenever she'd come to our house. But for two years, we didn't dare speak to one other.

The chance to communicate directly came as a result of a terrible accident in our family that took place during Ramadan one year. My first cousin, Mirwais, who was also a very close friend, had been riding with his father in a car when it struck a mine. Mirwais's father, my uncle, died along with several other passengers, while my cousin was considered lucky that he *only* lost his right leg. After he was released from the hospital, my family asked me to take care of Mirwais at his house at least until it was his turn to receive a prosthetic limb from the Red Cross. For the next several months, I spent every night at my cousin's house.

A couple of weeks after the accident, on the last night of Ramadan, a bunch of our friends came over to my cousin's house to try to cheer him up. We talked, joked, and—as discreetly as possible—gambled with cards late into the night. Then, at about one in the morning, as the party raged, I decided to turn in. I usually slept right next to my injured cousin, but since there were so many noisy friends around, I decided to go to the next room, which was separated from the party by only a dark curtain. As I held a small kerosene lamp to make my way into the dark room and started to pull the curtain aside, I noticed someone dash out of the room. I didn't know what to think. The only people in the house were our friends and my relatives. Why would anyone run away from me like that? But I was too tired to give this question any thought. I just curled up on the mattress, turned out the lantern, and fell asleep.

I was jolted awake sometime later by Mirwais from the next room. He was in agony—as he often was during those early days following the accident. He asked me to rub some medicinal oils onto what was left of his leg. When I finished massaging him, I returned to my room and once again, I saw a shadow run away as I pulled the curtain aside. This time I figured that it was probably some woman from Mirwais's family who was checking to make sure that us boys weren't doing something bad, like playing cards or drinking.

Five minutes after I returned to bed, just as I was about to fall asleep, I suddenly felt someone tugging on my foot. I sat up with a start and, squinting into the darkness, tried to make out the outline of the person before me. "Who's there?" I asked. My mouth was immediately covered by a hand, and I heard a girl whisper, "Shhhhh. Don't talk!" I turned on the gas lantern, and I saw Shahnoza crouching nearby.

"Let's go outside," she continued whispering. "I want to talk with you . . ." She took off before I had a chance to even lift my blankets. When I went out to the courtyard, I found her sitting on a small wooden chair with another chair nearby. She motioned to me to join her. There was a full moon, and her round face, plump body, and bright eyes were radiant. I had to pinch myself to make sure I wasn't dreaming.

When I sat down, Shahnoza said, "Najib, before this evening, I had always thought that you were a mullah or something. You were always so serious, and you'd always scamper off to the mosque for your prayers whenever I was over at your house. But I saw very clearly what you've been up to this evening . . . and now I realize that you are capable of doing anything!" She had a playful smile dancing on her beautiful full lips. "You know what I'm going to do tomorrow morning? I'm going to go straight to Mirwais's mother to inform her about the kind of nephew she's entrusted her poor, innocent son to."

If she was on the attack, I was ready to surrender immediately. "Oh please, don't say anything about what you saw tonight. All of the people who live here love and respect me, and I don't want to lose their confidence," I said in an exaggerated tone of fear. I had enjoyed a very successful night of gambling, and I pulled out all the money I had won from my pockets. The wad of bills spilled out everywhere since I hadn't had a chance to put it into any order after scooping up my winnings after each round. "Just tell me how much money I'll need to pay you to keep quiet."

"I'm not interested in your money. I have all the money I need," she told me with affected pride.

"So what do you want? Just say the word and I promise to get it."

"Things like money, clothes, and jewelry aren't interesting to me. . . . I'm interested in you," she said as she fluttered her long eyelashes.

I had to pinch myself again to make sure that I hadn't fallen back into a dream. "Well, I'm . . . I'm really interested in you, too," I managed to respond. "In fact . . . I love you."

"I love you, too! You know, I've been waiting two long years to say those words to you," Shahnoza said. "But I was always afraid to approach you since you were so serious around me."

"You know, I've wanted to talk to you for a very long time, too. But whenever you came over to my house or I saw you here, you were always surrounded by many women, and I didn't feel comfortable approaching you. I didn't dare talk to you under those circumstances . . ."

In the middle of these discussions, a lamp was lit in one of the windows inside the house. Shahoza quickly stood up, gave me a peck on the check, and ran back inside. But before she left, she asked me to sleep in the same room again the next night.

I couldn't sleep that night. I was thinking about Shahnoza—her sweet voice was still in my ears, and I could still feel her soft lips on my cheek. "What would happen the next night?" I was wondering. I kept repeating to myself: "I love you, I love you, I love you . . ."

❖ ❖ ❖ ❖

The next day was the beginning of Eid, when everyone wears new clothes. In the morning, I had some trouble adjusting my belt, so I asked one of my aunts to fix my pants before I went to wash up. When one of my young cousins went to retrieve my pants, they had a strong scent of fresh perfume. On my way to breakfast, I had to walk through the room where about a dozen of my female relatives were gathered, including Shahnoza, her mother, and her sisters.

One of the women immediately recognized the smell. "Najib," she exclaimed, "what a beautiful perfume you're wearing! Where did you get it?"

"I don't know," I responded, genuinely pleading innocence. "I asked my aunt to fix my pants this morning, and when I got them back, this is how they smelled."

All of the women started giggling and glancing over at Shahnoza in the corner. She blushed and put her head down.

On Eid, it's traditional to buy small presents for your closest friends and relatives. So I went to the bazaar and spent all the money I had won the previous night at cards. For my female relatives I bought flower-scented soap, shampoo, brushes, hair clips, perfume, hand mirrors, and plastic bracelets. I headed first to my house to give my mother and sister their gifts, and then I went to my cousin's house to distribute whatever remained. But I reserved the best presents for Shahnoza—I gave her perfume, a fancy hair clip, and a mirror.

That night, Shahnoza came to wake me up again, wearing the perfume I had just given her. I wasn't sleeping this time, though. We talked in the courtyard late into the night. At the end of our discussion, as we started to say good night, she took my hand. "Najib jaan," she said seriously, "I want to spend a lot of time with you and meet you like this often in the future. But this can't be just casual. I want you to promise me that you won't go off and marry someone else after we've been seeing each other for awhile. If we meet like this, I'm sure word will get out sooner or later. And my reputation will be forever tarnished if you don't marry me."

So that very night, now six years ago, I promised her that we'd get married.

We continued to have dates like this on and off for the next several years.

But like many people across Afghanistan, I saw my life, and my romance with Shahnoza, turned upside down when the Taliban captured our hometown. I left with my brother for Khwaja Bahawuddin when Taliban troops neared the city, and the next day she took off with her stepmother, father, and younger sister for Badakhshan province. Shahnoza's mother and a couple of other siblings remained behind in Taloqan. In Khwaja Bahawuddin, I quickly landed a job in a car-repair shop. I was very lucky. Most displaced people were forced to live in refugee camps set up by international organizations, while I enjoyed a steady source of income.

But I couldn't stop thinking of my dear Shahnoza. In the chaos of our rapid departure from Taloqan, I wasn't able to get any information about where she had gone. So I was thrilled when a few weeks later I found out that she and her family also had come to Khwaja Bahawuddin and had settled at the refugee camp. After they arrived and were going through the process of officially registering themselves as internally displaced people, I was eager to ingratiate myself with her family. So I decided to rent them a small house for three months and asked the landlord not to tell her family that I'd paid for it. "If anybody from her family asks about the rent, please just tell them that I'm your close friend and that you've lent me this house for free," I told him.

After I rented the house, I enjoyed much closer relations with Shahnoza's father. Since we were relatives, we always knew one another, but it wasn't until we were in Khwaja Bahawuddin that we really had a meaningful conversation. Her father would often invite me over to their house. And one evening as we were having dinner, he asked me, "I don't understand, Najib. Where are you spending your nights?"

"I work in the auto-repair shop in the day, and the owner lets me sleep there as well," I explained to him.

"Why are you sleeping there?" he asked me in great surprise. "As you know, this house has two rooms. Our family can all sleep in one room, and you can sleep in the other one. I'm sure your clothes are always filthy after a long day in the shop, so you can give your dirty clothes to one of the women here to wash."

I happily agreed. For the next six months, Shahnoza would do my laundry, prepare my bed, and cook excellent food. And almost every night, while the rest of her family slept, she would sneak off into my room, and we'd talk late into the night. But after six months, Shahnoza's father decided to move with his family to Iran. She hated the idea of leaving me for a foreign land. So she tried to talk her father out of it, but his mind was made up.

She was forced to resort to a different tactic. "You know, father, I really miss my mother," Shahnoza told him. "If we go to Iran, I think it will be very difficult for me to be so far away from her. Perhaps I'll just return home and live with my mother in Taloqan?" Shahnoza's father couldn't argue with this sentiment, so he began looking for a *marham*, a male escort, who might accompany her back to Taloqan.

The next evening, as we gathered together for dinner, I played my part exactly as Shahnoza and I had rehearsed it the previous night.

"Sometimes I find it so difficult living here in Khwaja Bahawuddin," I told her father as earnestly as I could. "I miss so many things from home—my family, my friends, walking around the Taloqan streets. I know that a lot has changed now that the Taliban have taken over, but I would love to visit at least for a couple of days."

Shahnoza's father took the bait. "Yes, my son, I know it's very difficult for you. This war has made it difficult for all of us. My guess is that it wouldn't be too great a risk to return to Taloqan for just a couple of days.

Your beard is long enough now, and if you put on a white turban, I doubt that the Taliban will bother you much. But I've heard some stories about how they occasionally grab young men off the street or from the mosques and send them off to the front lines. So try to be careful. . . . By the way, if you do decide to go back to Taloqan, maybe you could take my daughter with you? You probably haven't heard—she wants to return home to Taloqan while the rest of us head off to Iran."

I feigned ignorance. Shahnoza offered me a congratulatory smile.

So I did as I was requested. It was the middle of the winter, and we were experiencing an especially frigid cold spell. Although it was coldest at night, we were told that it was safer to travel under the cover of darkness. So one evening at dusk, Shahnoza and I took off on my friend's horse to Taloqan. Although we had many blankets, we were still shivering from the cold. She held me tightly—for warmth and to keep from falling off—as I controlled the horse's reins. The trip only takes a few hours by car, but we had to take back roads and paths through villages. We managed to arrive in Taloqan just before daybreak. While back in my hometown, I did little more than hide from the Taliban in my house for a couple of days, and then I attempted to make my way back to Khwaja Bahawuddin. This was the only time that I went to Taloqan while it was under Taliban occupation.

But my trip back was full of misadventure. When I was only a few miles outside of town, I was stopped at a checkpoint that had just been set up by the Taliban.

One of the young Pashtun soldiers with a long beard questioned me. "Where are you going?" He had a thick Pashtu accent when he spoke to me in Dari, and I had trouble at first following some of the things he said. I told him I was heading to Khwaja Bahawuddin since I worked there as a car mechanic.

"What's your nationality?" he asked. I explained that I was a Tajik from Taloqan.

"Why are you working with Mas'ud?" he asked me out of the blue. "Everyone knows that Khwaja Bahawuddin is a center of resistance. Who sent you here? You're a spy, aren't you?!"

I tried to explain the truth, but by then, he and five other soldiers who had come over to listen to our conversation were no longer interested in hearing my story. One of the other soldiers yelled, "Follow us!" Then the men began speaking in Pashtu among themselves.

They led me a few hundred yards away, over to a pool of water that was about four feet deep and twenty feet across. The pool was similar to many others that are used by villagers as a water catchment to provide drinking water for animals. It was surrounded by high trees, which helps prevent evaporation during hot summer days.

"Get into the water and walk over to the middle of the pool," the man who'd been questioning me ordered. I hesitated. But a couple of the soldiers raised their guns at me, and I realized I had no choice but to obey. I was sure that they would shoot me when I got to the middle of the pool. The water was indescribably cold, but I waded out to the middle in my clothes. I thought that at any second they would tell me to say my death prayer and send me into the next world. But instead they called out, "The moment you admit that you're a spy, we'll take you out of the water. Just inform this guard here when you're ready to confess." They then talked among themselves and left one soldier behind to guard me.

All night long, I shivered in the ice-cold water. I knew that if I confessed to spying, they would undoubtedly force me to endure even harsher punishments before killing me. So I just tried my best to survive the night. There were many times that I wanted to pass out from the cold, but I was afraid that if I didn't rub my body all night long, I could easily die of exposure. It was the most painful night of my life. In the morning, a thin layer of ice had formed in other parts of the pool.

Right after the dawn call to prayer, the young soldiers' leader came to the edge of the pool. He ordered me to come out of the water. My skin was blue from head to toe, and my teeth were chattering uncontrollably.

"Why was this man detained?" the commander asked the young soldier who'd been standing guard all night. "He doesn't want to admit he's a spy," the soldier responded.

The commander looked me up and down as I shivered in the early morning air. "I'll handle this investigation myself," he said. The commander took me back to the checkpoint where I'd been apprehended the previous day. He then inundated me with questions: "What's your name? Where are you from? Why were your traveling on this road so late last evening? Who are your parents? Where do you work?" and so on and so on.

As the interrogation continued, I saw people walking back and forth along the road gawking at us. Finally, a couple of women in dirty blue burqas came to my rescue. One of them was holding a tiny infant in her arms, while another was leading three small children. They came over to us and said, "Please commander, you have to help us. Our husbands are dead, and we have nobody to escort us on the long road north. Our homes have been destroyed, and we need to leave for our relatives' house. If nobody helps us to travel this long road ahead, I'm sure that we will all die. . . . Could you do us a huge favor and allow this young man to escort us on our journey?" The women were nearly begging, and their children were crying as they carried on and on with their pleas. They were making quite a ruckus.

"Quiet!" the commander finally yelled as he held up his hand. He looked back at me very seriously. "We've been unable to establish your guilt," he announced. "Therefore, I will allow you to escort these poor women and children to their relatives. It is your obligation to go with them until they reach their cousin's house. It is dangerous for women to travel unescorted."

"Thank you, thank you! May God protect you!" the women said.

I breathed a great sigh of relief and also thanked the commander for freeing me. I grabbed two of the young children into my arms, and we took off on the long road ahead. My friend's horse had been confiscated by the Taliban, but I was just happy to escape with my life.

→ → ← ←

As soon as the Taliban were defeated, I returned home. I got a job as a taxi driver while Shahnoza found work at a girls' school teaching mathematics. She didn't have any training as a teacher, but she had completed eighth grade and knew how to read and write. This education, along with some connections in the school's administration, proved sufficient for her to land a job.

We hadn't seen one another in more than a year and a half, since I left her in Taloqan on the night of my torture. When we finally laid eyes on one another again, our romance was instantly rekindled. I sat with her one night shortly after I returned and told her, "When I was living so far away from you, I thought about you every night when I fell asleep. You were the one who kept me going when I was depressed. And I knew that you were the one I wanted to spend the rest of my life with. So when do you think we should get married?"

Shahnoza was overjoyed. She'd been waiting for that question for many years.

We agreed that I would send my mother and sister to her house to handle all the negotiations. "I'm sure there won't be any problems . . ." she said with a wink.

That very same day, all of our relatives and friends suddenly seemed to have heard of our engagement. Of course it was well known that we'd been seeing each other for a long time, the only question was when we'd actually tie the knot.

Later that day I told my sister about my plans. And she ran off to tell my mother.

In the evening, I was watching Taloqan television by myself in my room. They were showing some Arnold Schwarzenegger film, I think. My mother came in but didn't interrupt the film. She just asked me if I'd like some tea, sat down next to me, and poured me cup after cup from my plastic thermos as I lost myself in the movie.

When the film finally ended and the channel was signing out for the evening, my mother said, "It's getting late, but before I go to sleep, I wanted to talk to you about something."

"Sure, of course, Mama," I said. "What did you want to discuss?"

"There's a rumor going around that you want to get married," she stated matter-of-factly.

"Yes, it's true," I said without emotion.

"Well, it's about time!" my mother nearly shouted. "Everyone knows by now that you're in love with Shahnoza. I'm sure that nothing could separate you two. Even if I were to object—which I certainly won't—I know you'd find some way or other to marry her. . . . Just go to the shop tomorrow and buy me some sweets, and then I'll go and begin talking with her mother."

But that night I could hardly sleep. I tossed and turned as I thought about my future. The next morning, as I was walking down the street to the shop, something happened to me. I'd been committed to Shahnoza for almost six years and there was no rational reason for me to start having second thoughts all of a sudden. But I started getting very anxious and began shaking all over. By the time I made it back home, I was in a total panic. I still don't understand why—maybe it had something to do with these nonstop wars in Afghanistan. Maybe that's what messed up my head. But for whatever reason, I just wasn't able to think straight.

When I came home and saw my mother, I just threw the sweets down on the floor. "I've been thinking about my marriage. And I've decided that I don't actually want to marry Shahnoza after all. I don't want you to take these sweets to her mother," I announced.

My mother was shocked. She had no idea what to make of my sudden change of heart. "What are you talking about? Everyone knows that you love Shahnoza. What happened to you?"

"I don't know. I just decided that I have no desire to marry her. None whatsoever! In principle, I have no problem getting married right now but just not to her. As far as I'm concerned, Shahnoza and the rest of her family can go to Hell! I hate them all!"

My mother was flabbergasted. "You must have lost your mind," she said. "You're either too brilliant for me to understand, or you're a complete idiot." She walked out of the room leaving me to stew in my own mixed-up emotions.

For one week, my mother didn't bother to broach the subject of marriage with me. I was still in my strange funk. I didn't want to talk to anyone about this, least of all to Shahnoza.

But then my mother started becoming anxious. "Look Najib jaan, if you really are intent on getting married, why don't you get engaged to the girl you've been dating?" she told me.

"Mama, I do want to get married," I told her. "But I've decided that I don't want to marry Shahnoza after all. She's just not right for me. Why don't you choose one of your nieces for me to marry?"

My older sister had married one of my mother's nephews ten years ago, so it was considered only fair that I, or at least one of my brothers, marry a girl from that family. I think my mother was not at all displeased with this unexpected turn of events. She enjoyed a close relationship with her sister and welcomed any ties that would bind them closer together.

"Are you sure this is what you really want?" she asked.

"Yes, I'm sure. I'm 100 percent sure. . . . If you ever want me to get married, you should take the sweets over to my aunt's house right now," I said.

So that's how I became engaged, only a few days later, to my first cousin Soraya. The engagement party took place at her house. There are actually several different types of engagement ceremonies here in Afghanistan, although my family usually practices only two kinds—*hejo-batqabul*, where a mullah leads the ceremony, or just a simple party that does not involve a mullah. If the mullah does not preside over the engagement, the future bride and groom have no right to see one another before the wedding. With a *hejobatqabul* ceremony, which is what was chosen for us, the engaged man and woman can see and talk with one other and even spend the night with each other. This is the rule only here in the city, where people are more educated; in the villages, no matter what kind of engagement ceremony you have, it's forbidden to see one another before the wedding.

A mullah came to our engagement ceremony and asked me three times: "Najib, son of Abdul Shafiq, do you agree to take as your wife Soraya, daughter of Daolat Shah?" The third time the question was posed, I said, "Yes." If you answer affirmatively right away, it's considered bad manners, as you'd be viewed as overeager. At the same time that the mullah asked me for my consent, there were two respected elders who were repeating the same question to Soraya.

But no sooner was the engagement party concluded did I begin to regret my decision. I thought about how wonderful Shahnoza was and what a fool I'd been to spurn her. From then on, whatever I would do and wherever I would go—whether walking on the street, driving my car, or sitting at home—I would always see her face before me. I had no idea what had happened to me; why did I suddenly get cold feet? After six years of romance and longing for Shahnoza, I suddenly began to despise her for a few weeks. And then on the day it became impossible to have her as my wife, my feelings for her grew much stronger than they ever had been before.

The day after Soraya and I had been officially engaged, I went over to her house. When we were alone, the first question out of her mouth was,

"Najib jaan, there's something I just don't understand. Everybody knows that you've been involved with our cousin Shahnoza for a long time. Why did you suddenly decide to marry me?"

I was silent for a couple of minutes as I thought about my response. "I really don't know," I finally stammered. "That's the way things turned out." I of course couldn't tell her that I was still in love with Shahnoza.

A few weeks after my engagement, I happened to be parked out near the school where Shahnoza teaches. A friend of mine was sitting in the back seat, and we were chatting as a woman in a burqa approached the car. By the time I noticed her, she was so close to my window that I didn't have a chance to look down to try to identify her by her shoes and stockings. I just rolled down my window, thinking that maybe she needed a ride somewhere in my taxi. But instead the woman flipped her burqa over her head . . . it was Shahnoza with her usually beautiful eyes bloodshot and full of anger. "Najib, you're not a real man," she said to me simply. Then she flipped her burqa back down over her face and started to walk away.

I got out of the car and tried to explain, to whatever extent I possibly could, my side of the story. "Please listen to me, Shahnoza!" I called out to her.

She turned around with her burqa still hiding her face. "Don't talk to me anymore!" she said through the mesh screen. "You are the kind of man who makes promises and doesn't keep them. Go ahead and marry whoever you want. I'm never going to get married—I will always be alone." I tried to talk to her, but she just hurried off behind the walls of the school yard.

About a month later, after I returned from a trip in my taxi to Badakhshan, I found Shahnoza and her mother sitting with my mother at our house. They were of course still our relatives in spite of my malicious behavior, but I was still startled to see them at my house. As Shahnoza and I made some polite small talk, it appeared that her bitterness had dissipated. When our guests got up to leave after a little while, my mother gave Shanoza a beautiful dress that she had sewed herself. By this time, it was dark and my mother asked me to drive them home. Shahnoza sat in the front seat while her mother got into the back. As we were riding, Shahnoza said the sweetest words to me. "Thank you so much for the beautiful dress your mother gave me. I'll be sure to wear it when I attend your wedding. At the party, you know that you can count on me to help you with whatever you might need. I'm sure that there will be a lot of cooking and cleaning to be done. I would be proud to be of service to you—no less than one of your own sisters."

I started to say something apologetic but she interrupted me. "Don't worry, I don't hold any grudges against you, in spite of all the promises you made to me over the course of so many years. It's all water under the bridge. That's all in the past now and it's time to move on."

After this, Shahnoza would come by the house from time to time and we'd chat. In a lot of ways, it was like the old times. But then one day as we spoke, she became very serious. "Najib jaan, what do you think? How am I ever supposed to get married now?" she asked me. "Taloqan is a small town, and everyone knows that we were dating for a long time. Women here love to gossip. Even at funerals, after an hour of mourning for the dead person, women will change the subject to savor some juicy piece of gossip. So even if I were to get married, sooner or later my husband would find out about what had happened between us. Then it would always be a source of contention in our marriage. It's much better if I never get married and just stay home with my parents. These days, with all the men who've died during the wars or are living abroad or can't afford a large dowry, there are many women who aren't married. It's not shameful to live your life without a husband."

It was only then that I realized that I'd totally ruined her life. I had given my word and then violated her trust. I became determined to do something to help. Not long ago, a friend of mine who recently returned here after many years in Pakistan asked me to help him get married. So I praised Shahnoza to the heavens. "She's an educated person, she's beautiful, and she's a very nice girl. You should definitely meet her!" I of course didn't breathe a word to him about our past romantic involvement.

So I organized an "impromptu" meeting one day at our house, and he did indeed like her. He ended up sending his mother to her house to propose on his behalf. But she rejected him straightaway. Shahnoza told me later that she was afraid of what would happen if my friend learned the full truth about us.

Even now, I'm still in love with Shahnoza. I still think about her all the time. But there's no escaping the fact that I'm engaged to another woman. I can't just call off the engagement now. I've already visited my fiancée more than a hundred times. And for Afghans it's considered a huge scandal to call off an engagement—it's just as bad as getting a divorce. I think that Soraya would be totally devastated if I were to end things. My mistake could easily lead her to commit suicide. Nowadays a lot of girls here in Taloqan kill themselves over far less.

It makes it all the more complicated that she's a close relative. There are too many ties that bind us together. For example, if I were to end our engagement, it could negatively affect my sister's marriage. In order to defend his sister's honor, Soraya's brother might use my calling off the engagement as a pretext to divorce my sister. Or even if he doesn't divorce her, he could make her life very difficult. Then what would happen to their seven children? There's just nothing I can do to undo the damage.

I have a very close relationship with my mother, but I can't talk with her about this terrible problem of mine. She often asks me what's wrong with me. I haven't been myself for a long time now. But since she was the one who made all of the marriage arrangements for me, I just don't feel comfortable sharing this deep, dark secret with her. I don't want to hurt her. I'm sure she'd be humiliated in front of her sister and all our relatives.

I've been engaged for over two years now, and my family is currently preparing for the wedding party. My mother has been sewing clothes for her future daughter-in-law, and my relatives have been discussing their various responsibilities during the wedding.

Whenever I'm alone, I begin to think about what I've done, and I'm racked with guilt. I replay my conversations and my actions over and over again in my mind. I just can't understand why I was so stupid. I try to escape from my twisted thoughts by surrounding myself with distractions. Every evening I invite friends over to my house, and we play cards and talk late into the night. If people want to go home or fall asleep before my eyes are ready to close, I poke them and force them to stay awake in order to save myself from my own haunted reality.

My friends used to ask me, "Hey, why did you break it off with that girl, Shahnoza? We all thought that you were in love and would marry her."

I always avoided the question. "I just didn't want to marry her, that's all!" My dismissive tone has always discouraged complicated follow-up questions. I can't tell anybody the truth about what really happened. I'm afraid people would just laugh at me.

I've considered taking Shahnoza as my second wife, but I have no idea how Soraya would react to this. Moreover, it takes a long time—and a large sacrifice—to gather together the resources for a new wedding party and for the bride price. I have already gone into debt to pay for my current fiancée and wedding party. My guess is that I wouldn't be able to collect the money for a new wedding for another four years or so.

And who knows if Shahnoza would even agree to marry me as a second wife after four years? In any case, I'd want to be sure that I could really provide for both of my wives and all our children. But isn't it crazy that I'm thinking about a second wife when I don't even have a first one yet?

Throughout our engagement, Soraya has repeatedly asked me why I decided to marry her and not Shahnoza. And I've never been able to give her a satisfactory answer. Then yesterday evening, when we were having an argument about something or other, she asked me yet again. This time I blurted out, "I really don't know why I decided to marry you. And I regret my decision every day. The truth is I'm still in love with Shahnoza."

Tears began welling up in her eyes. "If you love Shahnoza, then why are you engaged to me?" She buried her head in the pillow. For half an hour or so, I let her cry before I went over to her and began stroking her arm and back to calm her.

I would rather be left standing in that pool of ice-cold water than live with this daily torment.

CHAPTER SIX

Mahtabgul, Daughter of Zafar Khan

There was a time when I sank so low that my only possessions were the clothes on my back and an old, worn-out plastic mat.

It wasn't always this way. Growing up, my family wasn't rich, but we were able to provide for our basic needs, and all of my brothers and sisters received an education. My husband came from Taloqan. Maybe that's part of the reason I settled here so many years after he died.

My husband wasn't a relative. We fell in love when we were both living in the dormitories in Kabul. I came from an area near the capital called Parwan. We were married in 1974, and at the time, he was still a student in the pedagogical university and was studying to become a Dari literature teacher. The first four years of our marriage were the happiest time in my life. He was very kind and considerate. And he was quite exceptional; when I would head off to school in the morning to teach, he would do some of the housework and even look after the children. He always treated my parents and all my relatives with kindness and respect.

While my husband was completing his education, I supported our family financially.

Our economic situation was not good; a teacher's salary was hardly sufficient to support a growing family in those days. As a student, he became very active in politics and remained active even after he graduated in 1976. During that time, student activists on college campuses who favored a fundamentalist brand of Islam competed noisily against those who urged a socialist revolution. My husband was a member of one of the socialist parties at the university. But his party was not considered radical enough by the new communist government that seized power in 1978.

One day, at a protest at the lycée where he was teaching, police raided the gathering and arrested him and many other young activists. Dozens of students and teachers were beaten by the overzealous police force. In the midst of it all, they ended up shooting my husband in the arm. The government then accused him of being a reactionary allied with the mujahedin, although nothing could have been further from the truth.

By the time he was thrown in prison, we already had three children. I had given birth to a child every year for the first three years of our marriage: two daughters, Leilo jaan and Zebo jaan, and our youngest was a boy named Roshan. After my husband's arrest, the police came to our apartment and searched it from top to bottom. Our youngest child was only six months old when the police raided our place. I still remember how all our children bawled as the police tore apart our small flat. But they apparently didn't find anything worth their while because they left empty-handed and muttering something about "backward reactionaries."

I went from prison to prison in search of my husband. Finally, at the Jabal Saraj jail, they told me that they had some sort of record of him. "But he's not here right now," a surly prison guard begrudgingly informed me. "He was wounded when he was resisting arrest. They brought him here for awhile and then they took him to, let's see, Parwan hospital. You can probably find him there . . . I mean, if he's not dead already."

When I finally managed to locate my husband at Parwan hospital, I learned that he was in the surgical ward. As I approached the hallway where he was supposedly interned, my path to him was blocked by armed guards. I was beside myself with panic. "Let me see my husband! I need to see him!" I cried out. Out of desperation, I tried to force my way through the guards, but they refused to move. They kept my husband in the hospital for twenty-four hours. And the whole time he was there, I wandered back and forth near the hospital doors fearing the worst.

Eventually, after repeated requests, a kind young nurse told me that my husband was feeling better and had been transferred back to prison. This time they took him to Puli Charkhi prison. For the next two years while he was in jail, I would visit him once a week and take him whatever food we could spare. Unfortunately, this wasn't much, as there was hardly enough food even for our small children. It had been hard enough to scrape by on two teachers' salaries, but with only one breadwinner in the family, it became nearly impossible. Very often, the only food I'd be able to provide my children for the whole day was a small piece of bread.

When I would visit my husband in jail, I would bring him freshly washed clothes. I thought it was important for him to keep some semblance of dignity while surrounded by the filth and rats of the Puli Charkhi prison. He was held there for nearly two years, until 1980, shortly after the Soviet invasion of Afghanistan. For seven months, he lived at home with us. But he was no longer the same loving, considerate man who was taken away from me. He began to drink and smoke a lot and would just sit around the apartment all day. My husband had been crushed by his prison experience and was nearly a broken man. He had lost his interest in politics. But for some unknown reason, one dark morning at five o'clock, the police came for him. He was never a free man again.

Our financial situation sank lower and lower. I slowly sold off everything of value in our apartment in order to afford food for the kids. First I sold the curtains, then the window panes, the carpets, the plastic sheeting on the windows, then the dishes, the pots and pans, the mattresses, the pillows. The only thing that remained was an old plastic mat. This was the only possession that really belonged to our family. We would eat on it, sit on it, and sleep on it. By all rights, the plastic mat should have been thrown out long ago because it was practically worn all the way through. But I would continuously sew up the holes and do other repairs so that we could keep using it. In those days it was so difficult to survive, so difficult . . .

When my son Roshan was only five years old, he learned how to recite from the Koran. During Ramadan, he fasted and prayed five times a day, including at the crack of dawn. I was so ashamed that sometimes I couldn't even manage to scrape together enough money to feed him after the final prayer of the day, when it was time to break the fast.

When my children would ask me about their father, I would lie to them. I just told them that he had "gone abroad." I didn't want them to think that their father was some sort of petty criminal. I thought that this would have a terrible psychological impact on them. Instead, I described their father as a highly educated, kind man who loved them very dearly.

I remember one year at the end of Ramadan when everyone was celebrating the holiday of Eid. According to our traditions, at this time of year, parents are supposed to buy their children new clothes, give them money and other presents, and cook a lot of food for them and for guests. It's considered the father's duty to take care of all this. But my husband was still in prison. And I didn't have the money to buy new clothes or even cook celebratory food. When Zebo jaan saw all the other children on our street with their new clothes, she came home in tears. Little Zebo jaan was smaller than many other children her age because of malnourishment. "Mama," she asked with tears streaming down her cheeks, "when will Daddy come home? I miss him." I hugged her tightly and reassured her that her Dad would be home soon, God willing. In truth, she hardly even remembered her father. She was only four years old when the police dragged him back to prison for the second and last time.

Sometimes I would borrow money from friends and buy the children new clothes. I would always wrap the gifts with ribbons and tell them, "Look what your father sent you!" I still remember the wonderful glow in their eyes during these all-too-infrequent special occasions.

➔ ➔ ❧ ❧

Eventually, we found it impossible to keep living in that small apartment in Kabul. I had fallen deeply into debt, and I had no idea how I would repay my friends. At the end of 1981, with little more than the clothes on our backs and that one worn plastic mat, my three children and I moved back to my parents' house. Their house was already overflowing with poor relatives whose houses had been destroyed in the fighting in nearby villages. We were forced to share one small room with a relative's family from a neighboring village.

Back in Parwan, I got a new job as a teacher at my old high school. And with my miserable salary, I managed to continue to feed my children.

The next year, our economic situation improved slightly, as my older brother got a good job as a doctor in a hospital. Every day, at about eleven in the morning, I had a free period at school when I would rush home to prepare lunch for the kids. I could still rarely afford to buy meat, but at least I could cook them vegetable soup and buy enough bread to keep their stomachs full. One day, as usual, I was making soup. I fried some onions, added carrots and potatoes, and poured some water into the big pot. Seeing that I was busy cooking, my daughter Zebo jaan, who was only seven years old at the time, volunteered to go to the shop down the street to buy some bread. I gave her a little money and sent her off. "Hurry back," I called out after her. "Don't forget that you have to go to school soon." She went to school in the afternoon, while Leilo jaan went in the morning.

My daughter purchased the round flat bread at the kiosk down the street and headed home. As she was walking right in front of the local women's association, a firefight between some armed men broke out. The mujahedin were very active in Parwan at this time. My daughter tried to duck for cover, but it was too late. A stray bullet struck her right in the heart and she died instantly. She never let go of the bread. When I rushed out of the house to see what had happened, I found her body lying in middle of the muddy road, the pile of bread still folded in her lifeless arms.

At exactly the same moment, a missile fell on the girls' school where my oldest daughter was studying. Many of the mujahedin factions viewed schools, especially girls' schools, as instruments of communist ideology and as a direct assault on their radical Islamic worldview. So it was not by coincidence that the bomb landed right in the middle of the school.

As I ran out of my house to see my youngest daughter lying dead in the street, many other parents were rushing to the school. The explosion had shaken the entire town. There was pure chaos in the streets, and I was worried that my daughter's corpse would be trampled by the mobs of worried parents. I threw myself down on the ground and tried to protect her. Of course it was far too late to offer her the protection she really needed.

At that moment, I was sure that I had lost two daughters in one morning. I asked one of my brothers to carry my poor Zebo jaan back to the house. And I, still covered in my dead daughter's blood, took off running for the school. When I got there, what I saw confirmed my worst fears. My daughter's classroom had been reduced to a heap of rubble. Parents were wailing, and there were men climbing the ruins, trying to collect the dead and rescue the injured.

I threw myself on the ground, mourning my poor martyred children. And just then, little Leilo jaan ran from the crowd and grabbed my shoulder. "Mama, mama. Here I am." I looked at her in disbelief. I thought at first that I was seeing a ghost. She didn't even have a speck of dirt on her clothes, and she was holding a beautiful red apple.

"Mama, I was really hungry," she explained to me as she sobbed. "So I told the teacher that I was going to the bathroom, and instead I ran down the street to buy an apple. I'd just bought the apple when the bomb landed on our school." She hugged me tightly. "I'm so afraid," she cried. "Please, let's go home, Mama. Zebo jaan will be leaving for school soon. We have to tell her that she shouldn't come."
I didn't know what to tell my brave little girl.

In spite of all of my personal difficulties, I went back to the pedagogical institute for more training. I taught in the morning, and in the afternoon, I would study. After two years, I was promoted to vice principal of Muhammad Usman school in Parwan. After school, I would sit with my children and help them with their homework. Just because they didn't have a father in their lives, I didn't want them to be deprived of any opportunities. As my children fell asleep in the evening, I would stroke their hair and whisper softly in their ears, "As soon as this terrible war is over, you'll help rebuild your country. You're the future of Afghanistan. You're the future . . ."

My financial situation improved somewhat after I received the promotion. I was sometimes even able to afford to buy some new clothes for my husband, who was still in prison. I would try to visit him at least a couple of times a month. Every time I saw him, I was stricken anew by the sight of him behind those thick, steel bars. He told me that he was forced to sleep on cold cement floors and was barely given enough food to stay alive. He had grown as thin as a rail, and he had developed a heavy cough. One day, in the fifth year of his second imprisonment, I went to visit him. When I saw him, I was struck with a strong feeling that he was losing his will to fight and could no longer hold on. Sure enough, he died the next day.

✦ ✦ ✦ ✦

My daughter Leilo jaan graduated from school with various awards for her high level of academic achievement and immediately joined the teaching staff at my school. She had become a beautiful young lady, tall, with long, flowing black hair and light skin. Not surprisingly, she had many suitors who came to our house to ask for her hand in marriage. But I couldn't bear the thought of her leaving me for another family, so I would always refuse the offers. "I'm very sorry," I'd tell the mothers of would-be grooms, "but I've already decided that she'll marry one of my relatives." Leilo jaan had been teaching elementary-school students for five years when the Taliban captured Parwan in 1996.

By this time, my brother Abdul Ayoub had moved to Taloqan, where he was working as a doctor. When he heard about the Taliban offensive in our area, he sent an urgent message asking us to join him in the north of Afghanistan as quickly as possible. We decided to take half of our possessions and leave the rest behind. The things we abandoned, we never saw again. We joined many other fleeing refugees, who piled into large eighteen-wheel trucks. Our possessions were stacked beneath us as we traveled the long, dangerous road up north. Because there was such a massive flow of refugees fleeing the Taliban advances through the Salang tunnel, it took us three days to make the laborious trip to Taloqan.

My daughter, my son, and I lived with my brother's family for three years. I had heard a lot about Taloqan from my husband. And I had always dreamed of seeing his homeland. My brother gave us a small room in his house.

My brother was a very friendly man who frequently received guests. One of his friends was a young, handsome man named Anwar who was a pilot in the air force of the Northern Alliance leader, Ahmad Shah Mas'ud. His job was to transfer arms between Tajikistan and Afghanistan by helicopter. Whenever he was in Taloqan, he would come to our house and talk with my brother late into the night. One time, he happened to see my daughter walking around the compound, and he took a strong liking to her.

Anwar couldn't ask my brother directly about my daughter—that would have been considered offensive to his host. So instead he found another source: my son, Roshan, who was a soccer player and who sometimes played at a field in the center of town. One day, after Roshan's match, Anwar came up to him and started peppering him with questions.

"How old are you? Where are you from? What are you doing here? What do you want to do when you grow up? Have you ever flown in a helicopter? . . ." In this way, Anwar tried to soften him up for the questions that really interested him. "Where is your father? What does your mother do? How old is your sister? Is she married or engaged?"

Roshan told me all about this conversation, so I suspected that something might be afoot. Sure enough, when Anwar would return from his trips to Tajikistan, he would always bring gifts, like cases of soft drinks or video cassettes, for both my brother and for my son. He would even invite them over to his house for lunches and dinners.

One day, Anwar told Roshan, "You know, you have only one sister, and I would really like to marry a girl who is the only daughter in a family. Those kinds of girls are always so proper and well behaved. I really admire your family. And I like the fact that she is well educated."

Roshan recounted their discussion to me. He was very fond of his new "brother Anwar," but I didn't approve of the match. We knew next to nothing about him and absolutely nothing about his family.

Anwar was originally from Kabul, and at that time, it was too dangerous for his parents to come to Taloqan for the proposal negotiations. So one of Anwar's relatives, Dr. Baki who lived in Taloqan, decided to take charge of the necessary arrangements. Dr. Baki was one of my brother's colleagues, and they were close friends. He and his wife came to our house to officially ask for my daughter's hand. Dr. Baki's wife told me, "I need to let you in on a little secret." She looked around the room conspiratorially, clearly concerned that someone might overhear her. "Anwar had been engaged to his cousin before he saw your daughter. But since he first laid eyes on her, he's talked of nothing else. He returned the sweets and the flowers to his poor cousin, thereby calling off the engagement. Since that day, the two sides of the family have refused to speak with one another."

"He told me that he no longer wants to marry an illiterate girl from among our relatives. He wants to marry an educated girl."

At about this same time, my relations with my brother's wife began to deteriorate. We were stuck at home together all day, every day, and over time we found all kinds of little things to quarrel about.

One morning, shortly after one of our squabbles, my brother announced that he had found a room in a house nearby where my children and I could live. He gave us a few essentials—some dishes, mattresses, and pillows—and that same day we moved to our small rental house. The tiny, mud house was being rented out to a number of poor families. The conditions were very stark: there were dirt floors, tiny windows, and low ceilings. Because it didn't receive any direct sunlight, it was cold and dark inside all day. I couldn't prevent my disappointment from creeping across my face.

My brother caught my look. "Don't worry," he tried to assure me. "I'll be right down the street. If you need anything, please come anytime. I've paid three months' rent in advance." He gave me some food and spending money. I understood that we had become a burden on his family, but I still couldn't help feeling as though we'd been evicted.

As the negotiations regarding my daughter's future carried on, Anwar did more and more to try to influence the process. First he bought us a small generator to power the three light bulbs in the new house. Then he brought us a large drum of petrol so that we could run the generator. He'd give us all kinds of small gifts, which he would bring from Tajikistan. And he would invite Roshan to his house and show him action movies on his VCR.

His efforts were very effective. He offered me little reason to doubt that he was a stable young man and could provide for my daughter and their future children. But in the back of my mind, doubts continued to linger.

One day, before I had given my final approval, my daughter went to my brother's house to borrow a meat grinder. On her way back, a black Land Cruiser with tinted windows stopped on the road, and one of the men inside began talking to her. Anwar happened to be right down the street at the time. He saw what was happening, and without a moment's hesitation, he ran over and dragged the driver out of the car. He threw the man on the ground and, with his pistol drawn, shouted at him, "What business do you have talking to this girl? I'll kill you." He cocked his gun and seemed poised to pull the trigger. As my daughter sprinted back to the safety of our house, Anwar started to kick the guy sprawled out in front of him.

Anwar had indeed impressed us. He showed that he was willing to do whatever was necessary to defend my daughter and to protect her honor. It was only several years later that I began to play this scene over and over again in my mind. Why was it that nobody in the Land Cruiser came to the driver's defense? Of course it was a brave act, but given the way people were acting in Afghanistan at the time, what Anwar had done was almost suicidal. I began to wonder if the whole confrontation might not have been staged. But these thoughts never entered my head at the time— I was blinded by his charm and saw only his bravery and honor.

After this, I gave in and approved the match, accepting the sweets that had been pushed on me for months on end. And the next day, in accordance with our customs, I returned some sweets of my own when Dr. Baki's wife came calling. We arranged a modest engagement party, as we were planning a large wedding ceremony that his parents could attend.

It's undeniable that, in the beginning, Anwar was a very good man. He showed deep respect for me, my son, and my brother's family. He would praise me to the heavens. "You really are a heroine," he'd tell me. "You raised your children so well in the face of so many difficult circumstances. You lost your husband at an early age but remained determined to sacrifice everything to give them a proper upbringing. I bow down before you. It is a tremendous honor to be marrying a girl from such a respectable family."

Anwar promised that the wedding would take place shortly after the engagement party. But he kept postponing the date with the excuse that his parents wanted to attend but were unable to make their way from Kabul because of the fighting along the road.

After the engagement, Anwar would often come to our humble house, usually with his arms full of little presents like candies and beautiful, expensive fabrics for my daughter and for me. He quickly became like a part of our family.

✦   ✦   ✦   ✦

Before we even had a chance to have a wedding party, the Taliban invaded Takhar province. It was the summer of 1999, and we were forced to flee immediately. My brother's family went to Badakhshan province with my son and with as many possessions as they could cram into their small car. We were more fortunate. Helicopter pilots were permitted to take their families across the border to Dushanbe, the capital of neighboring Tajikistan.

It was my first time abroad, and we deeply appreciated the freedom and peace that we enjoyed in this foreign land. We lived in the center of town, so we had regular electricity, running water, and gas. Anwar hired a beautiful young girl to help us out with the housework. All I had to do was handle the cooking. But probably the best thing about Tajikistan was that we didn't have to wear our burqas in public. It had been far too many years since I had enjoyed this freedom.

A couple of months after we had arrived in Dushanbe, Anwar used some of his connections to help reunite us with Roshan. It was great having our family back together again. But after an extended search for work in Tajikistan, my son decided to leave for Moscow with some of his friends. Anwar gave him some money for the road, and Roshan called a few weeks later to tell me that he'd found a job selling cigarettes in the market and even had managed to pick up some Russian. His business became increasingly successful, and he would regularly send money back home for us. Eventually, he gathered together enough funds to pay a smuggler to take him to France. He got a job there selling flowers in a town outside of Paris. A few months later, he took off for England. But he was caught by the police when he tried to enter the country. After a long police interrogation, he was granted refugee asylum and was permitted to remain. Whenever I have access to a telephone, he tries to call me a couple of times a month. But I haven't seen him since the day he left us in Dushanbe.

Anwar's younger brother also lived with us in Dushanbe. But he didn't spend much time at home. What he seemed to enjoy most about living abroad was the chance to date girls, go out and drink alcohol with friends, and dance late into the night in the clubs.

During our time in Dushanbe, my daughter gave birth to a baby girl, Ahdiya. Three days after Ahdiya's birth, Anwar came to the maternity hospital to collect his wife and baby. He brought along a friend of his who filmed this joyous occasion with his video camera. As we would see again and again in the video, when Anwar met the doctors and nurses who had delivered the baby, he stuffed their hands full of money. Both he and my daughter were thrilled to be parents. Anwar was frequently out of town for his work, but when he returned, he would dote on his little baby. He'd sing her songs and bounce her on his knees.

Sometimes I would baby-sit the child when Anwar took my daughter out for long walks in the park or out to concerts. They'd go to the bazaar to buy clothes for themselves and their child. One of my happiest memories was celebrating the New Year in 2001 in the central square of Dushanbe; we saw a beautiful fireworks display and were surrounded by thousands of women and men dancing, drinking champagne, and enjoying the special night together. I never saw my daughter happier. We never wanted to leave Tajikistan.

But at the end of 2001, after the Taliban were driven out of Kabul, Anwar flew home. He was one of the first members of the Northern Alliance forces to enter Kabul, and when he arrived, he was swarmed by well-wishers. But ironically, the sweeping out of the repressive Taliban regime marked the beginning of the end of our happy family life.

The problems started after Anwar was reunited with his parents in Kabul. He told me later that his parents had been very disappointed in him. They complained that he was wasting all his money on his wife and her family, that he had helped my son find work in Moscow but hadn't helped his own brother, and that he didn't send sufficient money back home.

Anwar's parents had felt neglected as a result of his long absence from Kabul. So they decided to retaliate by criticizing almost every decision he had made over the last several years. Their biggest complaint was his choice of bride. They couldn't understand why he didn't marry the cousin to whom he'd been engaged. "What gave you the right to this kind of freedom?" his father would question him angrily. They demanded that he, his wife, and child return to Kabul immediately.

As the faithful son that he was, he obeyed his father's orders. He returned to Dushanbe from Kabul in early 2002 and demanded that we pack up our bags as soon as possible. "We're going home," he said gruffly.

When I sent word about our plans to Roshan, who was still in Moscow at the time, he called Anwar and urged him to allow us to remain in Dushanbe. "I'll pay all of their expenses—I'll rent them an apartment and buy them food. Just allow them to stay in Tajikistan. Everyone says that it's still unstable inside Afghanistan. Please don't force them to go back there so quickly. Why don't you wait awhile until the situation calms down a bit?"

But Anwar was already under his parents' influence. Echoing a conversation that he must have had with his father, he said to my son, "My poor parents don't even have their own house in Kabul. They're renting a small house, and instead of helping them buy a place of their own, I'm wasting all kinds of money on your family here in Dushanbe. This is not a question that's open for discussion. My wife and my daughter will return with me to Kabul."

While I understood that Anwar's parents didn't approve of his choice of wife, they were at least interested in going through the appropriate motions at first. When we returned to Kabul, we moved in with his parents. They had a house with a few rooms, but it wasn't nearly large enough to accommodate their huge family. Anwar had nine brothers and four sisters. And at the time, he was the only breadwinner in the family; the rest studied in school or in college or were unemployed. A few days after our arrival, they threw a big party for Leilo jaan and her daughter to welcome them to the family. Hundreds of their relatives, neighbors, and friends attended, and we were all treated to a very nice feast.

But only five days after this festive gathering, Anwar and his father got into a heated argument that my daughter and I couldn't help but overhear.

"Why did you come back home nearly empty-handed?" Anwar's father roared.

"I've had many expenses, father. I've tried to save up as much money as possible for you and mother."

"You knew very well that our house had been destroyed a decade ago. You should have been saving up money to help us buy a new house. We needed money for a house. But instead, you had to just waste all of your hard-earned money on some other family. You have no respect for your father. You're a selfish ass!"

The old, stocky man then began to beat his son. Anwar didn't try to resist. He just stood there with his arms folded across his head to protect himself from the blows. By the time his father was finished with him, Anwar was bleeding and his shirt was torn apart.

When Anwar returned to our room, Leilo jaan and I were in shock. We had heard the shouting, but we couldn't have imagined that the fight would have gone so far. Our family had always resolved our conflicts as calmly as possible. Unlike many men, Anwar never had so much as raised a hand to threaten his wife.

Shortly after we returned to Kabul, Leilo jaan became pregnant again. She began to get discolored blotches on her face like many pregnant women. But unlike in Dushanbe, where she had more than enough food and didn't need to perform difficult, time-consuming housework, she became little more than a servant in our new home. As the new wife in the household, her primary responsibilities were cleaning the house, washing clothes for the whole family, carrying water from the well, cooking, and washing the dishes as well as watching after her child. I tried to help her as much as I could, but I'd honestly grown too old and weak after too many years on this earth suffering through such hardship. After dinner and washing the dishes, my poor daughter was too exhausted to do anything more than lie down and fall fast asleep.

We felt like outsiders from our earliest days in Anwar's house. And this feeling only intensified over time. A few months into Leilo jaan's pregnancy, Anwar's father began to ask his son, "By the way, why does your wife's mother insist on living with us. You should just throw her out. Who needs her here anyway?"

One morning, when Anwar was out of town, Anwar's father confronted me as I was walking back to my room. "Mahtabgul, come over here," he called to me with a very sharp tone from across the courtyard. When I approached, he grumbled at me, "You know, your daughter has no respect for anyone in this house. She talks back to me, to my wife, and my daughters. What kind of upbringing did you provide your child?"

I knew very well that my daughter would never talk back to anyone. She was a humble and quiet girl around her elders. I began to understand that Anwar's father was determined to do whatever he could to break up their marriage. He no doubt had seen how Anwar had been doting on

Leilo jaan and their daughter, and I think that he and Anwar's mother were jealous.

I really didn't know how to respond to his accusations, but I was determined to defend my daughter. "I'm sure that she's trying the best she can," I said. "She works all day from early in the morning until late in the evening serving your family. But even if she was at her wits' end, I can't imagine that she would ever talk back to anyone. She's too well disciplined for that."

"See what I mean. Like mother, like daughter!" he yelled in a rage. "How do you have the nerve to talk back to me like that? You're living in my house, eating my food, and then you speak to me like that? And why do you bring up the fact that she's working all day long? This is her responsibility! Any Afghan daughter-in-law would serve her husband's family . . .

"Go and collect your things and leave my house right now! I don't want to ever see your ungrateful face here ever again! If you don't leave at this very moment, I'll call the police and have you thrown out."

I tried my best to maintain my composure, to show him that he didn't have power over me. But when I saw my daughter crying, I couldn't control myself. My eyes produced a fountain of tears as I walked out the front door.

I had a close friend I knew from many years ago when I had lived in Kabul. And I was sure that she and her husband would agree to take me in temporarily. So my daughter and I took a taxi to her house. We must have cried a thousand tears in that fifteen-minute taxi ride.

After we arrived at my friend's house, I had a long discussion with my daughter. She couldn't imagine living without me; we had never been separated for even one day over the twenty-seven years of her life. But I urged her to return to her husband. "I don't want you to break up your marriage and ruin your life because of me. We'll still be able to see each other from time to time. You have to go home to your daughter, your husband, and his family and be a respectful girl. Anwar is a good man— even if his parents are far from the most welcoming in-laws." I was worried about her reputation and what people might say if he were to divorce her.

→   →   ←   ←

Soon after I was forced to move out, Anwar changed completely. He must have finally fallen victim to his parent's malevolent schemes. He also began drinking heavily. He would make nasty comments about how ugly Leilo jaan had become after those blotches had formed on her face. When they slept together at night and she would try to cuddle up to him, he would push her away. "Move away from me," he would growl. "You're contaminated."

About this time, my son began sending money from London so I was able to rent a small room in a house for myself. I had already lived with my friend for several weeks, and I was afraid that I would soon become a burden on her family. She told me that I was welcome to stay as long as I liked, but I'd already learned my lesson about overstaying your welcome.

One day, Leilo jaan showed up at my door with her daughter hanging on one arm and a burqa hanging over the other one. Leilo jaan had a black eye, and tears were streaming down her swollen face. She'd clearly been beaten up. She was holding a plastic bag filled with her and Ahdiya's old clothes. Her stomach was already bulging from her pregnancy of seven months.

"My little girl, my little girl, what's the matter?" I said as I hugged her.

"This morning, for no reason at all, Anwar started beating me up," she managed to blurt out after several attempts to hold back her tears. "He told me that if I didn't leave the house right then and there, he would beat me up like a dog." He threw a few of my clothes into a bag, literally pushed me out the door, and locked it behind me.

"What can I do, Mama? His sisters and mother are constantly interfering in our lives. I don't know what they say to him exactly, but after he comes back from talking with them, he just yells and curses at me."

I held my daughter close and tried to calm her. "Don't worry, my daughter. They're bad people, but you need to be proud and maintain your dignity. You mustn't allow yourself to sink to their level. . . . You know that you are always welcome to stay here with me."

My daughter and granddaughter lived with me for the next seven months. In November 2002, Leilo jaan gave birth to another baby girl, Zarghona. I helped my daughter however I could while she gave birth and regained her strength, and I looked after the children as much as I could manage, feeding them, washing them, and cleaning up after them. Thanks to the money my son sent from London, I was able to pay for everything that my grandchildren needed. Anwar didn't contribute a cent. In fact, we didn't even see him at all for six months.

One time, my nephew, who was about the same age as Anwar, came to our house to visit. We received him so warmly that little Ahdiya became convinced that he must be her father. It had been so long since she had last seen him, she must have forgotten what he looked like. She jumped up on my nephew, wrapped her tiny arms around his neck, and said, "Daddy, I missed you so much. Now, I won't let you go. You're not going to leave the house without me." She kissed him again and again on the cheeks. My daughter cried for a long time after she saw this. It was then that she realized that she still loved her husband in spite of all the terrible things that had happened.

A couple of weeks later, there was a knock on the door. It was Anwar. He'd spoken to my nephew, who had recounted the story of his visit to our house. Although our relationship had been rocky since we returned to Kabul, I still remembered him fondly. I had convinced myself that his sharp change in character was the result of his parents' and his sisters' interference in his life. The side of his personality that he had shown us in Kabul was not the "real" Anwar, I thought. So when he showed up at our door, I greeted him warmly and tried to kiss him on both cheeks.

But clearly he was not in the mood for reconciliation. He was drunk and angry. "Stay away from me!" he shouted. He pushed his way into the house, sat down on the mattress on the floor, and started smoking a cigarette.

"What's going on with you?" I asked him. "Why are you behaving like this?"

"Where's your daughter?" he yelled.

"She went out for awhile. She's at the market," I told him.

"I hate your daughter!" he screamed at me nervously. "I want to give her a *taloq*. I want to give her a thousand *taloqs*," he practically shrieked. "I don't want to live with your daughter anymore. It's over. You understand?"

I tried my best to keep calm. "What has she done wrong?" I asked.

"What was her sin? My daughter has always been a loyal wife who has loved and respected you."

I felt the tone of my voice rising with emotion. "I just can't understand what's happened to you, Anwar. When we lived with you in Taloqan and in Tajikistan, you were always so kind and loving. In Tajikistan, you even hired a housekeeper so that your wife wouldn't have to work too hard. But since we joined your family here, you've become a completely different person. Why did you start treating her so badly? What happened to you?"

He wasn't in the mood for talking. "I told you that I don't want to live with your daughter anymore. That's why I came here—to rid Leilo jaan from my life forever. Now give me my daughter, Ahdiya . . . as well as that other one. They belong with me and my family." Luckily, neither of the girls were at home at the time.

I expected Anwar to return to the house any day to carry out the threatened divorce. But strangely, he never came back to recite the *taloq* directly to my daughter, as required by Islamic law to conclude a divorce. Maybe he had been so drunk, he had forgotten about our encounter.

When Zarghona was six months old, Leilo jaan decided that she wanted to return to her husband's house and try again to make the marriage work. "You know, Mama, it's been more than a month since Anwar came to the house and threatened me with divorce. Since he hasn't bothered to come back and follow through, it probably means that he really does want to live with me after all. It's not fair to force the children to grow up without a father."

I had seen the explosive anger in Anwar's face only a month before, so I had serious reservations about her plans. But I wanted to respect her wishes to do whatever she could to rebuild her family.

My brother, Abdul Ayoub, who was Anwar's good friend, happened to be in Kabul at the time. So I asked him to talk to Anwar and his family. After a long discussion, they agreed to accept my daughter back into their home. The next day, Ayoub and his wife accompanied Leilo jaan and both her children back to Anwar's house. I thought it wasn't a good idea for me to escort my daughter, as my last interaction with the family had been extremely unpleasant for everyone.

It was May 2003, and spring was in the air. Flowers and trees were blooming all over the city. Maybe this was enough to ignite a spark in their long dormant romance. For twenty days, my daughter and Anwar lived very happily together. Leilo jaan stopped by my house several times during this time and was practically swooning from her renewed love and affection for her husband. She told me that it was like the old days; Anwar was treating her with respect and affection and had even sobered up. During this time, Leilo jaan became pregnant for the third time. "Mama, I'm going to have many, many more children. Our house will be full of kids!" I was so happy for her.

But after twenty days, Anwar fell back under the influence of his parents and sisters and began to humiliate her again. He would say to her, "You're so stupid. You're as stupid as your mother. And so are all of your relatives. You're so ugly. I don't know why I ever married you." He would swear at her and beat her up.

It didn't help that Anwar was no longer employed. He had far too much time to stay home and torment my daughter and my grandchildren. Sometimes when I would speak with Ahdiya, she'd tell me, "Grandma, grandma. You know what Daddy says? He said my grandma Mahtabgul is a bitch!" She was so proud of herself. She had no idea what that dreadful word actually meant.

After Anwar found out that his wife was pregnant again, he flew into a terrible, alcohol-induced rage. "I don't want to have to feed another mouth," he complained. "Besides, I know that you're only capable of giving birth to girls. Either you go to the doctor and get an abortion, or I'll beat you so badly that your baby will fall out by itself."

"But I've always dreamed of having a big family," my daughter told him. "When I was growing up, I only had one brother and, for a few years, a sister. I often felt lonely because so many of my friends had many brothers and sisters. I want to give birth to this child. Please let me keep this child. Maybe this one will even be a boy!"

A couple of days later, my daughter came home looking pale and bedraggled. With a deep sigh, she told me, "Anwar has begun to abuse me again. He told me that he doesn't want to have another child. 'If I had enough money to provide for all of my thirteen siblings, then maybe I could consider having another child,' he told me. 'But now we just can't afford it.' He wants me to have an abortion.

"But, Mama, it's a terrible sin to have an abortion," Leilo jaan sobbed.

"Yes, my dear," I said. "It is. It's a sin against Allah. Millions of innocent Afghans have lost their lives over the last quarter century in these useless wars. Why should Afghan women kill more children? And beyond being a violation of God's immutable laws, it's also against the laws of our country. Who knows if one could even find a reliable doctor who would be able to perform the procedure safely?"

"You're right, Mama. But he's deadly serious about this abortion. He told me that he'd beat the fetus out of me himself if I refused to go to the doctor."

I didn't know how to respond. "Let's just pray that he changes his mind. It seems to me that after a couple more months, no one could possibly agree to perform the abortion because your pregnancy will be too far advanced. Let's just hope that he has a change of heart."

But Anwar didn't change his mind. Quite the opposite. He would try to deny her food with the hope that she would suffer a miscarriage. When she started to eat, he spat out at her, "Why are you eating like such a pig? You want to eat everything on the table so that there's nothing left for the rest of us?"

One time, my daughter asked her husband for some meat. Like all pregnant women, she was craving some substantial food. She whispered to Anwar, "Could you go out and buy me some beef?" She'd thought that her mother-in-law was asleep in the corner of the room. But she awoke suddenly when she heard this "outrageous demand."

"Look at this spoiled girl," she screamed at my daughter. "Do you think that we are all here just to serve your every whim and fancy?" His family allowed her to eat enough only for her to stay alive.

When the anticipated miscarriage didn't take place, Anwar sought out a more radical solution: he began searching for a doctor who would agree to perform an abortion. He went from one doctor's office to another until he found someone who was willing take the risk—so long as he was handsomely compensated. We found out later that this so-called doctor was only a nurse who had gone through a three-month medical training program in Pakistan. It's a big problem nowadays in Afghanistan; many people call themselves "doctors" after they've gone through only short training programs.

Anwar forced Leilo jaan to go to this charlatan, who somehow claimed that he could determine that the child would be a girl. In Tajikistan, I saw fancy machines that show the sex of a child before it's born, but this "doctor" only massaged her stomach to ostensibly figure out the child's gender. After this, Anwar became all the more convinced that an abortion was the right solution. The quack then prescribed her some sort of pills and gave her an injection. I have no idea what she had been prescribed but I do know that she began to feel queasy all the time after this trip to the "doctor."

After this episode, my daughter came to my house again and said that Anwar had become intent on following through with the abortion. I shouldn't have let her leave my house that day. I should have told her never to go back to that wretched Anwar. But I didn't. Instead, I only prayed to God that He would protect my daughter and her unborn baby. I think that Anwar might have suspected that my daughter would try to run back to me, so he forbade her to visit me for the next twenty-five days—the last twenty-five days of her life.

A few weeks later, Anwar and Leilo jaan went back to the so-called doctor's house, where he performed the abortion. I heard later that this procedure had cost Anwar about $50. He somehow managed to fork over this kind of money when he was complaining about the costs of raising another child. I was told later that the procedure involved sticking some sort of metal object up into her uterus until it struck the fetus. The fetus was discharged, and it turned out that it had been a boy. The doctor later said that it was already possible to identify his hands, feet, and even eyes. He then told my daughter that if she experienced any bleeding, she should return to see him immediately. Anwar took the fetus and buried it somewhere behind the surrounding walls of his house.

For the next two or three days, she bled steadily but not enough to be cause for alarm. As usual there was a lot of housework to be done, and she thought that the bleeding would soon cease. But on the third day, she collapsed in the middle of the yard while carrying heavy buckets of water. She had been bleeding and in terrible pain all night long. They took her to the Robiya Balkhi hospital. When the doctors examined her, they found that there were parts of the fetus still inside her and that she was bleeding heavily. The doctors tried to stop the bleeding and gave her an emergency blood transfusion.

For the first five hours that Leilo jaan was in the hospital, Anwar's family didn't bother to send me word of my daughter's condition. Five long hours! Finally, Anwar dispatched his youngest brother to my house to tell me that my daughter was very sick and had been taken to the hospital. I'd been working in the yard all day and was wearing a simple house robe, but without thinking, I ran out the door and jumped in a cab. When I got to the hospital, I found my daughter lying on the operating-room table, dead. Her body had been covered with a white sheet. I shrieked in horror and threw my arms around my poor daughter. Her body was already cold. I remembered the day that I held my poor little Zebo jaan in my arms after she was mercilessly cut down early in her life. But on that day, when I hugged her tight, her body was still warm. Leilo jaan was already cold.

Members of Anwar's family were gathered in the room where my daughter lay. They all offered their condolences. For a couple of minutes, I was in shock and wasn't even crying. But when I finally realized what had happened, I collapsed on the floor in tears. I began to beat myself over my head and tear at my face with my fingernails. A couple of Anwar's sisters came over to me, put their arms around me and said, "Try to be strong and control yourself. I know it's difficult for you, but it was your daughter's fate. It was Allah who decided to take her away from this earth."

"Take your blood-stained hands off of me," I yelled at them. "You killed her! You are all murderers!" I tried to grab the girls' hair and their ears. I wanted to tear them from limb to limb. But a couple of Anwar's brothers restrained me. So I had to resort to inflicting pain on myself. I tore at my skin, pulled out my hair, and pounded on my head.

One of my brothers, Omar Khil, who had recently moved back to Kabul, ironically worked as a doctor in that hospital. Anwar's family purposefully failed to inform him about his niece until it was too late. But when he did received word that I was in the hospital, he rushed into the room as I was beating myself on the floor. He tried his best to comfort me.

When the nurses came for Leilo jaan's body, I didn't want them to move her. "No! Don't take her!" I pleaded pointlessly. "You have to do something! Can't you revive her somehow!?!" I turned to my brother.

"You've saved hundreds of people's lives. Can't you do anything for my little girl?"

My brother separated me from my daughter's corpse so that the nurses could do their job. Leilo jaan was taken from the hospital to Anwar's house in an ambulance. I couldn't bear the thought of spending another minute with Anwar's sadistic family, so my brother and I took a taxi to my house.

Several of my relatives had already gathered to meet us and mourn with us. I was hysterical with anger. "Anwar and his family killed my dear little girl. She was forced to have an abortion. I'm absolutely positive that she was forced. He used to threaten her, 'Either you go and have an abortion or I will beat the fetus from your womb myself.' Pure and simple, Anwar is a murderer! It's so unfair that this murderer will be able to walk around as a free man—as my daughter lies in her grave. Isn't there any law in this world that can punish him?"

"My dear sister, if what you're saying is really true, and we can prove it, Anwar will assuredly be punished for his crime," my brother said to me calmly. "We have to prosecute him and make sure that he pays for his cruelty."

My male relatives went into another room in the house and had a long discussion about how they could most effectively send Anwar behind bars. They managed to piece together the story of how my daughter had died, and they brought their story to the police. The police arrested Anwar the next morning, a few hours before the scheduled burial ceremony. But his relatives went to the police at the same time to claim that Leilo jaan had died from cancer of the uterus.

Our versions were at complete loggerheads, and we were forced to prove that theirs was a pack of lies. So my brother asked my permission to allow the hospital to perform an autopsy on my daughter. According to Islam, it's considered a great sin to disturb a dead body. But I needed to know the truth so I gave my consent. As expected, the autopsy proved that the cause of her death was a botched abortion. There were no signs of cancer.

After the autopsy was concluded, they returned my daughter's body to me. When the body arrived, my house was filled with dozens of mourners. Everyone was shouting and crying in pain as my daughter's body was taken inside the house. I lifted the sheet from her face and yelled out, "Do you see what a beautiful daughter I had? Do you see what kind of child was robbed from me at the peak of her life? Anwar, I hope you rot in Hell!"

Later that same day, my son called from London. "How's my sister?" he asked innocently. I reassured him that everything was fine. I tried so hard to keep myself from bursting into tears. I didn't want to worry my only child when he was so far away. "Mama, I'm going to send some money home tomorrow. Can you do me a favor and make sure that most of it goes to Leilo jaan this time? She just had a second child and now a third one is on the way. She'll probably need money for her kids."

I didn't have the heart to tell him the truth. And even now, eight months after her death, Roshan still doesn't know about his sister's tragic fate. As far as he knows, Leilo jaan is living happily with her husband at his house. He sometimes asks me, "What's the matter with your voice? You sound upset about something." But I always make up some sort of excuse—that I have a cold or that I just woke up. I don't want him to worry; he loved Leilo jaan very deeply.

The court case, which was concluded only a couple of months ago, resulted in a ten-year prison sentence for Anwar. My brother took an active role in the prosecution, but I don't know the details of how the court case unfolded. Legal wrangling is left to the men in our society.

But I'm afraid that this is not the end of the story. Members of Anwar's family have been contacting us and demanding that we officially request a pardon for that swine. They say that if we fail to retract our complaint against him that they will "terrorize" one of my brothers.

I still can't help but blame myself for her death. I had so many opportunities to save my poor daughter. But I always misread the signs and trusted that it would all work out for the best—somehow.

I still have so many unanswered questions. The one that I have the most trouble understanding is this: If Anwar really wanted my daughter to have a safe abortion, he could have consulted with a real doctor instead of some quack. I have two brothers who are bona fide doctors, and they would have helped if it meant that my daughter's life was at stake.

I'm convinced that Anwar's real motive in forcing her to have an abortion was to kill *her*—not just her innocent baby. It was actually Anwar's whole family who conspired to kill her.

Within a couple of months of Leilo jaan's burial, I decided I had to leave my rental house; it was haunted with the memory of my failure to save her. I kept on looking at the door waiting for her to enter. That's why I came back here to Taloqan, to regain my wits and try to come to some sort of peace with my past tragedies. My brother still lives here, and he's been kind enough to allow me to stay here as long as I need.

What I really miss about Kabul is my grandchildren, who are still living there with Anwar's family. I wish that someone would bring them to me, and I could at least smell them and catch a whiff of my daughter's scent.

CHAPTER SEVEN

Nikolai Mironenko / Faizmuhammad

I was drafted into the Soviet army in the spring of 1983, less than a year after I graduated from high school. I was very worried about joining the army, especially since I had almost never left my native town in Ukraine. Shortly after I received news about the summons, my father came into my room as I sat on my bed staring absently out the window. He noticed how concerned I was and sought to reassure me. "Kolya, you know that your grandfather and I each fought honorably to defend the Soviet Union. Now it is your turn to serve our motherland. Being a soldier will make you a real man!"

My mother wasn't nearly as confident. A few days before I was enlisted, she sat down next to me on the couch as I was watching TV and hugged me tightly. "My dear Kolya," she cried, "please make sure that you take good care of yourself. You know that your father and your little brother and I will miss you terribly. It's not fair that they want to take you away from us. You're all skin and bones, and I think you're just too young to join the army. I really hope nothing bad will happen to you . . ." Now it was my turn to do the comforting. "Don't worry, Mama," I told her. "I'm sure that my two years of service will fly by, and I'll be back home before you know it. I've heard that I'll even get home leave after a year or so."

My father decided to throw a small going-away party for me the day before I left. He invited a few of my closest friends, neighbors, and relatives—and the vodka flowed freely. The table was overcrowded with my mother's delicious meat pies, as well as pancakes, dumplings, pickles, conserved tomatoes, sweets, and of course the mandatory *sala*, a Ukrainian specialty made from pig fat. There wasn't even enough room to squeeze my mother's freshly baked bread onto the table. Within an hour or so, all of our guests were very drunk. They sang, danced, and enjoyed the festivities late into night. It's really hard now to imagine that I once indulged in these types of vices—drinking alcohol and eating pork. But I'm sure that there were parties just like mine taking place across the former Soviet Union throughout the 1980s before young men were sent off for military training and, in many cases, on to Afghanistan.

I remember one of my father's toasts at my farewell party. "This is a toast to Nikolai," he said in his booming baritone voice. "My son, the next time we see you here, you will be a grown man. Everyone knows that the army turns boys into men, and that's what will happen to you. I'm sure of it!" But I noticed that a couple of tears had welled up in the corners of his eyes, and his usually strong voice began to crack. "We will think about you every day, my son. . . . Let's drink to Nikolai and to his safe return!"

The next morning, I packed a few remaining odds and ends, and my mother slid a few meat pies into my bag, which had been left over from the previous night's party. My father led me and my brother, Genadii, to the couch in our living room, where we sat down for a minute or two in silence. "May you travel with God," my father said just before we stood up. I went back to my room to retrieve my bags. I took a quick look around. It was a very strange feeling to be leaving behind the only house in which I had ever lived. "I won't see this place for at least another year," I remember thinking to myself. I never would have guessed that today, more than twenty-one years later, I would have yet to set foot in that house again.

My family escorted me all the way to the front gate of the local military headquarters. At least a hundred other young men were gathered with their parents and families, engaged in emotional farewells. Just before I turned away, my mother grabbed me one last time and began crying with the intensity of a mother who knows that she'll never see her child again. "Please take care," she whimpered. I had to try very hard to maintain appearances and not burst into tears myself.

I was taken by train to Kiev, where my head was shaved and I received my military uniform. It was then that I found out that I was being assigned to the battalion that is responsible for construction projects. Most of the other men in my battalion were also from small towns or villages where boys learned to build things from an early age. But nobody bothered to tell us that we were going to be stationed in Afghanistan. My guess is that they would have been afraid of deserters if we got wind of their plans. Already in 1983, only a few years into the war, word had gotten around that Afghanistan was a hellhole. So one night they quickly rounded up all the new conscripts and shipped us off to Termez, which is located on the border between Uzbekistan and Afghanistan.

I spent three months in Termez doing military training exercises. In my new battalion, there were soldiers from all across the former Soviet Union. But there was an especially large contingent of young men from the Soviet republics of Central Asia. The Soviet government probably thought that it would be easier for these people to understand and fight in neighboring Afghanistan because their forefathers were also Muslims and some of them even understood the local languages.

One day, a Russian helicopter pilot who was serving in Afghanistan happened to show up at our mess hall. We bombarded him with questions. "Is it as bad as people say it is? What are the Afghans like? Have you ever been attacked by mujahedin troops? Are all parts of Afghanistan as hot as it is here?" I was especially worried about the heat. By the time our military training was completed, it was not even summer, but I was already dying from the constant exposure to the sun in that desert outpost. We never experienced such high temperatures back in Ukraine. My pale face had already been sunburned, and it was only May.

At first the Russian pilot didn't say very much, but after a little while, he began to pour out advice. "Hey! You guys gotta cool it! Your questions will be answered soon enough—probably much sooner than you'd like. But let me just say this," he said turning toward me. "Yes, it's pretty goddamn hot over there in the summertime. And if you are unlucky enough to be assigned someplace near the mountains, the winters can be pretty damn cold, too. It's miserable. . . . As far as the Afghans are concerned, you have to watch out for all of them. You'll think that they're your friends, and then one day, out of the blue, they'll stab you in the back. You just can't trust any of them. . . . But the mujahedin are the worst. If you're captured alive, they'll torture you in all kinds of disgusting ways. . . . I've come across several of our comrades who have been tortured by these animals. Just a couple of hours ago, I had to bring back a couple of bodies in my helicopter. We won't even be able to show their faces to their relatives . . ."

The helicopter pilot regaled us with one horror story after another. None of us could say a word. When he was finally finished, one by one we slipped quietly out of the mess hall lost in thought.

When we learned that we would definitely be assigned to Afghanistan, some of the other young soldiers based in Termez used whatever connections they had to try to be sent elsewhere. They wrote letters home, and those who were from wealthy families or who had friends or relatives in the government were shipped off to calmer parts of the socialist world. A Kazakh guy who shared a bunk with me had an uncle in Moscow who was able to help him get a posh posting in Czechoslovakia. Like many other young men from poor families, I was not so lucky. I knew that my father had no connections or money, so I didn't even bother writing to let them know about my pending assignment. I knew that it would only make them worry.

✦ ✦ ✦ ✦

A few weeks after I had met the Russian helicopter pilot, I was sent to Afghanistan to work at the Kunduz airport just a few miles away from where I live now. It's probably hard to imagine today since almost all of the buildings at the airport have long since been obliterated, but the Soviets once had a fairly large military base there. I was one of the men assigned to construction duty. I was forced to carry heavy building materials all day long in the one-hundred-degree summer heat, and then several nights a week I was ordered to serve as a night guard. Our food rations weren't sufficient, and I was able to sleep only a little over four hours each night. Like many of my fellow soldiers, I developed large black bags under my eyes, and I was constantly exhausted. I recalled what my father had told me about military service. "So this is what makes you a man?" I thought. But on the other hand, I knew that I could have been assigned to far worse duties. "Oh well, at least I don't have to kill anyone on construction duty," I thought.

On a particularly hot day in July 1983, I was helping three other soldiers carry a huge timber beam across the airfield. My friend Sasha and I were on one end, and a couple of other guys were on the other side. As we were walking, Sasha tripped over a rock, and the wooden timber slipped out of his sweaty hands. In my weakened state, I wasn't strong enough to hold on alone, and the wooden beam fell right on my left foot breaking my large toe. I was treated by the doctor who was assigned to the military base, but he obviously didn't do a very good job healing me as I still walk with a limp. The pain comes and goes. Sometimes, I'm more-or-less all right, and then there are times when I'm in agony. Over the past few months, my toe has been killing me. But I don't have the money for an operation. Besides, I don't really trust any doctor here to be able to do anything about it.

My commanding officer sent me right back to work after the doctor released me, even though I was still in pain. "You've got nine other good toes, right? So what are you complaining about?!?" The commander always used to warn us recent conscripts that we would be considered traitors if we fell into the hands of the enemy. "If you're about to be taken hostage, you should have one last bullet in your gun for your own head," he instructed. "It would be a disgrace to the Soviet army if you were to be taken alive."

Although I never saw anything myself, there was a lot of talk that our commanding officer and other soldiers who'd been around for more than a year would sit around drinking vodka and smoking local hashish. I wouldn't be surprised if these rumors were true. Like many of the "veteran" Soviet soldiers, our commanding officer would have severe mood swings during which he'd be capable of doing just about anything.

One night, about a month after I'd been injured by the timber beam, I was serving my regular duty as a night guard. As a result of the pain in my toe, I had been sleeping even worse than usual. On some nights, I could hardly sleep at all. It was a terribly humid evening, and I remember struggling to keep my eyes open. At some point in the night I could no longer control myself, and I dozed off. The next thing I knew, three mujahedin had gagged me with one of their trademark black-and-white scarves, thrown a sack over my head, and were beginning to drag me away. I was terribly frightened and tried my best to squirm away, but the men were much stronger than I. They had, of course, taken my machine gun, so there was nothing I could do to stop them. Once they had dragged me about thirty yards away from the military base, my kidnappers pulled me down behind a small ridge and removed the sack from my head. I saw that there were five more men waiting for us.

They immediately led me down a long mountainous path, which was illuminated only by the stars and the nearly full moon above. My captors kept on pushing me to walk faster, but I wasn't accustomed to the rocky mountain terrain, and my toe was throbbing. One of the men kept on pointing to the side of the path and yelling something that I couldn't understand. But after awhile, I realized that he was trying to indicate places where the Soviets had planted land mines. This was actually my first time outside the confines of the military base. I was filled with a nervous energy, knowing all too well that my life could end at any moment.

Finally, we arrived in the village of Mangala shortly after daybreak. They locked me up in a one-room mud-brick house, which was nearly filled with hay, and left me all alone. I was expecting my executioner at any moment. "This is the end," I thought. I remembered what the Russian helicopter pilot had told me back in Termez. "The only question is how they'll kill me. Will they slit my throat, gouge out my eyes, cut off my nose, or chop off my limbs one at a time?"

About an hour later, I heard some men approaching, and then the door quickly flew open. I lay there shaking, in a cold sweat, my mind fixed on the tortures that lay in store for me. The first thing to greet my eyes as I looked up slowly was the leg that had kicked open the door. Then I saw a metal tray in the hands of a young mujahedin soldier. On the tray was a plastic thermos filled with tea, a glass, a cup of sugar, and some round bread. After putting the tray on a pile of hay next to me, the soldier walked out without saying a word, locking the door behind him. Paranoid thoughts shot through my head. "Maybe they've poisoned the tea or laced the bread with something that will make me violently ill." In spite of my fear, I realized that I was famished after the all-night hike and decided to take the risk. After taking a couple of small, tentative bites, I wolfed down the bread and poured myself one glass of tea after another.

After I finished eating and was still very much alive, I began wondering why they hadn't killed me yet. "Why are they prolonging my agony?" I thought. "Maybe they have some sort of strange tradition where they try to fatten up their victims for the kill—like animals? Maybe I should just kill myself and beat them to it." But I was so exhausted that I fell fast asleep on one of the piles of hay.

I must have been asleep for about three hours when voices outside the door brought me back to my miserable reality. Four heavily armed mujahedin, including an older man with a white beard, entered my makeshift prison cell. "This is probably my last minute on earth," I remember thinking. But instead, one of the soldiers handed me a *shalwar kameez* and a turban and motioned for me to change out of my Soviet army uniform. I did as instructed and handed over my uniform to one of the soldiers. As they led me out the door, I noticed some soldiers putting my uniform into a hole in the ground just behind the house and covering it with dirt.

We walked across the village in the direction of a river and then started climbing up a mountain trail. As we made our way up the path that rises above Mangala, seven Soviet helicopters suddenly appeared in the distance, heading in our direction. We happened to be standing near a few reed huts that had been assembled by farmers who grew wheat on these rolling hills. So we dashed into one of these structures, and through the reeds, we kept an eye on what was happening in the village below. Several Soviet jeeps pulled into Mangala, and a number of soldiers got out and went searching door to door as the helicopters continued to circle above. I realized that they were probably searching for me. I wanted to call out for help, but I knew that this would be useless. The roar from the helicopters was so loud that no one would have heard me. In any case, I was sure that my captors would have killed me instantly if I tried anything. At best, I might have been spotted by a Soviet helicopter pilot before the mujahedin killed me, and the Soviets would have doubtless launched an all-out attack on the people in the huts as well as on my captors. As all these scenerios ran through my mind, the trade-offs just didn't seem worth it. So I sat quietly in the hut along with my kidnappers for several hours as the Soviet soldiers continued their sweep of the village below. After the helicopters and jeeps had finally turned back toward their bases, we continued on our way.

About six hours later, I was taken to the home of Commander Amin, whose headquarters were in a mountainous area of Khanabad district in the eastern part of Kunduz province. I was immediately struck by Amin's charisma, his broad grin, and his very wide shoulders—much wider than mine, even though I was probably more than a head taller than him. He was wearing a beige *shalwar kameez* and a white skull cap, and his eyes were aglow with curiosity. Amin and my captors talked with one another for several minutes as I stood by quietly. Although I couldn't understand their conversation, it was obvious that the Commander was very pleased that I had fallen into his hands. He began looking very closely at my automatic weapon, which my kidnappers had brought with them. Amin then looked at me with a big smile, but all I could do was stand there like a mute.

Commander Amin invited all of us into his house, where we sat on mattresses on the floor. Then one thin young soldier brought in tea, sugar, dried fruit, and several plates of candy. As the young man with the candy stood by, Amin motioned for me to stand up. The commander then grabbed the candies from the plate and started tossing them up so that they would land on my head. As the candy was falling all around me, one of my kidnappers took a wreath of flowers that was hanging on the wall and placed it around my neck. This was the first time that I experienced this fantastic Afghan tradition of receiving honored guests. All of the mujahedin soldiers began smiling and talking to me in a kind tone. They also began calling me by my new Afghan name, Faizmuhammad. No one could ever explain to me why this name in particular was chosen, but it stuck.

Although I did not yet comprehend what was happening to me, it was clear that my abductors wanted to make me feel comfortable. It was only then that I finally realized that they weren't planning to kill me after all! They must have taken pity on me; they saw just a poor, thin, sunburned, eighteen-year-old boy with a limp.

That's how I began my life among the mujahedin.

✦   ✦   ✦   ✦

Over the past couple of years, several Westerners who have come to Afghanistan have asked me how I could have been "taken in" by the muja-hedin. Some people have even suggested that I was brainwashed by them. I don't have a good response to these questions. I guess I just felt comfort-able living with them. Commander Amin and his men received me as an honored guest and unfailingly extended to me their loyalty and respect. Amin in particular was eager to take me under his wing and make sure that I had all that I needed in order to be comfortable. The mujahedin's hospi-tality, bravery, and kindness made me feel at ease in spite of our initial dif-ferences in language and culture. Over the course of time, I came to understand and appreciate why my new mujahedin friends believed they were in the midst of an all-out struggle for survival.

At first, it was difficult to convey what I wanted to express, and I mostly had to rely on hand gestures. After awhile, I began picking up some Dari here and there and understood very well when my friends asked me to join them for "a little shooting." But I always declined; I never took part in any combat. Instead, I insisted on helping only with supporting tasks like cook-ing, carrying weapons, preparing the fire, or fetching water. It's very impor-tant to stress that I never killed a single one of my fellow countrymen. I am a peaceful man and can't stand the sight of death; my knees grow weak when I see even a little chicken being slaughtered.

Besides, I knew all too well that the vast majority of young men that the mujahedin were fighting were just like me—boys from poor families who didn't have the money to bribe or otherwise influence the right peo-ple. I'm sure the unfortunate victims of my new friends' guerrilla attacks had no desire to be in Afghanistan. But that was their fate. That was the fate of all of us.

A few months after I was captured, some of the mujahedin brought a badly injured Russian soldier back from the front lines. It was the first time in many months that I had spoken Russian to anyone, and it was very strange to be communicating in Russian again.

"What's your name?" I asked the soldier who was writhing in pain before me.

In spite of his anguish, the young man managed to look up at me with an expression of total disbelief. "It's Vladimir. . . . But who are you? What are you doing here . . . with these people?"

I told him how I had been taken hostage, but I was careful to avoid mentioning anything about my respect and admiration for my captors' cause. In fact, I said quite the opposite. "Really, you have to understand, I didn't have any choice but to go along with these mujahedin. They took me against my will." I was very worried that Vladimir would think that I was a traitor. In fact, I still worry that this is how everyone back in the former Soviet Union might think of me.

"Are you in a lot of pain?" I asked, eager to change the subject. I could see that there were a couple of metal shards lodged in his side and that he was having trouble breathing.

"Aren't there any doctors around here?" he pleaded.

Unfortunately there was nobody near our remote outpost who could help him.

Vladimir started coughing up blood. I tried to do my best to ease his pain. I gave him water and some medicine and tried to reassure him that he'd pull through. But there was nothing meaningful that I could do to help him. Within a couple of hours, Vladimir expired. I was so sad to lose my new-found friend. Like so many of the soldiers that I've seen die over the last two decades, he was just too young to leave this earth.

A couple of mujahedin soldiers and I buried Vladimir in a spot by our makeshift base. My guess is that to this day, he is one of the thousands of Soviet soldiers who are still considered missing in action. I learned later that I was officially listed as MIA for years on end. I can't imagine what a strain it must have been for my family as they agonized over what had become of me.

Shortly after Vladimir's death, I was introduced to a young man named Elias who spoke a fair amount of Russian. Elias became my Dari language teacher, and thanks to his patient instruction, my language abilities increased dramatically. After six months of intensive lessons, I could speak Dari more or less fluently. It was very exciting to be able to communicate without relying on my hands.

One evening after dinner, Commander Amin called me to his room. As I entered, I saw that he was seated alone on the floor. With a characteristically broad smile, he asked me to sit down next to him and began pouring me a glass of tea. On many occasions in the past, Amin had invited me to his room to lecture me about the mujahedin, their movement, Islam, and Afghan traditions. He would try to use simple words, but I was never able to comprehend his speeches fully.

But on this night, Commander Amin realized that I was finally able to understand almost everything that he was trying to explain to me. After an hour or so of discussions about Islam, Amin said to me, "Faizmuhammad, I am very happy that you now understand our language and that you've become our close friend."

"Thank you, Commander," I answered. "Your men have treated me very well, and I am very grateful for the hospitality, the bread, and the shelter that you have provided me. I consider myself very lucky to have so many generous friends."

"I'm very pleased that you feel so welcomed here. I've heard from my men that you are a great help to them," the Commander replied, still smiling. "But what I am about to ask you is something I've been meaning to discuss with you for a long time." Commander Amin's usual cheerful expression disappeared, and he began staring at me with his dark, penetrating eyes. "I think that it is now time for you to demonstrate your full loyalty to our cause. I would like to ask you to become our brother. . . . I would like you to convert to Islam."

Honestly, I'd had a feeling that this would come up sooner or later, and I had even considered bringing up the topic myself with Commander Amin. "I've now been with you for more than a year," I answered. "You have been like a father to me, and I can't begin to express how much I respect you. If you believe that it's necessary for me to convert to Islam, I will do as you wish."

Commander Amin was clearly overjoyed that I was so compliant. "That's great! You've made the right decision!" he told me as he patted me on the shoulder. "Since you will be here in Afghanistan for a long time, *Inshallah*,* I think it is very important that you become a Muslim. I am quite sure that you will receive much more respect as a result of your choice. Now you will need to learn more about the Islamic faith—how to recite prayers and study the Koran. And you will need to be circumcised. When I next travel to Pakistan, I'll bring you some books, and you can continue studying with Elias."

"As you wish, Commander," I replied.

---

* Arabic for "if God wills it."

I have always been grateful that Commander Amin encouraged me to convert to Islam. As a result of this decision, I have gained the respect and admiration of all my friends and neighbors. Almost everyone knows the "Soviet Muslim" here in town, as well as the dozen or so other former invading soldiers who have settled here and still live in northern Afghanistan.

I often wonder how I could possibly adjust to life back in Ukraine, where nobody would understand why I have converted. I know people would look down on me. They'd see me as some kind of outsider.

❖ ❖ ❖ ❖

Over the next couple of years, Commander Amin and I rarely discussed my planned conversion. During this time, I was traveling continuously from place to place with the mujahedin fighters under Amin's control, and occasionally learning about Islamic principles and prayers during lessons with Elias. When Elias would teach me prayers in Arabic, I would write them down in Cyrillic and repeat them whenever I had free time. I'd even recite the prayers five times a day alongside Elias. At that time, my mind was like a sponge, and I could absorb new languages easily.

In general, the mujahedin and I would try to operate after dark. It was considered too dangerous to move around without the cover of night. During our journeys, we would often stop in villages and eat at local residents' houses. Usually the local mullah or other community leader would host us, often providing us with a large banquet.

At one point, we stayed for an extended stretch of time in Ishkamesh district in the southwestern part of Takhar province. We were using this area as a base to launch random raids on Soviet positions. Then one day we received information that the area in which we were staying had been surrounded by Soviet troops and tanks. As we had done many times in the past, ten of us climbed up to a high point in the surrounding mountains in order to observe the advancing troops. There were Soviet trucks, tanks, and soldiers almost as far as the eye could see. We realized that they must have been conducting a major offensive and that we had no alternative but to flee deeper into the mountains.

We ended up walking in the mountains for several days in search of

Girl in Farkhar district, Takhar. © A. KLAITS AND G. GULMAMADOVA–KLAITS

Children studying in a school in a village of Chahardara, Kunduz.
© A. KLAITS AND G. GULMAMADOVA–KLAITS

Scene along the road to the Salang tunnel. © A. KLAITS AND G. GULMAMADOVA–KLAITS

Roghani Refugee Camp, Chaman, Balochistan, Pakistan. © LUKE POWELL, 2002

The Bagh-i-Sherkat IDP camp outside of Kunduz City. © A. KLAITS AND G. GULMAMADOVA–KLAITS

Makeshift house at the Bagh-i-Sherkat Camp outside of Kunduz city.
© A. KLAITS AND G. GULMAMADOVA–KLAITS

Boy selling bread along a central street in Kunduz city. © PILAR ROBLEDO

Turkmen woman in Qal-i-Zal, Kunduz. © A. KLAITS AND G. GULMAMADOVA-KLAITS

Hindu Kush from the air on a flight from Kabul to Mazar-i-Sharif. © JOHN PATTEN

Pashtun traditional dance, atan, at a wedding reception in Chahardara, Kunduz.

Meeting of village elders in Ali Abad district, Kunduz. © A. KLAITS AND G. GULMAMADOVA–KLAITS

Girls in a village in Ali Abad, Kunduz. © PILAR ROBLEDO

Children at the Bagh-i-Sherkat IDP camp outside of Kunduz City. © A. KLAITS AND G. GULMAMADOVA-KLAITS

Farkhar river, Takhar. © A. KLAITS AND G. GULMAMADOVA-KLAITS

Author Gulchin at the shrine of Hazrat-i-Ali in Mazar-i-Sharif. © A. KLAITS AND G. GULMAMADOVA-KLAITS

Former school principal in an Uzbek village of Imam Sahib district.
© A. KLAITS AND G. GULMAMADOVA-KLAITS

Local barge on the road between Kunduz City and Imam Sahib, used temporarily while the bridge was under repair. © A. KLAITS AND G. GULMAMADOVA-KLAITS

refuge. Because we were forced to flee in such a hurry, we didn't have any spare water or food. For more than two days, we walked and walked, but we didn't come across any settlements where we could receive food, and we didn't even run into any mountain streams that could quench our thirst. At this point I began to follow the example of several of the other soldiers: I tore up grass from the surrounding hills and began stuffing it into my mouth. Although I was famished, the bitter taste was nearly impossible to bear. But after a couple of days of eating only grass, I became increasingly accustomed to it. We usually had to sleep without the protection of even a cave, with nothing more than rocks to serve as our pillows. Several hours before dawn, we would wake up and continue on our trek.

The lack of water was probably the most difficult thing to bear. One of my friends was so thirsty that his tongue dried up completely, and he couldn't even talk. He began to panic, thinking that he might have permanently turned into a mute. We decided to feed him more grass in the hope that this would somehow help to relieve his pain. But this didn't help him. Eventually, he took out a small plastic bag from his pocket, turned away from us, and urinated into it. He then lifted the bag to his mouth and took a couple of gulps of his own urine. He turned back toward us with his eyes full of tears and croaked, "Now I can talk again." We all walked over to him and gave him big hugs.

Early the next morning, we entered a valley and walked by a small field where an elderly woman was sitting on a rock next to a grazing sheep. We saw that there was a village in the distance, but we knew that this territory was firmly controlled by Soviet forces so we were reluctant to enter. Perhaps we could have gone to the village the following night, but we didn't dare venture in that direction during daylight hours.

I didn't pay much attention to the woman sitting on the rock. I just continued walking down the path, hoping to avoid detection by the Soviet and Afghan army troops. But then I heard the old woman cry out, "Give me back my sheep! It's all that I have left!"

One of the hungry men in our small band had grabbed the poor woman's sheep. But the old lady didn't want to let it go without a fight and took a hold of the other side of her animal. "I'm a young man," the soldier said, "and I'm willing to die for the freedom of my country. And you won't contribute even one sheep to the cause? None of us here has had anything to eat for days. . . . As far as I'm concerned, you can go to Hell!"

But the old woman continued to hold on as tightly as her aged muscles would allow. She started screaming and begged him to leave her with her last possession. The soldier was so frustrated that he pushed the old woman down onto the ground, and blood started welling up around her mouth. She continued screaming and started cursing us.

I was nearly delirious from hunger, but even in my weakened state, I couldn't believe what I was witnessing. Almost all of the mujahedin with whom I had traveled had consistently displayed generosity and respect. But war and hunger can have a terrible effect on people. This was by no means the last time I saw how war can rob us all of our humanity. But there was nothing I could do to help the poor woman.

With the sheep in tow, we walked over to the foot of a nearby mountain where we discovered a small flowing stream. One of the soldiers slit the sheep's throat, and a couple of others began cleaning its innards, while I lit a fire. I wanted very much to eat, but the shrieking of the old woman was still ringing in my ears. I decided to join a couple of other men who went looking for some more firewood to keep the small fire burning.

Shortly after we left to gather wood, we heard the sound of rockets being launched. A number of them suddenly exploded. Maybe the Soviet forces had noticed the smoke rising from our small fire, or perhaps the old woman had informed on us. I still don't know how we were discovered. When the rockets came in, I ducked for cover behind a large boulder and stayed hidden there until several minutes after the firing had stopped. When we returned to our campsite, we discovered that one rocket had struck right in the middle, where the fire had been, and that three of our friends—including the soldier who had stolen the woman's sheep—had been killed. All of the fallen martyrs had been around my age. Their bodies as well as the sheep carcass had been blown to smithereens. Body parts were everywhere, intermixed with sheep's flesh. We couldn't possibly carry our friends' remains back with us, so we decided to bury them on the side of the mountain.

After we prayed for our departed friends, we continued on the mountain path—still famished and now terribly depressed. It took us a couple of days to find our way back into territory controlled by the mujahedin.

Yes, those times were very difficult. But I never considered trying to run off and rejoin the Soviet army. I always remembered the warning from my commander that it would be a disgrace to be taken hostage. I was afraid that if I were to return, I would be shot or at least sentenced to an extended prison term for desertion. Nevertheless, this experience in the mountains made me look upon the mujahedin movement in a slightly different light.

✦　✦　✦　✦

Commander Amin was often absent for long stretches of time when he and some of his most loyal troops would travel to Pakistan to retrieve weapons that were used to fight the Soviets. A couple of years after I had first talked to Amin about becoming a Muslim, he asked me if I would accompany him on a trip to Peshawar. The road to Pakistan was fraught with danger. It took us nearly a month to meander our way along mountain trails, traveling under the cover of darkness to avoid being detected by Soviet helicopters and airplanes. I was always afraid that I would step on a mine or fall off a cliff, but Allah was watching out for me. We carried with us wheat that we would fry along the road. We would drink water from mountain streams, and we would often sleep in small caves. The route was a common one for mujahedin rebels, and sources of water and shelter along it were well known to Commander Amin.

When we finally arrived in Pakistan and descended from the mountains, I was immediately struck by the heat. It was late summer, and Peshawar was sweltering. The Commander secured a room for me in a hotel that was used by many Afghan mujahedin soldiers. Amin had very important business to attend to, but he never invited me along. Instead he made arrangements for a mullah to visit me every day in my hotel room to instruct me in readings from the Koran, to teach me how to read and write Arabic, and how to recite my prayers. I was an eager student, and I knew that the more I understood about Islam, the more I would ingratiate myself to my friends and to the Commander. I'd guess that I learned more about Islamic practices in those three months than many people learn after three years of study.

While I was in Pakistan, I happened to meet a few other former Soviet soldiers who had also been taken prisoner. Several of them were also studying Islam, but very few of them had any interest in learning Arabic or reading from the Koran. They would spend most of their time smoking hashish. They would just go through the motions so that they wouldn't be killed by their captors. Then one day I met a Russian soldier who had decided to adopt a different tactic. "Why are you wasting your time with these Islamic lessons?" he asked me. "I've heard that if the mujahedin discover that we're not really interested in converting to Islam, sooner or later they'll hand us over to the CIA, and then we'll be sent to America. But you have to walk a fine line; if they think you're too independent, they'll just shoot you before they inform the Americans about you."

In spite of the unbearable heat, I have very fond memories of Pakistan. When Commander Amin asked me to return with him to northern Afghanistan, I at first resisted. "But I want to continue my Islamic education," I told him. He seemed very pleased with my commitment but nevertheless insisted that I was needed back at his base.

Just before we set out, Amin ordered all his men to take some sort of pill. I'm not sure what kind of medicine it was since the instructions were written in English, but it prevented us from feeling hunger for three days. We had a lot of equipment to transport, and the Commander didn't want us weighed down with excess food. Most of the arms were carried by donkeys, and everything else we carried on our backs.

During the hike, my toe started acting up, and I had to limp for most of the trip. On a couple of occasions, Russian aircraft flew overhead and dropped bombs on our caravan. As soon as we heard the planes approaching, we would drop our weapons and run for cover. Luckily, we didn't lose anyone during these raids, although six of our soldiers were slightly injured in one attack. The trip back took almost two months.

→   →   ←   ←

When we returned up north, we were temporarily based in Ishkamesh district. One evening, Commander Amin summoned me to his room and asked me to demonstrate all that I had learned while studying with the mullah in Pakistan. I recited some prayers for him and correctly answered several questions he asked me about the Prophet Muhammad's teachings. Amin was obviously thrilled with my responses.

"So now that you've become a devoted Muslim, how would you like to get married?" he asked me. "I'm sure that I'd be able to find you a very nice girl." I quickly agreed, although I harbored doubts about the possibility of a match. I really had trouble imagining that any Afghan would agree to marry his daughter off to me, a Ukrainian—even if I had converted to Islam.

The Commander and Elias and a couple of other men decided to approach the local mullah in the village in which we were living. The mullah had three daughters, but as I was told later, he was initially opposed to giving up any of them to me. But Commander Amin is a difficult man to say "no" to. "My dear mullah," he explained, "it is the obligation of all Muslims to help one another. Yes, I can understand why you wouldn't want one of your daughters to marry a Soviet infidel. But this young man is now with us; he has converted to Islam, and we should all consider him as a brother. He can recite all the important Islamic prayers, and he even understands their meaning. In the name of Allah, it is your obligation to sacrifice one of your daughters to marry this foreigner who has accepted our faith. I am certain that you will receive Allah's blessing in this world and the next if you help an outsider who has accepted the teachings of the Prophet." The mullah eventually accepted the Commander's request only after his third visit. And shortly thereafter, I became engaged.

It was at our small engagement ceremony that I first laid eyes on my fiancée, Rona, who was only fourteen years old at the time. In those days, she looked even younger, and I was shocked by her appearance at first. "She's just a kid," I thought. At the ceremony, she even giggled like a child. "This is the 'nice girl' who the Commander had lobbied so hard for me to marry?" I wondered. But I knew that it was Commander Amin's wish that I marry this girl, so I couldn't refuse. I also understood that if it had not been for the Commander's intervention, no Afghan would have ever allowed me to marry his daughter.

About a year later, Rona and I were married. It was a very simple wedding; I would guess that there were no more than 150 guests. We served everyone rice pilaf and there was a little dancing, but it was nothing very special. It was certainly not anything like a wedding party back in Ukraine. The biggest difference of course was that the men and women were entirely segregated.

I moved in with Rona's family after the wedding and was accepted with open arms. During the previous year, I'd managed to earn a little bit of money to buy some presents for Rona and her sisters. While we were still engaged, I would often come by Rona's house, and she and her sisters would cook me meals and wash my clothes. So in many ways very little changed after the formal wedding ceremony.

Rona is a kind and generous person. And I was very happy that there was someone waiting for me at home when I returned from work. But I was disappointed when my initial impressions about Rona proved to be fairly accurate. She often acted like a little child, for example, she would laugh at my foreign accent and tease me about the way I pronounced certain words.

A year after we were married, Rona and I moved to Khanabad district, where I managed to find work as a truck driver. The truck was given to me by Commander Amin after the Soviet withdrawal. I had always dreamed of working as a driver ever since I took drivers' education class back in high school in Ukraine. I would transport building materials, mud, dirt, sand, and sometimes, when there was fighting, I would even carry people in my Russian-made truck. It was in Khanabad that Rona and I had our first child, a girl. Unfortunately, however, Rona lacked knowledge about how to look after children, and our beautiful little girl died of pneumonia when she was only nine months old. Our second child was also an adorable girl. She actually looked a lot like me—she had green eyes, light hair and fair skin, and a snub nose that was a spitting image of my younger brother's. But she also fell ill and died at the age of nine months.

Thanks to the graciousness of Allah, our next three children survived. We now have a son who's eleven years old and two daughters. My youngest daughter looks a lot like our second girl who died. I'll bet that if someone saw her walking on the streets of Kiev, nobody in a million years would guess that her mother is Afghan. She even acts like a young Ukrainian girl; she loves brushing her hair in front of her small hand-held mirror and dressing up in beautiful clothing. My other two children are far calmer and never hesitate to help their mother clean and cook.

+ + ← ←

After the Soviets withdrew from Afghanistan in 1989, I began to correspond with my family back in Ukraine. Shortly after I had been taken prisoner, the authorities had notified my parents that I had gone missing. Almost everyone assumed that I had been murdered. In the first letter I received from home, my mother wrote how she always knew that I had somehow survived and was in good health. "I can't even begin to express my relief, my dear Kolya," she wrote. "Not a day has gone by that I haven't prayed for you. I'm overjoyed that my prayers have been answered." We had both been praying to the same God—although through the path of different religions—and He had heard us.

My mother's long letter was filled with news about our relatives and my friends. For the next several months, I would read and re-read the letter from my mother. Many times I'd even pull my truck over to the side of the road and read my mother's letter yet again. Every time I read it, I cried. I promised her—and I promised myself—that we would definitely meet in the future.

It wasn't until 1993, a full ten years after I had left home, that I was able to finally see my father again. He traveled all the way across the former Soviet Union to meet me on the Tajikistan border with Afghanistan. He was accompanied by Russian and Tajik border guards as well as a journalist who had come from Moscow.

As agreed, I crossed the Amu Darya with ten armed Afghan bodyguards who were usually stationed on the Afghan side of the border crossing. A couple of the men had actually fought under Commander Amin and were very happy to see me again. It was the responsibility of the Afghan border guards to make sure that I would not be grabbed by the Russian authorities and sent to prison. My bodyguards weren't taking any chances: their weapons were drawn, fixed on the Russian and Tajik soldiers. As our small boat slowly made its way across the river, I peered over at my father although my view was mostly obstructed by my bodyguards. As we approached the shore, I saw that my father had aged a great deal over the past ten years. He had wrinkles all over his face, and his eyes looked very tired.

The moment I got out of the boat my father grabbed me tightly. "Kolya, my dear son, I can't believe it's really you I'm holding in my arms. Look at you! You're alive! Almost all the boys you went off to the army with came home long ago. But there was never any sign of you. I can't believe that this is really you!"

"I'm very sorry that I caused you to worry so much about me, father," I said. "I wanted to write, but I didn't think it was safe. . . . This was just my fate."

After saying these few words to each other, my father and I broke down in tears. We cried and cried, and at one point I glanced around and noticed that the soldiers from both sides had lowered their weapons and several of them were in tears, too. One of the Russian soldiers then suggested that we sit down in his Russian jeep so that we wouldn't have to stand outside in the mud.

Once I finally regained my composure, I began to ask lots of questions: "Father, how is Mom doing? How's Grandma? How's my brother Genadii? I guess he's all grown up by now, huh?" But my father could hardly speak. He was too overcome with emotion, and we just broke down in tears again.

Finally my father said, "Kolya, we talk about you every day. There is a lot of news to report, but I don't know where to begin." He wiped some tears from his eyes and continued, "Yes, Genadii is a man now. He got married a few years ago, and he even has a son. They named him Nikolai, and the boy actually looks a lot like you."

"And how is Mom? Why wasn't she able to come here with you?" I asked.

But my father quickly changed the subject. "Your grandma died a couple of years ago, I'm sorry to report. We were all surprised because she was active right up until the day she passed away. And you remember our next door neighbor, Grandma Tanya? She also entered the kingdom of heaven last year. Your friend Sergei and his wife managed to emigrate to Germany a few years back . . ." He updated me on everyone, except my mother. It wasn't until several months later, when I received a letter from my brother, that I learned that our mother had died more than a year before. I guess my father didn't have the heart to tell me about her passing.

After a couple hours of tear-filled discussions, my father then put his arm around me and said, "Come on, son, let's go back home to Ukraine."

"What are you talking about, father?" I replied. "How would I live there? Everyone would say that I'm an 'enemy of the people,' a traitor. How would I answer them when they ask me why I'm still alive? It would be obvious to everyone that I'd fallen in with the mujahedin."

"But my son, times have changed," my father said. "The Soviet Union doesn't even exist anymore. Nobody will judge you—nobody will lay a hand on you. Let's go back home, my son. Let's go right now. I came here to get you. Please don't go back to Afghanistan. We all miss you too much! Besides, I've prepared all the paperwork to get you home without any hassles." He pleaded with me to return with him.

I tried to reassure my father that life in Afghanistan wasn't nearly as difficult as he imagined. It was my home, and I even had a family to worry about. At the time, my oldest son was only six months old. So I told my father, "I'm not just responsible for myself nowadays. I have a wife and a young child to provide for. Whatever I decide, I need to consult with my wife first. . . . I tell you what: why don't I bring my wife and son here tomorrow? If my wife doesn't want to go to Ukraine, at least you will have a chance to meet my family and take a photo of us that you can show everyone back home. In the meantime, please stay here for one more day until we reach a decision."

We agreed to meet again the next day at the border. The border guards and I took the boat back to Afghanistan, and I drove my truck back home alone. My wife and I agreed to go and meet my father, but Rona didn't support the idea of moving to Ukraine for good. She was afraid to leave Afghanistan and live in a land where she wouldn't understand the language, the religion, and the traditions. In spite of all the difficulties we were experiencing in Afghanistan, I, too, was reluctant to leave my adopted homeland.

The next day Rona, our son, and I, along with one of our cousins, set out in my truck toward the border. But this was a time of lawlessness in much of Kunduz province. Along a desolate stretch of road in the desert, several armed men stopped our truck and demanded that my wife's cousin and I get out and lie down on the road. The thieves then stole all of our money and beat me up with their Kalashnikovs. I was hurt very badly—I had deep wounds all over my body and across my face. Luckily, they didn't touch Rona and our little baby, who remained inside the truck. For many years, I have wondered who those men were who beat me up. Perhaps they were simple thieves, but on particularly dismal days, I sometimes wonder if somebody sent them on that mission.

I couldn't bring myself to allow my father to see me in that condition. Just the previous day, I had painstakingly reassured him that life in Afghanistan was safe and stable. I had told him that all of the propaganda about Afghanistan wasn't true—that I had gained the respect of people from all around. But there was no way to inform my father about what had happened. I found out later that he had waited at the border for two days before returning to Ukraine.

I was devastated that I had missed this opportunity to see my father. As it turned out, I never saw him again. He died a couple of years after our meeting at the border. But this is the way life goes—it can be very cruel. But I believe that whatever happens in this world is because of the will of Allah. We need to thank Him for all that we have, even in our times of grief.

✦   ✦   ✦   ✦

When the Taliban invaded in 1997, our village—like many parts of the front-line areas in Khanabad district—came under attack from helicopter and tank fire. During one of the attacks, my son was playing outside with a bunch of other children. As bombs fell all around them, the kids jumped down on the ground and lay totally still. Luckily, none of the children were seriously injured. But the bomb craters around the yard in which they were playing indicated that if my son had run off in the wrong direction, he would have been blown up. That's when we made the decision to leave Khanabad and move here to Kunduz.

Once the Taliban found out about my history, they treated me very well. They called me "the Soviet who converted to Islam" and even supported me financially. The Taliban were very rich—after all, Osama bin Laden had a lot of money—and they were willing to share their wealth with a few chosen Afghans and other honored guests from around the world. During this time, I continued driving my truck as well as a taxi. Under Taliban rule, I was able to support my family without any trouble.

But as soon as the Taliban were driven from power, I lost my job, and my life became very difficult. After six months of unemployment, I was left with absolutely no resources. It was only then that I started seriously contemplating the idea of returning to Ukraine. I even traveled to Kabul to apply for an Afghan passport so that I could travel abroad. But the passport officials told me that they couldn't issue me an Afghan passport in spite of the fact that I'd been living here for nearly twenty years. The official told me, "You're Ukrainian—you're not a citizen of Afghanistan!" I explained that I was a Muslim and that I had a wife and children living with me in Kunduz. But he refused to backtrack from his position. My guess is that he was looking for a bribe.

Before we ran into this bureaucratic snare, my wife initially agreed with me that we had little choice but to emigrate. But then she heard from someone or other that I would have many enemies back in Ukraine and that I could easily be murdered on the street. After this, she became completely opposed to the idea of leaving.

Fortunately, around this time I was able to find a job as a driver with an international aid organization. My $160-per-month salary proved to be enough to settle my debts and get us back on our feet. But unfortunately, a little more than a year later, this office closed down its operations in Kunduz, and I was forced to resort to driving taxis for little more than pennies. I hope that I'll be able to find full-time work as a driver or as a guard with another NGO.

I still think very seriously about whether I should remain here or leave for my homeland. But to be honest, I think that it would be difficult for me to live in Ukraine. Now, in so many different ways, I'm probably more similar to an Afghan than a Ukrainian. Besides, I have only one close relative, my brother, who is still alive. When I was still working for the aid organization, I called my brother with their satellite phone. He wasn't home so I spoke briefly with his mother-in-law.

"Why hasn't my brother been able to come here to visit?" I asked her. "I've reassured him that it's now entirely safe here. I really want him to meet my family." He had always danced around this question when we had corresponded by mail in the past.

"Kolya, your brother hasn't been receiving a salary for several months," his mother-in-law replied. "Life in Ukraine is very difficult nowadays."

As I hung up the phone, I remembered the famous Russian saying: "Life is always better somewhere else."

CHAPTER EIGHT

Bibi Maryam, Daughter of Atif

I've never attended a day of school in my life. My marriage was arranged for me in 1969 when I was fourteen years old. By that time, I had already been wearing a burqa for a couple of years. My husband, Hajji Muhammad Aman, who was from a neighboring village in Baghlan province, was about fourty-five and already had two wives. He treated me very kindly—he'd spend more time with me than with his other wives, and he'd buy me nice presents like expensive fabric for dresses and colored scarves. He would often call me when he wanted to be served tea or food, so I knew that I was his favorite.

I wasn't concerned about the age difference between us. I had already attended several weddings of relatives who'd been married off to much older men. The negotiations for the match were carried out by my widowed mother. My father had died when I was only five years old, and we continued living with his relatives. My mother was thrilled that I was able to bring in such a high bride price. She used the money to support my younger brother and sister for a couple of years.

Unfortunately, however, both of my siblings died a few years after my marriage from a strange, unexplained illness. The doctor claimed that they had typhoid, but the medications they were prescribed didn't help. The local mullah's prayers also didn't do anything to ease their suffering.

After my brother and sister died, the doctor claimed that they had been brought to his clinic far too late, and the mullah said that it was God's will.

Shortly after the mourning period for my brother and sister ended, my mother was forced to leave her in-law's house. She felt as though she was no longer welcomed there, now that all of her husband's children had died. She returned to live with her brothers and their families in her native village here in the Imam Sahib district of Kunduz province.

At the time I got married, my husband was working as a businessman and had enjoyed a certain measure of success. But after a few years, his business activities really took off. At the height of his financial success, he harvested large tracts of land, owned many shops and cars, and even made a pilgrimage to Mecca. He was able to support a large family: his first and second wives had five children each and I gave birth to three children—two boys and one girl.

Our lives were changed forever the day that the Soviet troops invaded our homeland. We lived near a main road, and I remember vividly the night that foreign forces passed through our village. Their heavy vehicles and tanks shook our large home. The lights were so bright that it looked like the middle of the day as they went by. We were terribly frightened. Only in the morning did we understand that the Soviets had invaded. No one seemed to have any idea why they had come.

Less than a year after the Soviets arrived, the new government became intent on robbing our family of its livelihood. They labeled us "rich bourgeoisie" because of my husband's landholdings and began dividing our property among poor people in the community. Of course they chose to implement their policies during the most profitable time of year—the harvest. My husband's men had worked hard all year to plant and tend to the crops, and we were looking forward to a rich yield of watermelons, wheat, and rice.

"Just go ahead and take everything," I heard my husband tell the government officials who arrived with their armed escorts to enforce the new policies. For the next two days, my husband didn't leave the house or talk to anyone. We all tried to cheer him up, but he would just swear at anyone who wanted to speak with him. So we all steered clear.

Two nights after my husband had lost everything, he quietly slipped out of the house without saying a word to any of his wives or thirteen children. He had run off to join the mujahedin resistance movement. Like many Afghan patriots from our area, he realized that he had no alternative but to defend his homeland from the godless foreigners.

Several weeks after he first left us, my husband returned home in the dead of night accompanied by several of his mujahedin compatriots. His white beard had grown scraggly, and his clothes were dirty. We were overjoyed to see him. The kids ran over to hug and kiss him. We asked him lots of questions, but he didn't want to talk about where he'd been or what he'd been up to. "Let me just say this," he told us, "the less you know about what I do, the better."

My husband gave me his dirty clothes, which I washed as the other wives prepared food for our guests. When I finally had a couple of minutes alone with him, I felt obligated to tell him how worried I was. "You know that you're not a young man anymore. Most of these other guys you brought over with you tonight are about half your age. Don't you have trouble keeping up with them? We're so frightened that something might happen to you." He just patted me on the head and returned to his guests.

A couple hours before dawn, my husband left with his friends. After this night, our late-night dinners with rebel soldiers became a regular occurrence. Even when my husband wasn't present, passing mujahedin soldiers would often come by our house to be fed. We would always manage to put something together to help the resistance cause.

☙   ☙   ❧   ❧

While our house was becoming something of a secret nightly refuge for the mujahedin in our area, my sons continued studying in school along with many of the children from our village. In 1982, my sons, Ahmed and Mirwais, who were ten and twelve years old, were entirely disinterested in fighting either for the mujahedin or the government forces. My husband's other wives also had three sons between the ages of ten and fifteen who lived with us. They were all content to stay as far away from the conflict as possible. But during this era, commanders were rounding up young men to fight either for or against the Soviets, and we were very fearful about our children's future.

One particularly cold winter night that year, my husband and several other mujahedin soldiers arrived at our house unannounced, as usual. My husband pulled us aside and told us that the men with whom he was traveling were high-level commanders in the mujahedin resistance. Apparently, they were the highest-ranking guests who had ever arrived at our place. To honor them, we slaughtered a sheep and cooked a mountain of food. When the mujahedin soldiers left several hours later, we were completely exhausted. "Let's finish cleaning up in the morning," I wearily urged the other wives and the girls who were helping us in the kitchen. Everyone agreed, and we all quickly fell fast asleep.

But only an hour or so after we had collapsed, our house was surrounded by government troops led by Soviet soldiers. One of our jealous neighbors must have turned us in. The Soviets really didn't understand who was to blame or who had visited whom. I was certain that it must have been our own local Afghans who had betrayed us.

The son of one of my husband's wives, Mansour, had left the compound to use the bathroom, I guess, and the soldiers began firing in his direction. They must have mistaken him for a mujahedin soldier. They probably didn't realize that our guests had long since retreated to their mountain hideouts. The poor boy was so frightened that he ran away to a small stream by the house and lay down along the banks.

As the soldiers moved into the house, all of us women quickly threw on our burqas and tried to run and hide. I just slunk behind a curtain in my room while my daughter, Sughra, who was seven at the time, got into a cupboard nearby. Our boys meanwhile tried to scramble away to safety by scaling the brick wall surrounding our compound. The poor kids didn't even have a chance to grab warm clothes to protect themselves against the icy-cold winter night. The boys didn't realize that the house had been totally surrounded and that there was almost no hope of escape.

I found out later that my twelve-year-old son, Ahmed, was shot in the shoulder as he tried to flee. He kept on running in spite of his injury, until he happened to run by Mansour, who was huddled on the stream's bank. Mansour yanked Ahmed down to the ground. They were protected to some degree by the cloudy night sky, but Mansour knew that it was not a safe place to hide.

"We've got to keep running!" Mansour whispered to his brother.

Ahmed tried to get to his feet, but the pain from his injury was too great. He just fell back onto the ground again. Blood was pouring from his shoulder.

"You just go ahead without me," Ahmed told him. Mansour tried to persuade his brother to try to come with him, but he couldn't. "You go and find a safe place to hide. I'm sure God will protect me," Ahmed told him. Mansour didn't want to leave his brother behind, but he felt that he had no choice. He ran off to hide behind a nearby oak tree at the edge of the rice field.

From that vantage point he watched a small band of Russian soldiers uncover my son next to the stream. As the soldiers stood with their guns trained on Ahmed's head, he raised his one good arm and screamed out, "I surrender! I surrender! Please don't shoot!" He was in tears—probably from both the pain and the fear.

But the Russians didn't understand Dari, or at least pretended not to, and began to beat up the poor boy. He didn't have the strength to even move. He just lay on the ground as the soldiers struck him with their Kalashnikovs and kicked him again and again and again. After awhile, his crying ceased. Mansour saw all of this unfolding before his eyes, but there was nothing he could do.

Three of the other boys, including my younger son Mirwais, also scattered in various directions. After the soldiers entered the courtyard, I heard an Afghan shout, "Nobody move! Surrender quietly or else a lot of blood will be shed!" Once they were inside the house, they didn't find the mujahedin fighters they were expecting. But it was obvious that we had hosted many guests late into the night. The government forces, as well as everyone else, knew what that meant. Our crime was obvious. We'd been so tired after our guests had departed that we hadn't even cleaned up the food from the *dastarkhan*. There were also parts of freshly slaughtered sheep—wool, head, knees, and so on—scattered about the yard.

Another soldier yelled out to no one in particular, "Why were you feeding the mujahedin? Don't you know that they are the enemy?"

The government troops and the Soviets began turning the house upside down looking for weapons. They quickly pulled each of us women from our hiding places and lifted our burqas to make sure that we were actually women. We tried our best to shield our faces with head scarves, which had been hanging around our necks, but the soldiers managed to see us anyway. We were so ashamed to be seen by all these strangers. In the end, after making such a mess and frightening us to our bones, they didn't find any weapons.

All of our boys, except my son Ahmed, were pursued by the troops and captured. Their hands were tied behind their backs as the soldiers led them to our house. They stood outside in our courtyard with their heads down, shivering in the frigid air, clearly humiliated by their capture. All of us women were screaming for fear that our sons would be killed by the soldiers or else die from exposure. I ran into the house to collect some warm clothes for the kids. Their clothes had been strewn everywhere by the soldiers, and I had to pick through the mess to find the right clothes to bring them. But when I went back outside, the cruel soldiers wouldn't permit me to distribute the warm clothes. They preferred to see the boys suffer.

As I stood with the pile of useless clothing in my hands, Mansour muttered to me under his breath, "My brother Ahmed was killed, and he's lying on the bank of the stream over there." He motioned with his head since his hands were tied. "I don't know if there will be much left of his corpse after the Russians beat him so badly." He quietly related the story of my son's death to all of us, including several Afghan soldiers, standing nearby.

Eventually some soldiers left to retrieve Ahmed's body, and it was obvious that Mansour's story was true. His body was mangled and muddy from being viciously stomped and kicked. All of us women fell to the ground at the sight of my dead son.

While a few soldiers stood guarding our sons, the others went back to the house to confiscate anything of value. They took all kinds of farming equipment, including our tractor and our truck. But we weren't thinking about our equipment at the time—we were most concerned about the fate of our children.

While rummaging through our possessions, they found a few spare shovels that they gave to some of the younger soldiers. Then the soldiers led our children away taking their war booty with them.

Without even considering the consequences, one of the other wives, Robiya, and I began to pursue the soldiers. In spite of the abuses we had already witnessed, we believed that the government soldiers were taking our children to prison.

As we trailed the rest of the soldiers and our children, Robiya and I tried to comfort one another. "At a certain point, the soldiers will probably order us to return to the house," she said to me. "If so, early tomorrow morning we'll dispatch some of our neighbors to search the prisons. After we bribe the right officials, I'm sure they'll soon be home." I reminded her that we also had some relatives who were serving in this regime who could help us free our children.

But after a twenty-minute-or-so march, our hopes were quickly dashed. As some soldiers stood guard with their weapons drawn, other soldiers untied the knots around our boys' wrists. They were then handed shovels and ordered to start digging. The slightly older boys began digging without talking back, but my son Mirwais began crying loudly. He was only ten years old, after all.

Seeing my son in such anguish forced me to leave behind any ounce of shame and decency I had left. I went over to one of the Afghan soldiers who appeared to be giving orders, and I started pleading for the boys' lives.

"What did we do wrong?" I managed to exclaim while choking back tears. "We only fed our fellow Afghans. If beggars come to our door, we feed them. It is our obligation to feed anyone who is in need. You know very well that this is our tradition.

"Look at them," I cried, pointing to the boys digging in the dirt. "They're only school children. Ask their teachers. Ask our neighbors. They're not part of the resistance."

"That's right," the commander scoffed. "During the day, they're school boys and at night they start rebellions." Walking away, he lit a cigarette as I pulled on his sleeve, begging him to spare the boys' lives.

I began to understand that it would be impossible to help all of the boys. And I couldn't imagine living without my only remaining son. His crying was unbearable for me. "I beg you. Please, at least spare the little one over there. Can't you hear how he's crying? Do you think that some-one who cries like that could be a resistance fighter? You already killed one of my sons. I left his dead body at home. Please have mercy on me! If this son dies, too, I'll have nobody to take care of me." I was shaking with terror, but I was determined to do anything in my power to save my remaining son.

The commander appeared to be swayed by my argument. He looked at me and saw the tears rushing down my cheeks, and then he wandered over to where some Soviet soldiers were gathered. Although I couldn't understand what they were saying, I saw them pointing at my son. After a couple of minutes one of the Russians said, "*Davai*"* and motioned for my son to be removed from the rest of the group. One Russian grabbed him roughly by the arm and, with one last kick, sent him away from the rest of the group.

Mirwais ran over to me, and I held him in my arms. He was trembling from head to toe, and we both cried feverishly. The other children and Robiya looked over at us. I felt so guilty that I hadn't been successful in saving the other children, but I really didn't know what else I could have done.

After another minute or so, the soldiers ordered me, my son, and Robiya to leave. We had all heard stories about how Russians would sometimes pretend to free POWs only to shoot them in the back as they were led away. And our worst fears seemed about to be realized when the barrels of their guns were planted in our backs as we walked. But as it turned out, they only wanted to make sure that we returned home.

We had nearly reached our front gate when we heard the sound of several guns being fired. Robiya looked at me with a panicked expression. "I pray those shots weren't for our children," Robiya said quietly. But we feared the worst.

For the next couple of hours before dawn arrived, we all sat in our house. We mourned the death of Ahmed and prayed for the safe return of our remaining children. We were hysterical with fear.

In the early morning, we went over to our neighbor's house and asked a couple of the men who lived there to help us find our children. We went back to the same spot where the soldiers had led our kids only a few hours ago. It was easy to figure out what had happened. When the hole the boys had been digging was no more than a foot deep, the soldiers began firing their weapons. The boys all fell to the ground, riddled with bullets, and died in a pool of blood. They had been digging their own shal-

---

* Russian for "come on."

low graves. Some of the soldiers who had killed them must have grabbed the shovels and just tossed some dirt over the bodies because there was no more than a thin coat of earth over them.

It's impossible to describe our horror. We screamed and began to tear at our faces, grab our hair, and beat ourselves.

The men picked up the bodies of the poor young martyrs and took them back to our house. The corpses of the four boys, including Ahmed, were laid out in the middle of our yard. Their bodies were disfigured from all of the bullet holes, and they were filthy.

When I remember that terrible sight, my heart breaks into a thousand tiny pieces.

One of the elders from the village conducted the funeral ceremony and gave them a proper burial. But other than the family next door who had helped us find and bury our children, nobody came to our house to mourn with us. Not a single person came with food for the next three days—as is traditional in our society. We had no appetite to eat anyway, but we were longing for the company and comfort of our friends and neighbors. But everyone was afraid. They were probably worried about what might happen to their children if they were seen with our family. We felt all alone in this time of greatest need.

⇥ ⇥ ⇤ ⇤

My husband came home after news of his sons' deaths reached him. After mourning with the rest of the family for several days, he announced to us that he had become too old and too tired to continue fighting. It was comforting to have him back home. But a couple of months later, when he was working in our courtyard, a government helicopter swooped past and shot him dead—in broad daylight.

This was the last straw. I had lost my oldest son and my husband, and I had only one son and one daughter remaining. After my husband's death, those of us in our family who had managed to survive gathered together to discuss our future. We decided we had no other option but to flee. We would split up the family and each of us would head back to the houses of our relatives. There really was no life left for us in our village. There were only horrible memories.

So that night, without telling any neighbors about our plans, we snuck out of the house on foot with a few of our most valued possessions. My two children and I walked for a couple of days to reach our destination, Imam Sahib, where my mother and other relatives lived.

When I had been better off financially thanks to my husband, I had always assisted these relatives. When some of them fled as refugees to Pakistan, I received them in our house along the road and gave them money and food for their journey. I thought that since I had done so much for them in the past, they would receive me with corresponding hospitality.

At first, we didn't have any difficulties living together. They did, in fact, treat us very warmly and provided us with whatever they could. But after several months of living in relative harmony, our relationship soured. Many of the problems had to do with my son Mirwais. He wasn't able to get along very well with his cousins. They would often pick fights with one another, and since Mirwais was bigger, he'd usually beat up the other kids in the family.

One day my son came into the house after playing outside. I had been sewing some mattresses as my elderly mother relaxed in the corner. My son was obviously in a bad mood but didn't want to talk about what had happened. After a few minutes, my cousin's wife came into the house with her screaming son who was a couple years younger than Mirwais. The boy's nose was bleeding, and he had a black eye.

"What happened?" I asked.

"You have a terrible son! He's like a dog!" my cousin screamed at me. "Look what he did to my poor child. What kind of upbringing have you given him? If you can't control him, why don't tether him to the ground so he won't bite and scratch my kids!"

As insulting as these words were, I was very angry with my son. It was clear that he must have been to blame—as he often had been in the past. I was about to beat him. But the moment I raised my hand, he looked up at me with tears in his eyes and said, "But, Mama, he called my father bad names. He said that my father was an 'enemy' and a 'traitor.'"

My husband's death was too fresh in my mind. My anger quickly melted away, and was replaced by sympathy for my poor son's wounded pride. Instead of slapping him, I just took Mirwais in my arms and hugged him. I tried to comfort him as he bawled, and I thought to myself, "That boy must have overheard something from his parents. How else could a young boy learn such hateful words?"

My cousin was infuriated that I had failed to discipline my son. She was beside herself to the point that she pulled me away from my son and began to beat him herself with her bony fingers. The next thing I knew, I was in a fistfight with my cousin, and she was pulling my hair. Everyone in the house heard our yelling. Her husband came in first and separated us. After he heard his wife's version of the events, he was furious with me.

Shortly thereafter, I felt that we were no longer welcome in my uncle's house. My mother was not in a position to come to our defense. She was too old and frail to carry any authority. So I had no alternative but to start living with different neighbors for short stretches of time. In return for their extended hospitality, my daughter and I would help clean their houses and cook bread for them. This is how my children and I lived for nearly two years—traveling from one house to another, taking advantage of kind neighbors' generosity.

It was very difficult for me and my children to live on the leftovers of others. After my marriage, I had become accustomed to a life of relative comfort. I couldn't understand why Allah had allowed me to fall so low, so quickly. I tried to think back to all of the sins that I must have committed. Every night I prayed to Him that my situation wouldn't get worse and thanked Him for all that I still had. Most of all, I was grateful that my two children were still healthy and full of life.

After a couple of years of living with my neighbors, my mother fell very ill. She told my relatives that she wanted to spend time with me before she died. I spent the last three days of her life sleeping by her side and trying to do whatever I could to ease her pain. During the mourning ceremonies, I lived in my mother's room at my relatives' compound. Our discussions were civil, but it was clear to me that they didn't like the fact that I had returned to their house.

After the forty-day mourning period was completed, my uncle made it clear to me that I wouldn't be permitted to remain in the house indefinitely. "You can stay here as a guest from time to time, but this cannot be your permanent house," he told me in no uncertain terms. "Nothing here belongs to you."

But I was tired of moving my family from house to house like an unwanted beggar. So I said to him, "Please, why don't you allow me and my children to stay in the room where my mother used to live? I think it's only fair since we have nowhere else to go."

"You can't stay in that room anymore," my uncle told me. "We've already divided up your mother's possessions. You had a husband. Why don't you take some of his land?" But of course my husband's land had long ago been taken by the government after the communists came to power. There was no land for me to claim.

I didn't know what I could do to change his mind; for one more week I lived in my mother's room crying myself to sleep every night as I considered my options. It was terribly stressful to live in my uncle's house. A lot of my cousins wouldn't even speak with me.

It was then that I decided that I needed to appeal to some outside authority to help me. A friend of mine who was literate helped me write a formal letter of complaint about this problem. She advised me to request that my uncle provide me and my family with three *jeribs** of land. I thought that this would be enough land for us to build a simple house and harvest enough crops to meet our basic needs. I took this letter to mullahs, government officials, commanders, and anyone else who might be able to assert some authority to help my cause. I was determined to do whatever I could to win just compensation. In order to provide a roof over my children's head, it's a shame to admit, I was forced to compromise my dignity.

Some of the authorities with whom I'd spoken began to negotiate with my uncle on my behalf. My stubborn uncle didn't want to yield a single yard of soil to me, but the authorities told him that he had to give me something. After a couple of days of bickering, he agreed to give me one-and-a-half *jeribs* of land right in the middle of their fields. That's why my house is the only one in this village that is built right in the center of a wheat field.

I had very few resources to build a decent house. So I put some fabric together, grounded it in the earth with some sticks, and we lived under a tent for several months. After awhile, just before winter set in, some of my kind neighbors sent their husbands and sons to help us build

---

* One *jerib* equals about half an acre.

a simple, mud-brick structure. But the wooden timbers in the roof were very thin. And I wasn't able to afford a lot of basic items such as windows and doors. Instead all I had to shield us from the cold were thin plastic sheets.

→ → ← ←

After I reached this compromise with my relatives, my relationship with them began to improve. We would sometimes even come by their house for meals, and Mirwais started to get along much better with the boys.

One day, about three years later, there was a wedding party in the village, which all of us were planning to attend. My daughter, Sughra, who was fourteen at the time, was a very close friend of the bride's. We had spent several months living in the girl's house when we had been cast out of my relatives' home. Sughra had been looking forward to the wedding for a long time. We had gone to the bazaar a few days earlier and had bought her beautiful fabric for her dress. She prepared her favorite dessert, *halvah*, to serve at her friend's party.

My daughter and I were running late for the wedding as she rushed to put the finishing touches on her dish and to apply her makeup. She was so stunningly beautiful that day. "Just be sure to keep your burqa on as we walk outside," I joked with her. "If a boy catches a glimpse of you looking like this, he might want to steal you then and there. Then what would I do?" Sughra just smiled and walked back to the kitchen. Just a couple minutes later, when she was still on the opposite side of the compound in the kitchen, I heard the unmistakable, dreaded sound of Soviet helicopters flying overhead.

Shortly thereafter, some mujahedin fighters burst into our relatives' compound. I found out later that they had arrived at the wedding and were of course encouraged by the host to take part in the festivities, which for the men, was taking place in a large field. When the helicopters began to circle above, the mujahedin—as well as most of the other guests—began to run for cover. As fate would have it, they ran straight into my relatives' house.

The helicopter pilot must have seen the mujahedin trying to escape. They fired two missiles in our direction. One missile fell to the ground and didn't explode, but the second landed squarely on the house and a huge explosion followed. It actually fell right next to the kitchen.

When I saw where the missile had struck, I ran across the compound to check on my daughter. The helicopter was still circling above, but I feared for my daughter's life and threw all caution to the wind. The kitchen had been heavily damaged, and there was so much dust in the air that I could hardly see.

"Sughra! Sughra!" I called out as loudly as I could, choking on the dust.

Finally I heard Sughra shrieking in pain. "Mama, Mama! I'm dying, Mama! I'm dying!" By the time I found her, she was covered in blood. Large pieces of shrapnel were lodged in her back, and she was bleeding profusely. I arrived in time to hear her last gasps of breath. "Help me, Mama. Help me, Mama," she managed to say as she died in my arms.

✦   ✦   ✦   ✦

Now I have only one child remaining. After Mirwais finished eighth grade, one of my neighbors, who works as a tailor, agreed to take him on as an apprentice. He eventually became skilled enough to sew men's clothes quite well. After borrowing some money from friends, he was able to open a small shop in the bazaar in the city of Imam Sahib. When he was twenty-one, he married one of my relatives, and they now have three children. His wife, Aisha, is a great help to me around the house. And she quickly learned to sew in order to assist Mirwais with his work.

But as soon as the Taliban captured Kunduz province, conditions became very difficult for everyone. Men and women all lived in fear that they would be beaten up by the overaggressive Taliban police. After the Taliban took control, I hardly ever left the house. Everything in the bazaar became very expensive, and fighting gripped the whole district of Imam Sahib. Our district kept on changing hands between the Taliban and opposition forces, and many local residents decided to flee.

My son was very worried that he might be drafted into the Taliban or into Mas'ud's army. But he especially hated the Taliban. One day, when he was working in his shop, some young Taliban policemen grabbed him and started beating him up with a wooden stick.

"What did I do wrong?" he asked them.

"Look at your beard. It's a disgrace to the Islamic faith!" a Taliban shouted. "Your beard is little more than stubble. Why are you resisting Sharia law? You know you need to have a long beard."

As they continued to beat him, he tried to explain that he was just wasn't able to grow a beard. "It's not my fault. This is as long as my beard can grow," he pleaded. "I haven't shaved in months."

After Mirwais was beaten up, his friend brought him home on a wooden donkey cart. His back was bleeding and he couldn't walk, but he insisted that he didn't want to see a doctor. I think he worried about the expense—money was very tight for us in those days. He lay at home for more than a week nursing his wounds.

When he was almost fully recovered, Mirwais announced to Aisha and I that he was planning to run off across the border to Tajikistan. "I've heard that it's pretty simple to cross the river and avoid the Russian and Tajik guards on the other side," he said to us. "There's nothing left for me to do here in Afghanistan. It's too dangerous with all these crazy Taliban around. Besides, I have some friends in the capital of Dushanbe who will help me out." At first I didn't want him to go. All of my family had already died, and I was afraid of being left by myself. But the more I thought about it, the clearer it became that it wasn't safe for him to remain here in Afghanistan. So I ultimately gave him my blessing. Before he left, I prayed to Allah long and hard that He would watch out for him and show him the proper path.

Mirwais left our house under the cover of night. He had made an agreement with some smugglers to take him across the river on a tiny raft. After a couple of months of living in Tajikistan, he started sending us letters and also money. Aisha had studied for four years in school so she was able to read me his letters. In one of the first that we recieved, Mirwais wrote: "My friends in Dushanbe have a very nice apartment in the center of town. They've helped me to find very good work. And I'm sure that my work will provide me with a steady income to support you very well." He was always vague about the kind of work he was doing. He just wrote that he was involved in some trading business.

Every month, as promised, Mirwais would send us money through friends and acquaintances. After a few months, we had accumulated enough money to build ourselves a nice, three-room house. The laborers we hired were even able to install doors and windows—things we had been living without for far too long. Later we were able to purchase nice clothes for Aisha and me and the children, and we even purchased some gold jewelry.

After about two years, my son's letters suddenly stopped, and the cash payments ceased. I became very worried about what might have happened to my poor son. I decided to visit a couple of my neighbors, whose sons were also living in Dushanbe. It turned out that they had continued receiving updates from their children, but these correspondences hadn't mentioned anything about Mirwais.

I was completely exhausted with panic. I could hardly sleep at night because my dreams were interrupted by vivid nightmares. Every day, I would go to my neighbors' houses and inquire if they had received any news about my son. And every day, they'd tell me that they'd heard nothing.

About four months after I had last heard from my son, I was at my wit's end. It had become something of a ritual for me to visit my neighbors and ask about my son. But on this day, I couldn't control my emotions any longer. As I sat in my neighbor Bibi Gul's house, I burst into tears and cried uncontrollably. The tension had just been too great, and I had to explode.

My friend tried to calm me. "Bibi Maryam jaan, please don't cry. I'm sure your son is all right."

"No, he's not. I'm sure that something must have happened. Maybe he died, and nobody wants to tell me. If he were alive, I'm sure that I would have heard from him long ago," I said.

Bibi Gul stroked my arm. "This must be so difficult for you. . . . OK, I'll tell you the truth then. . . . Mirwais isn't dead. But he's in prison in Tajikistan. Don't worry, he's all right. There are many other Afghans who are also in jail in Tajikistan. My son visits Mirwais often, and I'll tell him to get a letter out to you somehow or other. Your son didn't want you to know about this. That's why we've all been keeping our lips sealed."

I was relieved to hear this news. I had convinced myself that he was dead, and that I would never have a chance to see even his body.

A couple of months later, I received my first letter from Mirwais from his jail cell. "Dear Mama and Aisha," he wrote. "Please pray for me. I was imprisoned by mistake. I have enemies who framed me for a crime I didn't commit. Please pray that I will be released soon. All day long here in prison, I do nothing more than pray to Allah . . ."

About a year later, he wrote us the truth about his imprisonment. "Dear Mama and Aisha, I'm sending this letter through a trusted friend, and I hope that it will find its way to you. . . . I wanted to tell you how I became imprisoned. I was riding in a car with some Tajik and Afghan friends of mine who I knew were involved in drug trafficking. Our car was stopped by the police, who wanted to search our vehicle. My friends became very nervous. They said to me very quietly, 'Mirwais, can you take this small bag for a minute? If the police ask, just tell them that it's yours. If something happens, don't worry, we'll be sure to pay off the right people and free you.' It turns out that the bag was full of heroin. The police took us all into the police station and started interrogating us. I guess I trusted my friends too much. As we'd agreed, I said that the bag was mine and that the others in the car had no knowledge of it. But it turns out that they didn't hold up their end of the bargain. While they were released, I was thrown into jail, and I haven't seen them since. The judge gave me a twelve-year prison sentence . . ."

I'm happy that Mirwais is alive at least. We all count the days until he can come back to us. He's got eight years left before he's freed. I'm just hoping that I will see him again before I die. I still have horrible headaches when I think about my son's condition.

My grandchildren ask about their father all the time, and we just tell them that he's away on business and will return someday. "You have to be patient," I often tell my youngest grandson, who was only an infant when his father left. "When your Daddy returns, he'll bring you many beautiful toys!" This always calms him. Of course by the time Mirwais returns, my grandson will no longer have any use for toys . . .

CHAPTER NINE

Muhammad Sakhi, Son of Muhammad Yusef

When I think back to the days of my youth, I have trouble believing that I'm still living in the same country. I really can't understand how so many of us Afghans have managed to survive. I consider it a pure accident that I'm alive at all.

My wife, Fatima, and I were engaged when I was a senior in college and she was in eighth grade. We met for the first time at our engagement ceremony. I know that in the West, men and women date for a long time before they even consider getting married. And I know that sometimes they even have children together and don't bother getting married. But in Afghanistan things are very different. Almost everyone believes that it's the responsibility of parents to choose their children's future partners.

My parents and Fatima's parents were old friends—otherwise it would have been nearly impossible for my Pashtun family to consider a match with a Tajik girl. Our families were both living in Kabul at the time of our marriage, although both are originally from Kunduz. Fatima was actually my mother's choice. One day, when she was at her friend's house, she happened to see Fatima coming home from school and was really taken with her. After talking it over with my father, they made Fatima's parents an offer and concluded the negotiations within a couple of weeks. Fatima and I were both informed about our impending wedding once the deal was done.

Fatima was only fourteen years old when we were married in 1978. At the time, she had a short haircut and wore fashionable clothes like short skirts and tight jeans. It really was a different world back then.

I'll never forget our wonderful wedding party. It took place in a large restaurant in Kabul. Unlike today, women and men were able to celebrate together. Almost everyone wore Western-style clothes, and they were all in great spirits. My parents invited a well-known musical group and dancers to perform, and the guests celebrated late into the night. We were taken to and from the wedding in a long American Chevrolet that was decorated with beautiful white roses. And it was all videotaped by professional cameramen.

This was twenty-six years ago, and I don't know if there will be another wedding like that in the next twenty-six years. The restaurant has long since been destroyed. And many of our friends and relatives who attended the wedding have died or left Afghanistan.

My family warmly welcomed Fatima into our house. Unlike many parents of newly married sons, they didn't want her to sit at home and serve them. Instead, they encouraged her to continue studying in school. She took exams after eighth grade, and she was able to study in a special lycée during her high-school years. By the time she graduated from twelfth grade, she had given birth to three children. My mother, younger sister, and other relatives helped care for the children while she was studying. I was so proud of her and overjoyed to share our love with our children.

People in the West probably have trouble comprehending how we Afghans can spend our whole lives with perfect strangers who were chosen by our parents. But I'll tell you from personal experience that when I pray to Allah, I repeatedly thank my mother—who has long since passed away—for having the wisdom to select such an amazing wife for me. Fatima is not only my wife; she is a friend with whom I can share everything. We have a real partnership. When times have demanded it, she has supported me and the rest of our family. Some Afghan men would feel ashamed about this, but I am very proud to have such an educated, professional wife. Our love and commitment to one another has grown so strong over the years that we've become famous here in Kunduz.

We've heard that at wedding parties people sometimes say to the newly married couples, "Take care and cherish one another. We wish that your love will be as warm and deep as the love between Fatima and Sakhi!"

I graduated from the pedagogical university in Kabul with a major in psychology. While Fatima continued to study in school, I got a job teaching at my alma mater. After she graduated from high school, she also enrolled in the pedagogical university and became my student. I was so happy that Fatima was both my student and my wife.

In 1984, I was offered a full-tuition scholarship to study chemistry in East Germany. At the time, the Soviet-backed government in Kabul provided a lot of funds to send students abroad to socialist countries to further their education. It was thought that these young people would return to their homeland and serve as the intellectual vanguard for our country's recent socialist revolution. Although I was reluctant to leave my family and children behind, we all knew that it would be best for my future if I were to get an education in the West. My parents and brothers and sisters had recently moved back to Kunduz, so I sent Fatima and our children to live with them.

During my first year in Germany, I took intensive language lessons at a university in Leipzig. Then I began studying chemistry at Martin Luther University. While I missed my family a great deal, I was deeply committed to my studies. I wasn't very interested in talking a lot with my fellow students or hanging around in beer halls; I spent most of my time in the laboratory conducting experiments. In addition to the annual stipend I received from the Afghan government, I won a scholarship of 270 marks per month from the German government as a result of my high level of academic achievement. Among the twenty-three students who received the scholarship that year, I was the only foreigner.

I became a sort of celebrity when a widely-circulated student magazine wrote a big profile about me and my life back in Afghanistan. After that, students would sometimes stop me on campus and say, "Hey, aren't you that Afghan guy they wrote about in the magazine?" In 1987, I received my Master's degree with highest honors. Just before I graduated, my advisor mentioned that he thought that I could probably receive my Ph.D. in chemistry if I were to remain there for just a few more years. "Your research is so strong that I'm confident that you'd be able to write up and defend your dissertation in short order," my advisor told me. So I stayed on in Germany until 1989, returning home for good only a few months before the Berlin Wall fell.

Throughout my five years in Germany, I came back home every summer for vacation. I did my best to economize while I lived in Germany, so that I could bring home cash, Western clothes and electronics, and, most important to me, a variety of books. After a couple of years studying there, I managed to save up enough money to buy a used Mercedes, which I drove home through the Soviet Union.

After I completed my studies abroad, the Ministry of Education offered me a position as a deputy minister in Kabul. But I wasn't interested in an administrative position, and even more to the point, I didn't want to spend any more time apart from my family and relatives in Kunduz. Furthermore, I longed to return to the classroom and to have direct interactions with students. I was eager to pass along everything I had learned to the younger generations back home.

So I accepted a job as director of the Kunduz pedagogical university and managed to carve out enough time from my busy schedule to also teach part time. After a few months of working in the university, I was appointed Director of the Department of Education for all of Kunduz province. But even with my various responsibilities, I didn't give up teaching part time; I would have missed my students too much. I felt that if I were to undertake only administrative tasks, I would grow weak, and I'd forget all that I learned. For nearly three years, until the communist government fell from power, I held two positions—head of the Department of Education and professor at the pedagogical university.

After I got the job in the Department of Education, Fatima used to like to tease me. "Now that you've reached this high position at such a young age, what's left for you to do in the future? Is this all you're striving for in life?" she would laugh. I was full of optimism that I could achieve anything I wanted. I had great relations with teachers, school principals, and government officials all across the province. "If I go to the mountains, sit on some rock somewhere, and call out for help, I'm sure that the rock itself would provide for me," I used to tell Fatima. In spite of all the wars and conflicts that were consuming the rest of the country, I had high hopes for my future.

In the summer of 1986, when I returned from Germany on vacation for the second time, Kunduz city was in turmoil. Every day, we witnessed some sort of violent abuse carried out by the mujahedin. They were intent on destroying all the symbols of government authority. They would bomb government-run schools and hospitals and terrorize the families of government employees. Sometimes murdered teachers were strung up on electrical wires and young students were found dead in the streets.

Our family lived in a large two-story house in the center of Kunduz city. Like many Afghan families who live in close quarters with their relatives, my family shared a house with my two brothers, their wives and children, as well as with our parents. During this time, it was common for mujahedin to come to people's houses in the dead of the night to demand food, clothing, or money. On many different occasions, since we were relatively well-off, our family was forced to prepare food for the combatants and give them new clothes and shoes. But the mujahedin were not satisfied with this level of "contribution."

One humid summer night, when we were all fast asleep at about one in the morning, someone began knocking loudly on our front gate. One of my brothers eventually opened the door, and several armed men rushed into the courtyard. "Everyone freeze!" they yelled. We all woke up from our sweaty slumber but were too frightened to move.

A few soldiers burst into my bedroom. As one of them held a gun to my head, the others turned the place upside down. Fatima and our children were in tears as our clothes and valuables were sent flying in every direction. After a couple of minutes, one of my brothers, who also had worked for many years as a teacher, was led into my room by a few other gunmen. My brother and I were ordered to stand up straight against the wall with our hands on our heads.

Finally the commander in charge of the operation, Ibrahim Sarsafed, entered my room with his revolver drawn. "We know that you work for the government!" he screamed at us. "Why are you supporting these infidels? Don't you know what we do with people who work for the communists?" he said as he pressed his revolver against my forehead.

My whole family had gathered in my bedroom to witness this terrible scene, and the women and children were howling. Just when I was sure that my brother and I were about to be shot, my elderly father put his frail hand on Ibrahim's gun and begged him to spare his sons' lives. "Please, commander, I will give you whatever you want in order to free them. Everything in this house is yours. Please take whatever you like!"

The commander's tone softened as he went into bargaining mode. "Whose Mercedes is parked out in the courtyard?" he asked. It was the car that I had scrimped for two long years to buy.

"It's yours. Really it's yours," my father said quickly. "Please just leave my sons in peace. That's all I care about."

But the commander wasn't satisfied with taking only the car. "Everyone knows that you're a very wealthy family. So if you're really serious about seeing your children alive again, I suggest that you also give me $5,000."

"Commander, sir . . . we don't have that kind of money, I'm afraid. We are simple people. My children work as teachers—they're not businessmen," my father pleaded.

"Well I guess you don't really value your children's lives then, do you?" Ibrahim said as he pointed the revolver once again at me.

"OK, OK, we'll get the money for you," my father said imploring Ibrahim to leave us in peace. "But I just don't have those kinds of funds right now. Please just come back tomorrow, and I promise to gather the money for you."

The commander agreed. "That's fine, but we're going to take your sons with us . . . as an insurance policy that you'll keep your word."

As a couple of soldiers tied my hands together to escort me out to their car, one of them noticed that I was wearing a very nice watch. He grabbed it and casually put it into his pocket. I was heartbroken. When Fatima and I got married, her father had given me this watch as a symbol of his trust and faith in me. I hadn't taken it off since the day I was married. After this, I swore to myself that I would never again wear another watch . . .

The day after I was abducted, my father went around to friends and neighbors borrowing money to pay our ransom.

Meanwhile, Ibrahim's troops brought my brother and I to their secret military base, which was located in a house in Khanabad district, about a half hour from our home. I thought that they were going to interrogate us, but they actually weren't interested in talking. Their only objective was to induce pain and fear. For the next twelve hours or so, we were beaten by our kidnappers. They repeatedly struck me with their fists and the butts of their Kalashnikovs, until I turned black and blue all over. They broke one of my arms, and at one point they knocked me completely unconscious. My brother and I had no idea whether we would ever see our families again.

The next afternoon, after my father turned over the money that had been demanded, Ibrahim's troops drove by our house and threw us out of their car as it was still moving. Some people from our family quickly rushed out of the house to retrieve us. The first thing I noticed as I limped back into my house was that my Mercedes was gone.

After this experience, I thought long and hard about why so many countries, especially the United States, were helping these backward primitives. Why would the United States, with its long history of education, liberty, and democracy, support this ruthless rabble who didn't even know what a human being was, much less how to treat one with respect and dignity? Like many others, I understood very well that the U.S. was buying the mujahedin weapons and missiles and giving them money so that they could torment those of us who were educated. I just couldn't fathom why.

✦ ✦ ✦ ✦

I will never forget the first day that Fatima wore a burqa. It was 1990. Every day we heard news of the mujahedin advancing across northern Afghanistan, pushing back the government's troops. They had taken control of neighboring Takhar province, then Khanabad district, and we knew it was just a matter of time before Kunduz would also fall. Fatima had a very difficult time with the burqa at first. "It's so stifling!" she would complain. "If I have to wear this thing all the time, I'm sure I will die from lack of oxygen. And I can hardly see a thing when I'm inside it." It was tortuous for me that I was actually encouraging Fatima to wear it. In my mind, the burqa had always been a symbol of backwardness and a bygone era. But it was becoming too dangerous for women to walk around the city without one. So I told her, "We have to make a choice: it'll either be death or the burqa. If you want all of our family to stay alive, you'll have to wear it. I'm very sorry."

In addition to asking Fatima to wear a burqa, I decided to take other precautions. I had brought many books back from Germany, and I was afraid that the mujahedin soldiers, who wouldn't be able to distinguish a scientific book from a political one, would find them and punish me as a "communist." So I took almost all of my books outside into the courtyard, poured some petrol on them, and watched them go up in flames. I cried and cried. I had only a few books remaining after this—which I couldn't bear the thought of parting with and for which I managed to find a good hiding place.

Then, a few days later at three o'clock in the afternoon, the government forces retreated a few miles from town to the Kunduz airport, while the rebels entered the city. The nicest houses in town were quickly captured by commanders who wanted to set up bases for themselves. So, within a few hours of their arrival in Kunduz, some mujahedin soldiers broke through our front gate. As Fatima, my children, and I stood in the courtyard, soldiers started rummaging through all of the things I had brought from Germany. They grabbed anything they could lay their hands on—dishes, clothes, our stereo, TV, VCR, and lots of other things.

I stood by powerless, praying to Allah that they would only take my things and not harm my family. After a few minutes of watching our family's possessions being carted away, a commander then walked through the front gate. He had a Kalashnikov in his hand that he pointed at me. Then he fired his gun in every direction—in the air, toward our house, toward the street, everywhere—except, thank God, at me and my family. As the shots rang out, we all fell to the ground and put our hands over our heads. He emptied an entire magazine of thirty bullets from his Kalashnikov. Many of the bullets struck my house, and the holes still remain to this day.

When the deafening noise from the gun mercifully ceased, he yelled at us, "Get out of here right now and never come back!" We left our house with only the clothes on our back. Fatima happened to be wearing some of her gold jewelry and managed to keep it hidden from the looters underneath her burqa. As we walked across town to my cousin's house, Fatima and our children were in tears. I tried to maintain a stoic expression on my face, but after a little while I started crying, too.

A short while later, the government's forces recaptured Kunduz. But when we returned to our house, there was absolutely nothing left. There wasn't even a single cup remaining in the pantry so that we could drink some tea. That night, we slept on the cold, hard floor.

→   →   ←   ←

When the mujahedin finally came to power for good a couple of years later, educated people like us were treated like anti-Islamic infidels. All of the high-level government officials were immediately dismissed from their jobs. Although I knew that the mujahedin were fighting against the communists, I didn't think it was fair that I should be labeled as one. In fact I had never believed in the socialist revolution—or in the fight against it. I was always interested in my scholarship and my students and considered this entirely distinct from siding with the Russians.

I've seen in Afghanistan how education has been used as a tool by those in power to help implement their political agendas. And the mujahedin were more guilty of this than most regimes. In my opinion, there shouldn't be any relationship between politics and the natural sciences. Chemistry is chemistry, whether it's looked at through the lens of Marxism or Islam, whether it's examined by intellectuals or mullahs. Chemistry and other natural sciences should be unchanged by political winds.

When the mujahedin gained power, those teachers and professors who had taught history and political science had the most difficulty. The curriculum was radically overhauled to support the political ideology of the new regime. During communist times, there was always discussion about the struggles of the working classes and the proletariat. But under the mujahedin, even elementary school textbooks prepared students to fight against infidels. A typical line in one of my child's new Dari language book would go something like this: "Ahmad gave a glass of water to a mujahid. Ahmad is a good boy. It is good to help the mujahedin." And in the new mathematics elementary textbooks, there were examples like:

"One hand grenade plus one hand grenade equals two hand grenades." Or "Three Kalashnikovs plus one Kalashnikov equals four Kalashnikovs." I was shocked to learn many years later that these textbooks were actually published with funds provided by the American government as an instrument to further their fight against the communist regime in Afghanistan. This is how education was hijacked and turned into a political arm of this militarized regime.

The mujahedin robbed us of everything—both physically and psychologically. They were intent on changing the way we all lived. They said that men should grow beards and that we should no longer wear Western clothes, since this dress was considered "un-Islamic." It was impossible for women to leave the house without a burqa. And we always lived in fear of random violence. Armed men wandered the streets of the city and murdered people at will.

The heavy damage you see in Kunduz today is a direct result of mujahedin misrule. Kunduz city now bears little resemblance to the old days. As recently as the early 1990s, there was electricity in all public buildings. Schools were in good condition, and children sat at desks and chairs rather than in fields, on floors, or in tents. Students even had a chance to take advantage of well-stocked libraries and laboratories. Likewise, government departments each had their own official cars at their disposal.

When the mujahedin took control, they took everything for themselves—both public and private property. When commanders would loot schools, they didn't just take desks and chairs—they would also grab window panes, window frames, doors, and even the timber beams from roofs. They also chopped down almost all the city's trees, which is why there are such terribly dusty conditions nowadays.

I was still teaching chemistry in the pedagogical university when the kleptomaniacal mujahedin regime was tearing apart the country. One day, a commander—who was also a mullah—burst into my classroom when I was conducting my lesson. The first thing that he saw was a human mannequin on a side table that was used by my colleague in the biology department to teach anatomy. "What is this?" he screamed at me. He grabbed the model in his hand and marched up to the front of the classroom where I was standing. I started to mumble something about teaching human anatomy, but he demanded that I shut up. He then grabbed the pointing stick, which I had been using in my lecture, from my hand and began to beat the mannequin. "You see this body," he said to my students. "This is Lenin! This is from Lenin! *Allah-u-Akbar! God is great!*" he yelled as he whacked the model again and again. My students quietly filed out of the classroom in fear that the mullah's wrath would soon turn on them.

The mujahedin could never figure out how to establish a workable political system. One day a commander would announce one policy, and then his deputy would go ahead and implement something entirely different. Small disputes between military rivals would often lead to open gun battles on the streets and the deaths of dozens of innocent bystanders. One time I happened to be walking down the street when a couple of women in burqas were being arrested for "immoral acts." They were dragged to a field near the center of town, where the Spinzar factory is located, and were stoned to death by a group of soldiers. Hundreds of bystanders gathered around to witness this perverse version of Islamic justice.

And remember, this is several years *before* the Taliban came to power. During this time, I started writing poetry. I guess it was my way of psychologically escaping from a harsh and unforgiving reality. The poems were usually about happy times and places very far away. Usually I would share my poems only with Fatima. Other people saw me as a man of science, and I was afraid they'd laugh at me.

Throughout all this, most of the schools, at least in the cities remained open, but there were no salaries for teachers and other government employees. Since us teachers didn't have any income to speak of, it quickly became difficult to buy enough food for our families. A year after we had last been paid, a group of us teachers decided to see the Kunduz provincial governor, Qori Rahmatullah, to try to resolve the issue. But the governor was far more interested in ranting and raving than in listening to our complaints. "I know all of you. You were all sympathizers with the previous regime! There's no use for you anymore! All of you better get out of here right now!!! If you don't leave my office this very second, I'll replace each and every one of you with a computer!" But he couldn't even pronounce the word "computer" correctly—it came out something like "kamputar." Many teachers in Kunduz now laugh when we recall that terrible day. We still eagerly await the time when "kamputars" will finally come to our schools—and we become obsolete! By the way, Qori Rahmatullah is now head of the customs department at one of the main border crossings between Afghanistan and Tajikistan. Everyone says that he's become fabulously wealthy as a result of the fees he imposes on legal, as well as illicit, cross-border traffic.

➔ ➔ ↞ ↞

One year I happened to be walking through the center of town when the mujahedin were celebrating their independence day, the anniversary of the withdrawal of Soviet troops from Afghanistan. The mujahedin commanders had erected a wooden viewing gallery on the side of a field as boys and men paraded and danced before them. There were no women in sight.

After a couple of minutes, I was about to walk away when I saw one of my neighbors sitting nearby. "Hey teacher," he called out. "Why don't you join us?" He was relaxing with a group of men under a makeshift wooden structure covered by a tarpaulin sheet. As I sat down, we watched some young men dancing *atan*—a Pashtun national dance in which men form a large circle and clap at regular intervals. As is traditional, the dancing was accompanied by musicians playing the flute and drums. One of the high-level commanders in Kunduz at the time, Commander Amir, wanted to make an ostentatious show of his generosity. So he walked up to the musicians with a pile of bills and placed two million afghanis in their collection box. Then, a few minutes later, not to be outdone by his colleague, a different commander, Mirzoi Nasiri, gave the musicians three million afghanis.

It was then that I started to think about my own life. "Hey Sakhi," I remember saying to myself. "Why did you waste twenty-one years of your life studying in Afghanistan and Germany? Your salary—which nobody even bothers to pay you—is only 100,000 Afghanis a month. It probably would have been much better if you'd just concentrated on learning how to play the flute or the drums. Then at least you could earn enough money to feed your family."

I had similar thoughts many times after that. There was no place for my scholarship and my teaching in this pseudo-Islamic world. To be honest, I still harbor some of those same regrets.

I was desperate to find some sort of solution. I had almost no money, and I needed to provide for my family. Then I thought about a good friend of mine named Sayid, who was planning to immigrate to Pakistan with his family and hoped to go on from there to the West. I recalled that he owned a small garage that was located along one of the main roads that runs through town. So I asked Sayid if he wouldn't mind lending me his garage for awhile.

He was perplexed. "What do you need a garage for? You don't have a car anymore," he asked me.

I explained to him that I wanted to convert his garage into a small shop.

"It's no problem, Sakhi. As long as I'm abroad, you can use the garage as long as you like. I hadn't really thought about what I'd do with it anyway. . . . And I tell you what, if I make it to the West, the garage is yours."

A couple of years later, I received a letter from Sayid. He was living in New York City and had just gotten a job as a taxi driver. He told me that I could keep the garage for as long as I liked.

At home, we had almost nothing left. I needed desperately to find some capital to start my business. Fatima and I spoke about the problem, and we agreed to sell off the last of her gold jewelry. With the money that we earned from the sale, I went to the bazaar and purchased hundreds of pounds of wood, a large scale, and an axe. I brought the firewood to my newly converted shop and threw all of it on the ground. I tied up my waist. Then I cut up the firewood into small sticks, weighed them, and tied them into nice, evenly sized bundles. The wood was the right size to fit into any wood-burning stove used either for cooking or heating. I was able to sell this precut wood at a healthy profit.

That's how I began my new career as a firewood salesman—with a Ph.D. in chemistry from Martin Luther University.

The most difficult part of my new job was that initially I didn't have sufficient experience wielding an axe. You can still see the nasty scars on my hands, which betray my clumsiness. Only a few weeks after I opened the shop, I hurt myself so badly that I wasn't able to work for several days.

I sold firewood in my shop for eight long years. The money proved sufficient for my whole family to live quite well—certainly a lot better than many other teachers in Kunduz. It wasn't until Fatima got a job at an international aid organization after the fall of the Taliban that I was finally able to sell my shop. Her $250-a-month salary has given me the luxury of leaving my axe behind forever, God willing.

While I worked in my garage in the afternoon, in the morning I continued teaching chemistry at the pedagogical university. I was rarely paid, and when I was, it was far less income than I could earn through my shop. But I just couldn't give up my job as an educator. I taught because I enjoyed opening the minds of young people; I sold wood because I needed to survive.

One day, when I was in the midst of teaching a class, the door opened and in walked the provincial governor (of "kamputar" fame) along with the President of Afghanistan, Dr. Burhanuddin Rabbani! I told all of my students to stand up, which they did immediately. But Dr. Rabbani motioned for the students to be seated. "Please, my colleague, continue with your lesson," he told me. President Rabbani was a highly educated man who had a Ph.D. in Islamic studies. It always baffled me that such an intellectual could preside over such tyranny and chaos. So I continued my lecture for a few minutes. Then Dr. Rabbani interrupted me. "Might I ask you a question? Where did you study?"

I told him that I'd received my Ph.D. in Germany.

He asked me a couple of other questions and then inquired, "And tell me, what do you do in your spare time?"

"Well, let me put it this way," I answered him. "If you have any extra firewood at your home, I can demonstrate to you how I can cut it into nice even pieces that will fit into any stove." A couple of my students started to laugh. "In fact, I sell firewood in the market in order to feed my family."

Rabbani seemed surprised by my answer. He was probably expecting me to say how much I enjoy reading or researching. "I'll tell you what," he said. "I will return here after three days, and we will speak more about the conditions of teachers here in Kunduz." But I never saw him again.

✦ ✦ ✦ ✦

In 1997, the Taliban captured Kunduz. Many of us expected the Taliban to implement big changes. We had all heard about how they were intent on re-creating a society that reflected the times of the Prophet Muhammad in the seventh century. But what was most remarkable to me was how little actually changed when political power swung from the mujahedin to the Taliban. Almost all of us men already had beards and were wearing *shalwar kameezes*. The only difference was that we were forced to wear turbans as well. Life for women, however, did become much more difficult. They could no longer leave the house at all without a male relative serving as a *marham*. Almost all of the schools as well as my university were closed down. Only madrassas were permitted to remain open.

Likewise, the Kunduz television station was shut down, and music was banned from the radio and elsewhere. The day after I heard the announcement that the Taliban had banned music I thought to myself, "Hey Sakhi, do you remember how at one point you regretted becoming a teacher and wished you'd learned to play the flute or drums? Well, thank God you're not a musician now. You'd be completely unemployable!"

Then, a few months later, my friend told me that he'd heard that it was easy for musicians from Afghanistan to be granted political asylum in the West. And I thought, "Yes, it would have been so much better if I were a singer or another musician and could emigrate abroad! I could be living in the West like the famous singers Hangama, Parastu, Farhad Darya, and many others." My chemistry training certainly wasn't helping advance my life in any tangible way.

We also learned very quickly about the Taliban's prohibition of photographs. I had collected hundreds of photos over the years: pictures of my children and other relatives, photos of my friends in Germany, pictures of me and Fatima during our wedding and shortly thereafter. We also had lots of photos from a wedding we had attended over the border in Tajikistan before the Soviet Union broke apart. These pictures showed Fatima and I dancing together; she had short sleeves, and her face and hair were uncovered. If the Taliban found these photos, we knew that there would be terrible consequences. We had no alternative but to destroy the most incriminating ones, which showed us dancing and wearing Western clothes. So one evening our whole family passed around the most "blasphemous" photos to one another. We each took one last, long look at them and tried to capture them in our mind's eye. I was last in line, and it was my job to tear them apart. When they were in shreds, we put them into our stove and burned them. Fatima and I cried all night long as this piece of our history was stolen from us.

But we still possessed certain other items that would implicate us in the eyes of the Taliban: the photos that we didn't destroy, some of my old books from Germany, our old wedding video and audio cassettes, as well as a television set I had managed to buy with the profits from my firewood sales. I wrapped up all of these things in several layers of plastic bags and buried them in various parts of our courtyard. When the Taliban were forced out several years later, we dug up these items. But unfortunately the pictures and books had wilted as a result of the ground's moisture. The television also didn't work. The only thing that survived was the audio cassette from our wedding.

Once my university was closed down, I worked from early morning until evening at my firewood shop. From time to time, women and girls in their burqas would walk by my shop and greet me discreetly from beneath their veils. I assumed that they were my former colleagues or students.

Then, one day shortly after the Taliban arrived, a woman came into my shop, sat down before me, and began to cry.

"My teacher, I can't bear to see you working like this." It was the voice of Safina, one of my best students. Usually, she was entirely self-assured, so I had trouble placing her at first. She must have been visiting a friend or a relative because she had never passed by my shop before, as far as I know.

"Don't cry, don't cry!" I said to her. "I'm a man, and I have the strength to work and earn an honest living."

"But look at the bruises on your hand," she cried. "Oh teacher, you shouldn't be working here! You should be in a classroom somewhere and not in the market. Why don't you leave for another province or another country where the Taliban aren't in control?"

"Why should I go anywhere else?" I asked her. "My relatives and my family are all here. Besides, these calluses and scars on my hands are honorable, and I'm proud of them."

I began to look around nervously. There were always Taliban roaming around, looking to enforce their interpretation of Sharia law. To see an unescorted woman sitting in a stranger's shop could be grounds for serious punishment.

"My daughter, you'd better get out of here," I told her. "If some Talib sees you here with me, he could easily kick and beat you before my eyes. If this happens, I won't be able to do anything about it. This would be a great shame for me. I really couldn't bear to witness such a sight. I'd have no alternative but to . . . to take this axe and break open my own skull."

"But teacher, I can't stand to see you suffering like this!" she said. "Tell me, what can I do to help you?"

"You want to know how you can help me?" I asked. "The best thing that you can do for me is to stand up right now and walk away from here."

As she got up to leave, I told her, "Please, my daughter, have faith. There will be light at the end of this dark tunnel. I know it. As the Koran says: 'Every long night eventually yields to dawn.'"

In spite of my outward optimism, these were in fact very depressing times for me. I was sickened by the fact that my own children didn't have a chance to study in school—not even a school whose the lessons were shaped by mujahedin ideology. Fatima and I tried our best to teach them what we could, but it couldn't replace a formal school education.

All of my children are talented and beautiful, but I have one daughter, Shokira, who is particularly stunning. She was always the best student in her class, and she had a hunger to learn about everything. I had always been convinced that she would one day be a leader in Afghanistan.

But those dreams were all shattered about a year after the Taliban took control of the city. One day, a local Taliban commander came to our house on behalf of his son to ask for Shokira's hand in marriage. He offered a far better price than was the going rate at the time. But of course I didn't want to accept. I voiced every possible excuse I could think of: "She's too young" (although she was actually eighteen at the time); "I want her to marry one of my relatives"; "my wife isn't ready to give her up . . ." I of course couldn't tell him the real reasons for my objection—that I wanted her to further her education one day, after the Taliban were overthrown, and that I didn't want her to be married to a commander's son.

After engaging in a more-or-less normal negotiation process, the commander suddenly stood up. "Look, I'm requesting that you offer your daughter to my son. If you fail to fulfill my request, then I will have to resort to less amiable terms of relating to you."

Based on the way he spoke to us, we became convinced that if we didn't accept, he was liable to kill us all. Fatima and I discussed the problem for a long time, but eventually we realized that we had no choice but to consent.

Shokira's wedding felt more like a mourning ceremony to me. Music was not permitted, and most of our guests sat in silence throughout the gathering. Fatima and I couldn't help but notice the contrast between our wedding and our daughter's wedding; it couldn't have been starker.

The girls' schools had all been closed, but my brave Fatima wasn't afraid of anyone. She talked to a bunch of our neighbors and told them, "Why don't you send your daughters over to my house, and I'll teach them? If anyone asks, I'll just tell them that I'm teaching the kids about the Koran." We bought a small chalkboard, which we set up in one of the back rooms in our house, and every day thirty girls and some of their younger brothers would come over to learn about the Koran—as well as other school subjects. These children took exams after the Taliban left and the schools were finally reopened, and they placed into much higher grades than their former classmates.

I hated the Taliban. They murdered people on the street and hanged them on posts; they kicked and beat women in front of crowds. I never attended the weekly torture ceremonies that the Taliban sponsored at the soccer field, but it became a commonplace question to ask, "So what happened down at the field today?" And then they'd say, "They shot a guy for murder" or "they stoned a woman to death for infidelity" or "they lashed a woman while she was lying on the ground." Every time I heard these stories, my heart would break.

But as horrible as life was under the Taliban, I just couldn't imagine running away anywhere. If we were to flee, it could be even more dangerous for my family along an unknown road. Besides, I felt that there was no place for us to go. I didn't want us to become a burden on distant relatives in Pakistan or Iran.

Kunduz became our prison. It was as if I were stuck behind bars with my whole family.

✦ ✦ ✦ ✦

After September 11th, the world finally understood the mistakes it had made in Afghanistan. America realized that it had been a huge miscalculation to support the mujahedin and then turn a blind eye to Taliban abuses. They mercifully freed us from those cursed Taliban, but in the process caused us many anxious days and nights.

In November 2001, after Mazar-i-Sharif and other areas in the northeast had fallen to Northern Alliance advances, thousands of Taliban soldiers decided to regroup in Kunduz. During this time, you could see Taliban who were Chechens, Arabs, Pakistanis, Uzbeks, and many others right here on the streets of Kunduz city. All night, American B-52s circled overhead, dropping bombs. Loud bangs were heard across the city as deadly payloads were delivered.

One night, a huge explosion struck so close to our house that all of our windows and mirrors were instantly shattered. We all thought that the bomb had fallen right on us and that we would soon be dead. For about ten nights, we were subjected to such intensive bombing that we had no idea if we would survive to see the next day. The battle in Kunduz ended a lot faster than most of us had feared. Many of the enemy combatants were from Pakistan, and they were allowed safe passage to return home. I think that this agreement is what brought such a quick conclusion to the fighting up north.

Thank God we managed to survive another close brush with death.

When the Taliban and the terrorists fled Kunduz—or blended back into the local population—we felt as though we'd been freed from an indeterminate prison sentence and finally had a chance to rejoin the world. We were full of optimism for the future.

After the agreements in Bonn in December 2001, President Karzai began to lead the interim government. But our hopes for the future were quickly deflated when we saw on television Karzai's first official meeting with all of the twenty-nine new cabinet ministers and other high-level government officials. Among them were many familiar faces—they were the same leaders whose hands had been soaked in the blood of Afghans and had caused all of us so much suffering. There were many people we saw who should have been prosecuted for crimes against humanity, rather than rewarded with government posts. The most obvious example that comes to mind is General Abdul Rashid Dostum, who has only a sixth-grade education. Four times his forces attacked Kunduz during the early- and mid-1990s, and they engaged in bloody battles with General Ahmad Shah Mas'ud. Dostum's troops looted our houses and forced women to walk barefoot all the way to Taloqan. There are many others in Karzai's cabinet and in other elite posts who also deserve to be sent off to prison in Guantánamo.

The government immediately pledged that they would appoint highly educated and well-trained people to the most important positions. I was buoyed again with optimism—it was a good decision after all that I hadn't become a flutist! All of my studying and my knowledge of chemistry were not useless; my education was going to help me gain a position in which I could contribute to the rebuilding of Afghanistan.

But as we have seen, the Karzai government has been in power for more than two years, and it has done little to promote educated people to prominent positions of authority. Not much has really changed—at least outside of Kabul. Professors at my university receive only $90 per month on average, while teachers in school receive only $40.

Fortunately, though, Fatima was able to find good work, and I was able to quit my job selling firewood. But I wasn't content to just sit at home after my lessons. Fatima would come home very tired after putting in a long day at work. So I would help clean up around the house and would cook dinner before she came home. Many of our friends and neighbors are surprised when they hear that I help out around the house. But I consider it only fair. In a successful marriage, each person needs to contribute however he or she can.

Just two weeks ago, I got a job with the German military forces, which recently moved to Kunduz as part of the international peacekeeping forces. They didn't hire me as a highly educated chemistry professor, but rather as a simple translator. Nevertheless, my salary is many times higher than I can earn at the university. I felt as though I needed to take advantage of this opportunity in order to save some money for our future.

Six months ago, my second daughter, Suno, was married. Her husband is not a rich man, but he's well educated—and that was most important to us. He studied law in Czechoslovakia, and he's very well mannered. Suno had been studying in the pedagogical university, and they must have met there. His parents came to our house several times to propose, and we asked our daughter if she, in fact, wanted to marry him. Only because she agreed did we accept the proposal.

They're now living very happily together. Suno's husband doesn't have any objections to her working outside of the house; she's both a school teacher and an editor for the Pashtun service of Radio Liberty at the Kunduz radio station. At the end of each broadcast, they announce Suno's name, and I always tell whoever's nearby, "Hey, that's my daughter!" In addition, from time to time, she writes beautiful stories for the local newspaper. We are so happy that she's able to live like a free person and pursue her interests, while at the same time living with her husband's family.

However, my first daughter, who married the commander's son, isn't so fortunate. From a financial standpoint, she's certainly not suffering. But her family doesn't allow her to leave the house. She has three mothers-in-law, and she doesn't get along very well with any of them. Occasionally, her husband allows her to see us, but these visits are far too rare.

⇝   ⇝   ⇜   ⇜

We see and we know that there are international peacekeeping forces around. But thus far, they're only in northeastern Afghanistan and in Kabul. Most Afghans, including me, don't believe that this peace is stable. So long as these criminal officials are occupying high-level government posts, we all know that this is not a real peace—it's only an illusion.

This is why women here in Kunduz, including brave women like Fatima, are not yet prepared to take off their burqas. They are still fearful. The women—and their husbands and fathers—know that government officials from the city and provincial level all the way up to Kabul are drenched in blood.

Another sign that the criminal commanders are still in control is the rapidly expanding opium and heroin trade. Every step of the process—the growth, harvesting, transportation, and processing of opium into heroin—is overseen by those who have political power. And in this way, they manage to exercise control over the whole society. These elites are in contact with worldwide drug cartels, which transport the heroin all around the world, even to the shores of America. The heroin production and distribution is inextricably linked to terrorism and an extremely cor-. rupt government system.

I hope that the world community will pay attention to this serious problem before it's too late. Some of the biggest ringleaders in this narco-trafficking business need to be arrested and prosecuted in a neutral third country. If narcotics production can be eliminated from our land, we will rid ourselves of whatever terrorists remain behind. Drugs have had a terrible corrupting influence on our society. Once they have been eliminated, we will all be able to build a brighter future.

It will take a lot of time and work to rebuild the shattered infrastructure of Afghanistan after twenty-three long years of war. But what is less talked about is how to rebuild our shattered psychology. An entire generation has been lost to these useless wars. Middle-aged Afghans never had a chance to experience youth. Young people never had a childhood. If one were to diagnose the entire Afghan population, we could say that all of us—our children, our youth, our elderly—all of us suffer from some sort of psychological problems as a result of these wars.

CHAPTER TEN

Humaira, Daughter of Said Nuruddin Khan

t's the dust here in Kunduz that really gets to me. It's so hard to keep my five children and my house in decent shape. When I used to work as a teacher, the first thing I'd do when my students came to class was to check their hands to make sure that they were clean and that there was no dirt under their nails. I feel like much of my life has been spent fighting a losing battle against dirt.

Many years ago my father reached a high rank in the army. Although he left the military several years before I was even born, I've always thought that his army background is what gave me my fighting spirit. I've never hesitated to tell people what I really think—regardless of whether they have guns, are with the Taliban, mujahedin, communists, or are just ordinary thugs. What's the worst they could do to me? Kill me? Well, if I didn't say what I felt then I might as well be dead anyway.

My parents were married in 1955. At that time, my mother was only thirteen years old and my father was forty. My mother gave birth to six girls— I was the third—and three boys. But all of my brothers died shortly after they were born. One fell victim to tetanus and the other two to measles. I discovered many years later that my father's relatives had endlessly lobbied him to marry again after my brothers' deaths. "Can't you tell that this woman is damaged goods?" they'd say. "She can't even bear a healthy son for you!" But my father always responded, "If Allah had wanted me to have a son, he would have saved one of the boys who was born to me. It's not my wife that's defective. It's just my fate to have only daughters."

Until the age of thirty-five, my father served in the army. He had risen in rank very quickly, but as a result of some conflicts with his superiors, he was forced to resign. But my father wasn't the type of man to sit around the house and mope. He was always active. And when he lost his job in the army, he immediately went back to school to study agronomy. After his graduation, he began working for the Spinzar factory, which controlled cotton fields across Kunduz province and was by far the largest employer in the area. He specialized in locust control and eventually became well known in northern Afghanistan for his innovative techniques in battling locusts.

My father would love to tell stories about his youth in Kunduz in the 1920s and 1930s. Apparently, Kunduz has always been a dirty place. He used to say that when you'd walk down the street, fleas and other bugs would jump up on your legs and bite you. According to him, there used to be a famous saying among Afghans in that era: "If you want to die, go to Kunduz."

When I was growing up, my father would often take me to the bazaar. He was a famous person in town, and he would spend far more time talking with acquaintances than shopping. I was always so proud to be the daughter of such a respected man. But while we were in the market, I'd often see a scary old man who had a long, white beard and a heavily wrinkled face. I could tell that my father also didn't like this odd-looking man since he wouldn't even bother greeting him.

One day, after he noticed that I was staring at the old man, my father turned to me and asked, "Do you know who that guy is?"

I shook my head.

"His name is Nazar Muhammadi Chubi."*

"What do you mean—'made of wood'?" I asked my father.

"They call him that because he's a murderer. They say that his heart turned into wood as a result of his crime."

When we got home, he told me the legend surrounding Nazar Muhammadi Chubi.

"A long time ago there lived a man in a small, mountain village who

---

* *Chubi* means made of wood.

was very religious," his tale began. "Year after year, he put aside small amounts of money so that he could make his once-in-a-lifetime pilgrimage to Mecca. When he finally had enough for the trip, he was an old man with a white beard. One day, he took his trusted old horse out of the stable and, with a few provisions, left for the long trip to Arabia.

"Along the road, he happened to stop for the night in the town of Imam Sahib. As he had done in every other town along his journey, he went straight to the mosque just in time for the last prayers of the day. All the worshippers were pleased to welcome a man who was on his way to Mecca. They brought him food and tea, and the mullah invited him to spend the night in the mosque's guest room.

"That man we saw today in the bazaar, Nazar Muhammad, was among the men gathered in the mosque that evening. After everyone else had left for home, he stayed behind to chat with the out-of-town guest. He managed to find out everything about him: where he was from, what his profession was, and, most importantly, how much money he was carrying.

"Later that night, Nazar Muhammad snuck back to the mosque in the middle of a huge rain storm. Nobody saw him enter the old man's room with a long knife. As soon as he got to the man's mattress, he pushed the knife's blade up against the unfortunate traveler's throat.

"The man pleaded, 'Why do you want to kill me? I didn't do anything to you.'

"'I need your money. I'm gonna kill you for your money,' Nazar Muhammad told him.

"The old man managed to turn his head toward the door of his room. It was wide open, and it was raining cats and dogs. But nobody was outside. All he saw were bubbles formed by the rain in large puddles.

"'Then just go ahead and take my money. Somehow or other, Allah will show me the road to Mecca even if I don't have any means,' he said.

"'No, that just won't be possible,' Nazar Muhammad said. 'I have to kill you or else you will go and tell everybody about this.'

"'Oh Allah, help me!' the old man cried out. 'You are my witness. You see everything. I have dreamed my whole life of seeing your holy city. And now I am going to be murdered.'

"'Where is your Allah? Is He here to help you?' Nazar Muhammad shouted blasphemously as thunder clapped in the distance. 'There is no one to witness my crime.'

"The old man pointed out the front door and said, 'You see those bubbles in the water? They are my witness. They will bring you to justice.'

"Nazar Muhammad laughed. 'What a stupid man. Bubbles are his witness!' And then he killed the old man and took his money.

"In the morning, nobody from the village could understand who could have possibly murdered the traveling man. They had no way to contact his family, so they decided to bury him there in Imam Sahib. Since he was on a pilgrimage when he died, the local mullah gave him the title of 'Hajji'—someone who has successfully completed his pilgrimage to Mecca. He was called a martyred Hajji—*Hajji Shaheed*—and his grave has become a holy site.

"Nearly five years after Hajji Shaheed was murdered, the crime still remained a mystery. The police had been utterly baffled, because Nazar Muhammad had cleverly covered his tracks.

"Then one night when Nazar Muhammad lay down in bed to go to sleep, it began pouring outside. It rained as heavily as it had on the night he committed his foul crime. He lifted his head up from the pillow and noticed through his window that bubbles had formed in the puddles of rain. He couldn't help laughing uproariously.

"His wife awoke with a start. 'What is it? Have you gone mad?'

"He kept on laughing and his wife kept asking him what was so funny. 'What the devil is wrong with you?!?' she asked him angrily.

"'Oh it's nothing,' he said when he had finally collected himself sufficiently to talk. 'I was just thinking about a fool that I once knew. . . . Let me tell you a story. You know, I've never told anybody about this before, but it was such a long time ago, nobody will even care now. . . . Many years ago I killed some stupid guy who was on his way to Mecca, and I took his money. It was this money that I used to start up my businesses. I have no regrets. . . . But it's this rain that made me remember him. When I was just about to kill him, he told me that the bubbles in the puddles of rain would be his witness and would bring me to justice. Of course no one's caught me yet. What an idiot!' With this, he turned over and went to sleep.

"Nazar Muhammad's wife had been unhappy with her husband for a very long time. He'd waste his money, and he'd often beat her.

"She thought to herself, 'My husband is a terrible person. Not only does he abuse me, but he's also a murderer and a thief.'

"So the next morning, she left the house before her husband was awake and went straight to the police and told them what he'd told her.

"The police arrested Nazar Muhammad and beat him again and again while he was in detention in order to force a confession. But no matter what they did to torture him, he refused to repeat the story that he had told his wife. Finally, they took boiling oil and began dripping it on his head. Nevertheless, he still wouldn't talk. For the next two years, they held him in prison. But eventually, the police had to let him go because they had no concrete proof of his involvement in the murder.

"By the time Nazar Muhammadi Chubi was freed from prison, his wife had long since run off—nobody knew where she had gone. She had feared that her husband would try to take revenge.

"For the rest of his long life, Nazar Muhammadi Chubi has always been bitter. He grew so thin that his body became more like a stick figure than a real person."

After my father first told me this story, my family adopted the habit of traveling every year to Imam Sahib to visit Hajji Shaheed's grave at the time of our Nawruz—or new year—celebrations. Many other families would also picnic in this peaceful place for Nawruz, although I doubt that many of them actually knew the story of his tragic death.

✦　✦　✦　✦

I was never very interested in politics. But in my high-school days in the late 1970s, it was impossible to steer entirely clear of some type of political involvement. Afghanistan was in turmoil after President Daoud was overthrown in 1978. The new communist regime tried to impose its will across the country, but in many cases it was met with stiff opposition.

When I was in the tenth grade and the communist leader Hafizullah Amin was president, my classmates and I were forced to take part in a big parade. School children have often been trotted out by whatever regime has been in power in Afghanistan to show that their policies both benefited and were supported by the youth. We showed up in the central field of Kunduz near the Spinzar factory in our school uniforms. By the time we'd arrived, there were already thousands of people gathered in the field. Truckloads of young men who, we were told, were Spinzar employees from around the province, had been brought in recently from the surrounding villages to fill out the crowds.

We stood out in the baking sun for hours, forced to listen to one boring speech after another. Then the most famous speaker, Abdullah Amin, the brother of President Hafizullah Amin, took the stage. He was a high-level government official responsible for administering the northeastern part of the country. I will never forget his fiery speech. "Comrades!" he yelled through his microphone. "I have assembled you here today so that you will join the revolutionary fight! There are certain elements in our society that are especially resistant to the new regime, and I think you all know who they are. The center of the reactionary movement is in the Shi'a Hazara areas in Baghlan, Hazarajat, and Bamiyan provinces. I am commanding all of you young Spinzar employees who are gathered here today to fight against these backward counterrevolutionaries. . . . You should not have an ounce of mercy for these enemies of the people. You should wipe out all of them! . . . Their heads belong to me, but their possessions are yours!"

Several weeks later word began to spread about what had taken place in the areas of Tala and Barfak in Baghlan province. People say that most of the local men had already escaped into the mountains by the time the attackers arrived. But many women, children, and elderly people had remained in their homes. Many of those who remained behind became the victims of unspeakable atrocities. Their houses were burned to the ground, women and children were beaten up, and pregnant women even had their stomachs slit open. This was a direct result of those incendiary words from Abdullah Amin. I heard them with my own ears, and I knew that from that day on politicians of any stripe were to be distrusted.

The next year, when I was in the eleventh grade, the Soviet Union invaded Afghanistan. While anticommunist forces had long been opposed to girls studying in school, the invasion from these so-called "infidels" gave fresh momentum to their campaign. "Do you really want to allow the godless Russians to see your daughters?" mujahedin leaders would ask men in the mosques.

It quickly became unsafe for female students and teachers to walk to and from school without a burqa. While some girls in outlying villages had worn burqas for many years, it wasn't something that I, as a city girl, had to do. But within several months of the Soviet invasion, my oldest sister and I were wearing burqas on our way to our lessons.

One day, returning home from school, we found a note on our front door. "Said Nuruddin Khan," the note read. "I would advise you to control your daughters' behavior. If we discover that your children have gone to school again, you are liable to find them dead in the street." The letter wasn't signed, but it was obvious that it had been written by the mujahedin. Our burqas had not been enough.

That evening, when my father returned from the mosque, all of us kids were sent directly to bed. As soon as we were in our rooms, we opened our windows to eavesdrop on our parents' conversation.

"What should we do?" my father asked my mother with great consternation. "This is already the third time they've posted this kind of note on our door. I have to admit that I already found two notes, and I destroyed them because I didn't want to scare you and the kids. But now I'm worried that they're really going to kill our daughters."

My mother couldn't understand. "What did our daughters do wrong? Why would anyone be opposed to our children going to school?"

"Their argument is that they want to protect our Afghan girls from the foreign invaders. They say that it is our duty as parents to keep them home during the jihad."

After listening to their conversation for a couple of minutes, I couldn't restrain myself any longer. I marched into the room where my parents were sitting. "I want to study," I said firmly. "And all of my sisters want to continue their education, too."

My father looked at me long and hard. Finally he said to my mother and I, "Birth and death are in the hands of Allah. We have no power to alter His will. . . . I cannot live with the idea of my daughters remaining at home, illiterate. You have to keep going to school, no matter what. May Allah protect you!"

So the next morning, as usual, we walked to school in our burqas.

But now, we decided to take extra precautions. Each time we took a different route, walking through neighbors' yards and through back alleys so that nobody could identify us. For the next several days, we would look all around to see if someone was in pursuit. Studying by this point had become more-or-less useless. We couldn't even concentrate on our lessons, sitting in fear that the afternoon walk home could be our last.

Then one day a mujahedin commander, who had once been a close friend of my father's, came to our house.

"So I've heard from my men that your daughters are still going to school," he said to my father.

"Yes, it's true," my father answered. "But there are some people who obviously aren't very happy with this. I've discovered several notes on my door threatening to kill my children if they continue their studies."

"I've recently been informed about this," the commander said. "And I can assure you that it won't happen again. I know that you have no sons and that you need to educate your daughters. I will never forget the kindness you've shown me in the past. I remember many years ago, when your young daughters would serve me tea when I sat in this very room. I would never want anything to happen to them. Please accept my apologies for what has occurred."

So all of my sisters and I continued going to school without fear of reprisals. The fact that I am educated stems both from my father's courage and from his faith in God.

→   →   ←   ←

I had always been a very good student, and as a result, many of my classmates would come over to my house after school for help with their homework. This was possible only because I didn't have any brothers, and my father was too old to be a threat to my teenage female classmates. If I'd had brothers, rumors would have doubtless circulated about the "real" purpose of the girls' visits to my house.

One day, when I was in the twelfth grade, one of my classmates, Asifa, came by my house for assistance with her physics homework. She was accompanied by her younger sister, Kamilla, and her mother. I looked at their mother with a puzzled expression because I had never enjoyed a particularly close relationship with Asifa in the past. And I knew that their mother was a housewife who rarely ventured out onto the street.

Asifa, noticing the look on my face, explained, "At first my mother wanted us to go to the house of another girl, Nasiba, because she's friends with her mother. And she thought that since we all studied together, Nasiba could help me with my physics homework. But I persuaded her to take us to your house because I know you understand physics much better than Nasiba. She'll wait around for me to finish up my homework, and then we'll go over to Nasiba's house."

This explanation seemed rather odd, but I didn't really think about it too much at the time. I welcomed their mother with traditional Afghan hospitality. I brought her tea and sweets and made sure that she had everything she needed. Then I took out my notebook and physics book and we began studying. I answered all of Asifa's myriad questions and explained the homework assignment to her. But throughout our discussions, I realized that my classmate's mother was staring at me intently. I began to feel so uncomfortable under her probing gaze that I even started to sweat.

It was then that I began thinking back to Asifa's strange explanation for her mother's presence. "Why is it that she never brought her mother here before?" I asked myself. "What was her real motive in coming here?" I noticed that even Asifa wasn't paying very close attention to what I was talking about. Instead, she and Kamilla were discreetly alternating their glances between me and their mother.

When our work was completed, my mother and I escorted them to our front gate. A few minutes later, one of our neighbors rushed in with a handful of chocolates. She told us that the guests who had just gone had left behind several boxes of chocolates next to our front gate.

We were all very confused. We supposed that this gesture indicated that our guests wanted to create a "sweet" relationship between our families. But as I learned later, this meant that I apparently had just passed Asifa's mother's little test, and now she wanted me to marry her oldest son. My classmate had praised me to her mother, saying that I was very clever and an active student. Her son was also studying physics in a university in Kabul, so her mother thought that we'd make a good match.

Over the course of the next several months, Asifa's mother often came to our house with marriage proposals. At first, my mother told her, "I hardly know you at all. What kind of guarantee do I have that your son isn't already married? Or that he's not some terrible person who will beat Humaira for no reason or who won't let her continue her education?"

A few months later, my would-be husband, Habib, returned from Kabul after graduation. It would have been an ideal time for a marriage because I had just completed high school. But my mother remained opposed to marrying me off to a relatively unknown family. So she invented a new pretext. She said to his mother, "You know, military tradition is of great importance in our family. My husband and his father both served in the army with great distinction. Until your son has served at least two years in the army, we will not be able to approve this match."

My mother thought that this would be enough to put an end to these discussions. But apparently Habib had already been considering military service. So while I was studying at the pedagogical university here in Kunduz, he joined the government army and fought for two years against the insurgent mujahedin.

When Habib's military service was nearing its end, his mother began coming to our house more and more frequently. By this time, my mother was starting to get worried that I wouldn't be able to find a better suitor. I was almost twenty at the time, which is considered practically an old maid here in Afghanistan. Furthermore, Habib's mother had been so persistant that she began to think that his family must be a good one. This is the reason that my mother finally relented.

Only after the agreements were made did Habib's parents bother to inform him about the impending wedding. His mother later told us about his response after his father broke the news to him, "I'm ready to marry any girl who my mother chooses for me. I, of course, honor my parents. I remember my mother's words before I went off to study in Kabul—'Don't think about marrying one of your classmates. I don't like those city girls. I will choose your future wife.' Of course I will keep my promise. I know that if my mother and father approve of a girl, I will like her, too."

It was two months after I had been promised that I first laid eyes on my future husband. As part of the engagement party, the male relatives on both sides of the family gathered at our house, and then the next day was set aside for a women's party. Many of my relatives gathered for the festivities, including my older sister and her family, who were living in Mazar-i-Sharif at the time.

As we were preparing food for our guests, my sister asked me if I had ever met my fiancé before. I was shocked by the directness of her question. I wasn't living in Kabul or somewhere where relationships between men and women were more liberal. "I swear to God that I have never seen him before. I've been told that he hasn't even set foot in Kunduz for a long time," I told her earnestly. I didn't want her to think that I was a bad girl.

The men's party was set aside for a Thursday after the evening prayers. Twenty men from my fiancé's family—including my fiancé himself—entered our courtyard. Before coming into the house, they all lined up to wash their hands with a pitcher of water. At this time, one of my cousins who had seen Habib before ran into the kitchen giggling. "Do you want to know what your future husband looks like?" she asked playfully elbowing me in the ribs. She pointed out the kitchen window and across the courtyard. But I was too embarrassed to look up.

Then my sisters and other female cousins began to gather beside us in the kitchen.

"Look at that first guy with the mustache," one of them called out laughing. "There's your future husband! Look, look, look—before he goes into the house!"

Everyone burst out laughing. Then, when I finally mustered the courage to raise my head, the girl said, "No, I'm just kidding. That's not your fiancé, it's actually the fourth guy in line."

"No, that's not him," another one teased. "It's the short guy who's fifth in line."

"No, it's the guy with the big nose and the ears that stick out," another whispered conspiratorially.

"Don't tease Humaira," another cousin said as seriously as she could manage. "It's that really fat guy."

They all burst out laughing uproariously.

But I'd had enough of this silliness. "I don't want to hear any more about it. I'm not interested anymore. Whoever my husband is, there's nothing I can do about it anyway."

Then my cousin grabbed me by one of the braids in my hair and said,

"OK, I'm not joking anymore. You see that last guy in line—that's your future husband."

By that time, I was so embarrassed that my sisters and cousins said I looked like a tomato. All I could do was sneak a short glance at the man I was supposed to spend the rest of my life with.

I was pleased with what I saw. He was tall, with big eyes, and a full head of dark black hair.

After our guests had eaten, all the men left except my fiancé and a couple of his younger cousins. To my great surprise, Habib then walked over to the room where I was sitting with my female relatives. As is customary, everyone stood up when he entered the room. I assumed that he would greet all of my relatives first and then speak with me last. But he'd seen a photo of me before, and after quickly surveying the room, he came over to me directly. He gently took my hand in his and began to ask me some simple questions. But I was too embarrassed to look up at him or even to mumble anything back in reply.

That's the only time in my life that I can remember being left completely speechless.

✦ ✦ ✦ ✦

We got married shortly after I graduated with a teaching degree from the Kunduz pedagogical university. I immediately got a job as a geometry and algebra teacher in the local high school, while my husband began teaching physics in the pedagogical university.

After the wedding, I moved in with my husband's family in their compound. I tried to do whatever I could around the house to ingratiate myself to my new family. After I came home from teaching, I would work tirelessly around the house, cooking and cleaning. I got along excellently with all of my husband's younger sisters and brothers, as well as his parents.

Habib's parents had been relatively wealthy; they had bought a few houses in Kunduz as well as a couple in Kabul. Over the course of the next few years, they encouraged several of their married sons to take up residence in their own compounds. That's how we came to inherit a beautiful two-story house that was located a few minutes away from his parents' house.

While the mujahedin caused a lot of trouble for educated people in the 1980s, we were able to escape any serious harm. However, the fall of the communist regime in the early 1990s was accompanied by many difficulties for our family. In 1992, my mother-in-law died and my husband lost his teaching job. Everything was in chaos. Kunduz was being bombed again and again by one faction or another. It was a very difficult time for everyone—except maybe for the commanders who got rich from their looting.

My husband became depressed after he was forced out of his job, and he told me that he needed a change. "We have four young children. How are we supposed to feed them?" he asked me one day. "I have some friends across the border in Tajikistan who told me that they can help me find work as a trader. Maybe after I get some money together, I can arrange to bring you and the kids over, too." So I was left alone to take care of our children, while my husband left to start a new career.

But at that time, the situation in Tajikistan was not much safer than in Kunduz. After the Soviet Union fell apart, Tajikistan quickly descended into its own bloody civil war. Shortly after Habib arrived, he was traveling somewhere in Dushanbe, the capital, with his close friend Omar Khan and ten other Afghans. It was late in the evening, and they were traveling in two separate cars on a remote back street. As they drove along, my husband spotted several armed men standing next to an army jeep with government license plates and tinted windows. They flagged down both cars, and all the passengers were ordered to line up out on the street.

The soldiers collected all of the Afghans' documents. At the time, many Afghans had been assisting the mujahedin forces in Tajikistan in their fight against the government. The armed men asked them a couple of questions that suggested that they thought that my husband and his traveling companions were part of the opposition. My husband was convinced they'd be shot then and there.

While the soldiers looked through the documents, one of them shouted out, "Which one of you is Omar Khan?" My husband's friend stepped forward. "It says here in your passport that you were born in Farkhar, you son of a bitch." Many of the government and paramilitary forces were from a southern district of Tajikistan also called Farkhar. Before the Soviet Union took control of Tajikistan and closed the border with Afghanistan in the 1930s, relatives would cross between both Farkhars. The soldier took my husband's friend from the line and asked him, "Who else is from Farkhar?" Omar Khan paused for a moment and then pointed to my husband. "He comes from Farkhar, too—he wasn't born there, but he's lived there for many years." Then they removed my husband from the line as well.

As they began leading the other men away, Omar Khan turned to the soldier who'd saved him and asked, "Can't you do something to help these other men, too?"

"Nope, I can't do anything about them," he said.

They led the rest of the men about fifty yards down the road, to the site of a half-constructed house. There were big pits in the ground where the earth had been dug up. The men were led over to the side of one of the pits, and their hands were tied behind their backs. Then they were shot dead.

As dangerous as it was for my husband in Tajikistan, there were still more business opportunities there. He managed to build a relationship with a couple of Iranians who wanted to export macaroni and laundry detergent. After this, year after year, his importing business slowly grew. Within a few years after his arrival in Tajikistan, my husband organized a company that was importing large quantities of food and household items from Iran, Turkey, and Turkmenistan and reselling it at a large profit. His biggest import items included macaroni, cookies, tea, sugar, flour, cooking oil, butter, soap, laundry detergent, and shampoo as well as thermoses and cups.

While my husband was building his business across the border, I stayed behind in Kunduz with our young children. My husband managed to come back home from time to time, bringing money so I didn't have to worry about feeding and clothing my children. But like everybody else in Kunduz at that time, we suffered terribly as a result of the fighting between Generals Dostum and Mas'ud. At first airplanes and helicopters would bomb the city. There were many reports about the terrible crimes that Dostum's troops committed when they captured new areas; they would steal from people's homes, murder men and boys and rape women.

At one point in 1995 the fighting became so fierce, that my husband decided that we needed to leave Kunduz immediately. At that time, we had four children—the oldest girl, Maliha, was eleven and our only boy, Fayoz, was ten, and I was five-months pregnant with our fifth child. Although I was in no condition to flee from home, we knew that it wouldn't be safe to remain in Kunduz as Dostum's forces were quickly approaching. It was impossible to get over the border because we had yet to acquire the proper documents, so my husband came back from Tajikistan to help us flee to neighboring Takhar province. We decided to take our most valuable possessions with us: our expensive carpets, jewelry, beautiful dishes, and various antiques. For over two weeks, my children, father-in-law, and I lived with my father-in-law's friend in the Bangi district of Takhar as the battles around Kunduz raged.

The entire time we lived in Bangi, I lived in fear that something would happen to my husband, who had returned to Kunduz with some of his relatives. "Why did he have to go back?" I kept thinking. I was torturing myself with my fears and my overactive imagination. We never left the house we were staying in. Our host had warned us that there were a lot of land mines strewn around the village, so my children and I didn't set foot outside the compound. The two weeks we were in exile felt more like two years.

But eventually my husband came back to Bangi to retrieve us. "Things have quieted down considerably back in Kunduz, and I think it's safe for all of us to return," he told us. "Let's start gathering our things together." We were overjoyed with the news. None of us wanted to be away from home any longer than necessary. But when I was standing close to my husband as we talked, I looked down and saw a little louse running down his shirt. I grabbed it immediately and asked, "What in the world is this?"

"Oh that," he grinned at me. "Don't you know? It's a mark of war. . . . We didn't have a chance to change our clothes or wash since I last saw you. So what do you expect?" War or no war, I couldn't stand seeing my husband so dirty. "Before you take another step inside this house, I want you to go directly to the bathroom and scrub yourself clean. You want to give our children some sort of disease?" I asked him angrily.

We assembled all of our possessions and we were ready to return home. But the biggest obstacle was finding transportation. There were so many displaced people who were also returning home that we couldn't find any free cars. After many hours, my husband finally managed to flag down an overloaded truck for us. The truck must have been used to transport mud or bricks, because it was filthy. Nevertheless, many families from Kunduz were already onboard with all of their goods. The truck was so full, it sagged down nearly to the ground. The jolting three-hour crawl to Kunduz was terribly uncomfortable. I was worried that the trip might bring about a miscarriage. My elderly father-in-law, who was suffering from rheumatism, was also in terrible pain. But we all knew that there was no other way home.

By the time we arrived back in Kunduz, Dostum's forces had retreated to Mazar, but Kunduz still couldn't be considered safe. There were armed troops all over the city running around looking for war booty, some obviously more interested in taking revenge than in keeping the peace. General Mas'ud's troops who had "liberated" Kunduz were joined by common thieves who entered people's homes at will with the excuse of rounding up Dostum's forces or locating weapons. As we witnessed the disorder on the streets of Kunduz from the back of our truck, my husband and I began to discuss whether it would, in fact, be safe to remain in our homes.

We decided that it would be best if we didn't bother to unpack our bags. "Just take some of your jewelry and other valuables and put them back in the house," my husband instructed. "Everything else you should just keep in the courtyard. I'm going to have a look around the city and find out what the situation is. And then we'll decide on our next step."

As soon as we arrived home, my father-in-law went upstairs and crawled into bed. He was completely wiped out from the trip. I was busy organizing our possessions in the courtyard when I heard a loud knock on the front gate and the voices of some strange men speaking Dari and Pashtu. I walked over to the gate to look through the crack, and I saw several soldiers gathered in front of our house. They were carrying guns, their clothes were ragged, and their beards and hair were a mess. "Open up the door!" one soldier yelled threateningly.

I was too afraid to open the gate myself, so I whispered to my son, Fayoz, who was standing nearby, "Go inside and tell your grandfather to come out here and talk with these soldiers." But my father-in-law was not feeling well, and it took him a long time to make his way out of bed and downstairs to the front gate. By the time he shuffled his way into the courtyard, one of the soldiers had jumped over our surrounding wall, walked over to the gate, and opened it up for the rest of his fifteen or so fellow soldiers. They immediately grabbed my father-in-law, threw him against our surrounding wall, and began beating him with the butts of their rifles.

"What took you so long to open the door? Are you an infidel? Are you with Dostum's forces?" they screamed at him as they beat him. Before he could even answer, they said, "Where are your weapons? Go get your weapons for us or we'll kill you!"

As soon as I saw the soldiers come into our courtyard, I quickly gathered together the gold jewelry I had just put back in my bedroom. I also noticed my husband's guns hanging right by the front door. "What will they do if they discover these weapons here?" I thought. So I grabbed the guns and hid them in the bathroom behind a burqa that was hanging on a nail.

After I finished, I rushed over to the window just in time to see my father-in-law being beaten in our courtyard. I couldn't bear to see this happen. He was so sick that he could easily have been beaten to death. I had to do something. So without even thinking about the consequences, I threw on my burqa and climbed the narrow stairs to the roof of our house. As I stood on our mud roof where I could be heard both on the street and in the courtyard below, I started yelling, "Hey you down there with your dirty heads and bare feet!" All fifteen of the soldiers looked up at me. I also noticed that a couple of men on the street stopped to marvel at this strange sight. "What do you want from us?" I continued. "Who the hell do you think you are to come here and beat up this poor old man? Every regime that's been in power here—the Shah, the communists, the mujahedin— everyone respected him and honored him as a community leader. But you ugly, dirty people think you can just come in here and beat him up? Tell me who you are! Are you part of Dostum's army that has come back here to torture us again?"

The men all stood frozen in total shock. Thank God I was endowed with a loud voice that was able to get everyone's attention. The soldiers stopped beating my father-in-law and just looked at one another.

I kept carrying on, "Did you stop to think about why it took so long for my father-in-law to come to the gate? Actually, I came to the gate first. But I couldn't possibly open the gate for strangers, could I? You're men

230 + LOVE AND WAR IN AFGHANISTAN

and you should speak with men, not women. . . . Look at the person you're beating up. He's in poor health. Nobody around here will ever forgive you if you keep hurting him."

As my haranguing continued unabated, one of the soldiers eventually called out, "Hey, sister, please come down from there and stop your yelling. It's our responsibility to search people's houses for illicit weapons. We're going to continue our search, and then we'll be on our way."

"Why would you think we have weapons? We're innocent civilians," I screamed in response.

"We saw all these bundles here in your yard. We received information that they were actually stolen goods. That's why we came here," he said.

"What nonsense!" I screamed in response. "Isn't it obvious that this stuff belongs to our family? We just returned from Takhar. We were fleeing the fighting—like everyone else. We didn't even have a chance to put our things back in the house when you showed up!"

A few of the soldiers went inside the house to look for weapons in spite of my assurances that they'd find nothing. I continued using the only weapon in my arsenal—my loud voice. "Why did you people come here to bother us? Can't you see that we just returned to Kunduz? Why don't you leave us alone so that we can live our lives in peace and quiet?"

I climbed down from the roof as they searched the house—the basement, our bedroom, and so on. But they had yet to search the bathroom with the hidden weapons when I got downstairs. So I decided to go directly to the living room, which was located on the way to the bathroom, to continue my tirade. Eventually, the soldier who appeared to be in charge of the operation turned to me and said, "Look, we've all gotten headaches from your obnoxious voice. You've managed to get under all of our skins. Congratulations! We're going to leave your house now. So just cut out your yelling!"

Then they left, without checking the bathroom, and we slammed our gate behind them. Luckily, my father-in-law wasn't seriously injured. We took him back up to his bed to bandage up his wounds.

About an hour later, my husband returned. After I told him what had happened, he said, "If they came here once, they're probably going to be back again. It's just not safe to remain in Kunduz anymore. . . . Why don't we all move to Tajikistan?"

At first, I was very skeptical. "But your father and my parents are very old. What will happen to them if they grow even more ill? I really don't want to be separated from them. What will happen to our house? How will the kids cope with the long trip? How can I live in another country?"

But for each of the million questions I asked, my husband had a ready response. "This is the bottom line," he finally said to me very seriously. "The truth is that I have no idea if our family will even survive if we decide to stay here in Kunduz."

I thought about what he'd said. A day or two later I reluctantly agreed to leave.

→   →   ←   ←

When we crossed the border into Tajikistan, it was a bitterly cold evening. We had to take the official small motor boat that belonged to the Tajik government to cross the Amu Darya. The wind was howling, and my four children were shivering. I was very sad to be leaving Afghanistan behind. I couldn't even begin to conceive of what life would be like in another country. We were also traveling with another refugee family from Mazar-i-Sharif, who seemed to be just as fearful about the road ahead.

After we passed through the customs checkpoint, we discovered that there were no taxis available. Everyone seemed to have gone home for the night. The bus driver who had taken us from the boat to the border crossing offered to take us home for the evening and then drive us in his own informal taxi the next morning to Dushanbe. His wife prepared very good food for us, and we were happy that we were finally in a warm, safe environment. By this time, the war in Tajikistan was mostly confined to other parts of the country, outside of the capital and nowhere near this border crossing.

Our bags didn't fit inside the bus driver's car, so he had to attach a small trailer to the back of his vehicle. The trip to the capital, Dushanbe, should have been only three hours, but when the roadside police spotted our trailer, we were stopped again and again on the road. All our documents were in order, but they focused on the trailer. "What's this trailer for? Do you have the proper permits to have a trailer?" and so on. The trip took six hours in total, and we had to give out innumerable small bribes to the police so that they wouldn't search through every single one of our bags.

We spent our first few days in Tajikistan at the bazaar, buying fashionable Western clothes for me and my children. I also went to the beauty salon, and they managed to make my straight hair very shiny and wavy. We especially enjoyed the park in the center of town, where the kids played on all the amusement-park rides. Since my husband's business was going very well, we had enough extra money for quite a luxurious lifestyle.

A few weeks after we arrived in Dushanbe, my husband announced that he had purchased a four-bedroom apartment for us. Our new neighbors, many of whom worked in the nearby maternity hospital, were very kind and welcoming. The fact that I was six-months pregnant at the time made them especially interested in hearing about our adventures and how we had escaped to Tajikistan. My kids also quickly became friends with the young people who lived in our apartment house. I heard that our neighbors would tell their children, "Try to treat those new children kindly. They came from a country that is in the middle of a terrible war."

But many of the Afghans who were living in Dushanbe at that time experienced serious conflicts with their neighbors. It was commonly assumed that Afghans who came to Tajikistan were successful businessmen and that their wives had a lot of gold jewelry. So there were a number of incidents of masked gunmen coming into Afghan apartments to steal all of their valuables. One of my Afghan friends told me about a thief who had plugged in an iron and threatened to burn her husband if he didn't hand over all his valuables.

We were lucky. Except at night, we never even bothered to lock our front door. There was a Tajik family who lived above us and an ethnic Russian family below with whom we enjoyed especially good rapport. Since our family was much better off than many of our neighbors, I never hesitated to give away money or food when any of them were in need.

As I was pregnant, it came in handy that I had quickly built a close relationship with many of the hospital staff. My doctor, an older Russian woman named Antonina Pavlovna, was also my friend and neighbor. She would frequently give me check-ups and would always help me skip ahead in line. One time when I was standing in line in the corridor of the hospital behind ten or so women, Antonina spotted me and said very loudly, "My Afghan daughter, what are you doing standing out here? Come in and I'll check you right now."

I didn't speak Russian very well at the time, but I caught the gist of what she was saying. As I approached, she suddenly remembered that she needed to finish examining a woman who was already in her office. "But as soon as I'm done with her," she told me, "you'll be next." I waited in the corridor, and glancing down the hallway, I saw the other pregnant women casting hostile looks in my direction.

At first, no one said a word. Then a pregnant Tajik woman looked up at me. "Look at the beauty queen," she said contemptuously. "You know it's only because your husband makes a lot of money that you can skip ahead of us. Aren't you ashamed to dress this way when so many people back in your homeland are so poor? They are all barefoot, with nothing to eat, and nothing to wear. But look at your clothes and your hair—you're trying very hard not to look like an Afghan, aren't you? . . . And now take a look at that Russian infidel and how she seems to love and respect you. 'Come in my Afghan daughter.' How is it possible for an Afghan woman to have a Russian mother? 'My daughter, my daughter,'" she said with biting sarcasm.

This was the first time I encountered such resentment against Afghans in Tajikistan. I was very fortunate that I didn't face this kind of hostility very often during my six years in Dushanbe. Some of my Afghan friends said that they felt very unwelcome there, but I think that a lot of it had to do with the way that they interacted with other people. I tried to treat people warmly, and I was generally treated well as a result.

→   →   ←   ←

Over the next several years, my husband's business continued to expand, and we lived in the lap of luxury. We bought another apartment nearby for visiting guests, as well as a fancy imported car.

But this prosperity was not fated to last forever. Our problems began around 1999. At that time, my husband entered into a partnership with a group of Tajiks who had close ties to the government. For several months, the relationship between my husband's company and the Tajik company, Nazokat, was working out very well. With the Tajiks' connections in official sectors, he was able to get around cumbersome bureaucratic procedures and avoid paying bribes. Ultimately, my husband decided to invest $33,000 in their company. But only a few months later, the Tajiks claimed that their business had gone bust and they officially declared bankruptcy. My husband didn't believe that this could possibly be true, but given the people he was dealing with, there was no way he could seek recourse with the authorities. Their people were in power, and nobody was going to undertake an investigation on behalf of some Afghan. That's when things started to unravel.

My husband was devastated that he had lost so much money. He was so upset about it that I began to worry about our future—for the first time in many years. But after my husband realized how troubled I was, he tried to reassure me. "You shouldn't worry, Humaira jaan," he told me. "I've just imported a large amount of food by train from Iran, and as soon as we sell it, we'll be back in good shape again."

But later that same week, his business was entirely wiped out when there was a strange explosion at his warehouse. Everything that he had just imported was destroyed. It took the firefighters hours to extinguish the flames, due to all of the highly flammable cooking oil that was in storage. The authorities concluded that the fire was an accident caused by an electrical short circuit. But my husband believed—and still believes—that he was a victim of foul play. There was stiff competition among many of the traders, even the Afghan traders, and he wouldn't have been surprised if any number of people had been to blame. Whatever the cause, $70,000 worth of goods were destroyed in one terrible night.

Much of the money that went up in flames at his warehouse was not his own. Several other businessmen—both Tajik and Afghan—had invested in his company, and he had to figure out a way to repay their loans. From this time on, we were visited by his creditors frequently. My husband always tried to hide the fact that these people were coming to our house since he didn't want to worry me.

Over the course of the past several years, he had constantly given me money for shopping and other expenses. But instead of spending it all, I managed to save nearly $3,500. At the time I didn't understand that this money would hardly put a dent in my husband's massive debt, but I gave him everything I had.

During the rest of our time in Tajikistan, my husband became increasingly jumpy. Anytime the doorbell would ring, he'd leap from his chair and rush to the door. He developed a nervous twitch, and at night he'd walk around the apartment smoking cigarette after cigarette, even though he'd never smoked before. Finally one evening he came home and said, "Humaira, I have to tell you something. I can't sleep at home tonight. I'm afraid for my life. I've been told that some people are going to come by tonight to collect their money. But I don't have a penny to my name."

That evening at around eleven, our doorbell was rung repeatedly. The children and I were watching a movie, and my children were clearly frightened by such a late-night visit. But I was determined to show the people on the other side of the door that I wasn't afraid. So I got up and opened the door. To tell you the truth, I was entirely fed up with all of these people coming to our house all the time asking about money. I wanted to find a solution—one way or another.

There were three young Tajik men standing in the corridor. They all looked like weight lifters.

"Where's your husband?" one of them asked me rudely.

"He's not home right now. And who are you?" I asked.

The one who'd spoken first said, "My name's Aziz. We're with Commander Suhrob."*

"So what do you want from my husband?" I asked.

"Your husband owes us $5,000. Every day he promises that he'll pay his debt, but he just never manages to produce the money."

"OK, so let's get right to it." I said. "Tell me what you want. To get your money back or to kill him?"

"We want to get our money back. But he's been lying to us! We're beginning to doubt that he even has the money."

I sighed. "Let me tell you what the situation is. He wants to pay everyone back, but he can't right now." I then explained to them exactly how my husband had lost all of his money. "I'm sure if you give my husband

* General Suhrob Kasymov was a famous commander in charge of an elite brigade of Interior Ministry troops.

more time, he will find a way to get back on his feet and settle his debts. . . . But your coming by here all the time isn't very conducive to clear thinking on his part. Besides, if you keep showing up like this, my husband will never spend another night here. Is this what you want?"

The men spoke amongst themselves for a couple of minutes. Then Aziz turned back to me and said, "You know I really appreciate that you've been honest with us. Because of your honesty, we're going to cut your husband some slack. He'll now have two months to repay the debt. But this time, the date is fixed. There's no going beyond these two months."

Early the next morning, when my husband returned home, he asked with great concern if his creditors had visited. "Yes," I said as casually as I could. "But I sent them away for the next couple of months. You won't have to worry about them for awhile."

"What did you say to them?" he asked me with great surprise.

"Well you know I was just so sick and tired of them bothering you, not to mention the rest of us, I just told them the truth."

After this incident, my husband decided that we had no choice but to sell both our apartments as well as our car. In fact, we sold off almost all of our possessions—most of our furniture, much of my jewelry, and most everything else of value. We moved into a small rental apartment. But even with all of that money, my husband was able to pay back only some of his debts.

It wasn't until we put our apartments up for sale that I began to understand what it meant to be deep in debt. When we lived in Afghanistan, we were never rich, but we had always been comfortable. Then, when we came to Tajikistan, we lived in absolute luxury. My husband had been able to provide us with everything we wanted. And then, suddenly, it was all gone. It was very difficult psychologically to have to start counting pennies. I began to lose a lot of weight and to worry constantly about our future.

✦   ✦   ✦   ✦

We were still living comfortably in Tajikistan when the Taliban captured Kunduz in 1997. All of us Afghans in Dushanbe were deeply concerned about what would happen to everyone back home. The saddest topic of discussion was the Taliban's new edicts: preventing girls from studying in school, requiring men to have beards, banning music, and so forth and so on. Although I was very happy that my children and I weren't forced to live under this horrible regime, I worried every day about my parents, my sisters, and their families, as well as Habib's relatives.

In early 2001 we received a letter from Habib's younger brother who had remained behind in Kunduz all these years. He wrote that the Taliban had begun confiscating empty houses that belonged to Afghans who had left the country and that our house had become an object of their rapacious interest. "If you don't return to Kunduz soon, I'm afraid your house will become state property," Habib's brother wrote. He also reported that my father-in-law had fallen into very poor health.

My husband was alarmed by his brother's news and decided to return to Afghanistan quickly. He crossed the border into a part of the country that was still under the control of the Northern Alliance and eventually found a group of men who were traveling to Kunduz.

Shortly after my husband arrived in Kunduz, he wrote a letter to one of his closest friends in Dushanbe. The person who had been asked to deliver the letter had never been to Tajikistan before so he had trouble tracking down my husband's friend. Somebody suggested bringing it to me so that I could pass it along. The letter was brought to me one evening at around ten o'clock.

I had been anxiously awaiting news from my husband ever since the day he had departed. And here was a letter from him in my hands—the only problem was that it wasn't addressed to me. After thinking about what I should do for a couple of minutes, I decided to just tear open the letter. The suspense was unbearable.

In the letter, he wrote, "I've arrived back in Kunduz and have been greeted with one piece of news that's worse than the next. First, I learn that Humaira's father has just died. Then I find out that the Taliban have claimed ownership over our house. And when one of our conniving neighbors found out about this, he went to the Taliban headquarters and negotiated the purchase of our house. Now the house legally belongs to him. All of the possessions we left behind or hid, including Humaira's gold, are nowhere to be found. . . . I still have no idea how I will possibly repay my creditors back in Dushanbe. The debts are just way too large. Things are grim indeed . . .

"But please, whatever you do, don't tell Humaira about this letter. She's alone in Tajikistan with our kids, and I'm really afraid of what her reaction will be to all of this awful news. I know her very well—she's liable to catch a taxi to the border and come back to Kunduz herself. The Taliban are terrible people, and it would be very difficult for her and the children to be here. I'll find a way to break the news to her myself after I return to Dushanbe."

It was really too much horrible information to bear at one time. I wanted to talk about it with my oldest son and daughter with whom I have a very close relationship. But after I read the letter, I went to the next room, where all my kids were gathered, and found them all deeply absorbed in some old Soviet comedy on television. I saw how they were lying on their pillows, totally relaxed, and laughing out loud. I just couldn't find the strength to disrupt the festive mood. So I went back to my room, sat on the sofa, and thought about the future. Then I decided to call one of my friends in Dushanbe who had also been our neighbor in Kunduz. The moment she answered the phone, I spilled forth my tragic news.

For some strange reason, I focused most of my attention on my lost jewelry. I guess all of the other news was too difficult to make any sense of and I wanted to discuss something far less meaningful.

My friend said that she'd come over to our apartment first thing in the morning to discuss it more. I cried and cried when I saw her. "We had everything—I didn't have a care in the world," I said to her sobbing. "And now look what's become of us."

I told her that I was seriously thinking about returning to Afghanistan. She tried to talk me out of it. "Humaira, Afghanistan is in terrible shape now. If you go back, it'll be very difficult for you to live there. And it will probably be even more difficult for your children. They've gotten used to the freedom of life abroad; they dress, think, and even speak differently than young people in Afghanistan. After all, they've been here six years!"

My friend was right of course. But I wasn't able to think very clearly then. I decided to call my sister in Mazar-i-Sharif whose husband had a satellite phone. As luck would have it, my mother happened to be visiting my sister at the time. I was relieved to have the opportunity to speak to my mother. But my happiness quickly turned into even greater anxiety when I heard how my mother's voice trembled as she spoke. I thought she sounded seriously ill, and I was overcome with the desire to be with her. She had no sons to take care of her—just six daughters—and I knew that I could be a big help to her.

It isn't like me to give in to depression when faced with adversity. I have to act, to do something. And my husband did indeed know me very well; after that phone call, I made up my mind to go back to Afghanistan. And I wasn't about to sit around and wait for a male escort.

Nevertheless, there were several obstacles to our return. The biggest problem was that I needed to sell off all of our things in order to pay for the journey. But I had to be very careful. My husband still had many creditors who would frequently come by our house. They would not be happy to hear that our family was planning to move back to Afghanistan. They knew very well that if we left for good, they might never see their money. I was afraid that if they were to get wind of our plans, they would kidnap one or more of our children or do something to me. So, as I sold off our goods to our neighbors, I just explained to them that we were moving in with some friends on the other side of town and that we wouldn't need any of our furniture after we left our place.

I was in such a rush to leave that I sold all our things at rock-bottom prices. If I could have gotten $100 for a carpet, for example, I ended up selling it for just $25. I just wanted to gather money quickly for the trip home.

With the money I raised, I went directly to the Tajikistan Ministry of Foreign Affairs to acquire the mandatory exit visas. But when I called from the front desk of the Ministry to make an appointment, the guy on the other end started yelling when he heard my accent. "You miserable Afghans! You waste all my time. I don't want to have anything to do with you people." Then he hung up the phone.

I stood at the front desk for a couple of minutes in shock. I didn't know what to do. Then a couple of fashionably dressed Iranian women walked in and called the same person I had just spoken with. I could tell from their conversation that it was far from a hostile call.

I grabbed the receiver and dialed the number again. But before I could even finish a sentence, he interrupted me again. "I thought I made myself clear. I don't want to talk to any Afghans!" I screamed into the phone, threw the receiver back down, and burst into tears.

The Iranian women tried to comfort me. "Madame, please don't cry. It's OK." Even the Tajik woman who worked on the other side of the reception window was moved by my tears. She came out of her small room from behind the window and said to me, "You shouldn't cry. I'll talk to him myself. Just relax."

She picked up the phone, and I heard her say angrily, "Why are you yelling at her? She's just a simple person who wants to go back home to her family. And all you can do is make her cry!"

The woman at the Ministry offered me invaluable assistance. First she brought me tea and asked me to sit down with her. After a few minutes, she sent one of her colleagues inside the Ministry to take care of all my paperwork. I sat there for about an hour, gave her the necessary fees, and was issued the proper documents. I'll never forget that woman's kindness.

✦　✦　✦　✦

There's a famous Afghan proverb, "Women are sinful until they're in their graves." Actually, the monitoring of women's behavior extends beyond even their death. In Afghanistan, people aren't buried in caskets like many places in the world. They are covered in white fabric and placed underground. Over the course of three days, some people will come back to pray and check on their departed relatives. In some rare cases, animals will have managed to unearth the body, and the corpse is found lying near the surface of the ground. If this happens, it means that the woman was sinful, and it brings great shame on her family.

I knew that everyone back in Afghanistan would judge me by my actions. After all, I was setting out on a long journey without even consulting my husband. But I had made up my mind, and I didn't want to tell a soul about our plans, not even my brother-in-law who happened to be in Dushanbe at the time. I knew how quickly rumors flew through the Afghan community in Tajikistan. I didn't want word to get back to my husband or, worse, his creditors before my children and I made it back into Afghanistan.

When we arrived at the border, we all got out of the taxi, and I peered across the river into Afghanistan. It was then that the doubts started to creep over me. "Here I am with my five children all wearing Western clothes," I thought as I looked at my beautiful kids with me. "My sixteen year-old-son, with his fashionable haircut, was our sole male escort. And we're heading back into a country controlled by the Taliban!"

We waited around for awhile as the Russian border guards finished their three-hour lunch break. The sun was blazing hot on this late spring day, and my kids and I found a shady spot beneath a large oak tree to relax.

When the Russians finally returned to work, we had to pass through security. Just after we entered the small customs house, a male Russian border guard started sweeping his metal detector over me searching for weapons. "Aren't there any women around who can carry out this check?" I asked him, very embarrassed. But he told me there were no women on duty that day.

I was carrying a few metal objects in my pockets—a watch and some of my daughters' metal hair clips—which set off his machine. He immediately reached into my pockets to grab for them. I was terribly ashamed. In our culture, a stranger shouldn't even look at a woman, much less search a woman's pockets. I looked all around me. "Please, can't you stop?" I asked the guard plaintively. "This is the rule, lady, there's nothing I can do about it. This is my job," he replied.

After this humiliation, they began to search our bags. The guard searched absolutely everything—our clothes, small gifts for friends, and all of the other odds and ends we had in our possession. I was nervous that he might notice the small bulge in the bottom of my suitcase. I knew very well that the Taliban had outlawed photographs, so I had removed the stitching from the bottom of my suitcase, placed some of my most prized photographs there, and sewn the bag back together. The pictures showed me and my kids wearing shorts and jeans and short sleeves, without headscarves, of course. He found the bulge in my suitcase, and I said to him worriedly, "Please don't open that up. I'm not trying to hide these photographs from you. It's the other side of the river that I'm worried about." But he wouldn't listen. "You think it's easy to hide things from us? You think I'm that dumb?" he said as he tore open the suitcase stitching with a knife. When he found the photographs, he began to look at them with great interest, one at a time.

I had heard that the other side of this border crossing was then in the hands of the Northern Alliance and that it wasn't until you went farther down the road toward Kunduz that you'd be confronted by the Taliban. Knowing that I didn't have to face the Taliban immediately offered me a certain measure of comfort. So my family and I boarded the same boat that had brought us across the river six years before. Like the last time that I had been on this boat, I felt a strange jumble of emotions as we sputtered our way across the Amu Darya. The moment we climbed onboard, my oldest daughter and I put on our burqas. She had never worn one before. "Mama, how do people see with these sheets over their heads?" she asked me. The younger girls giggled at the sight of their mother and sister in such strange costumes. The novelty wore off quickly, however.

As soon as we crossed the border and showed our documents, one of the Afghan border guards said, "Oh, these are the children of Teacher Habib." He ordered a couple of his soldiers to help us carry our bags up the hill to where the taxis wait to pick up passengers from Tajikistan. I didn't recognize the border guard, but I knew that if he was acquainted with my husband and had been willing to assist us with our bags, I could ask him for a favor.

"I don't know what to do," I said. "The Russians tore open the hiding place for my photographs, and now I'm sure the Taliban will confiscate them and punish us. . . . Now I don't think I have any choice but to tear them up."

"Why don't you just leave them with me?" the border guard kindly offered.

I quickly agreed. I also gave him some cassettes of Tajik music that I was sure wouldn't make it all the way to Kunduz. I didn't see the photographs again for another two years, long after the Taliban had been overthrown. And when we did recover them, it turned out that more than half of them were missing. What anybody would want with our family photographs is totally beyond me. And nobody remembered the cassettes at all.

While we were waiting for our documents to be stamped at the border, I started speaking with two young men who had crossed with us. It turned out that one of them was a former student of my husband's at the pedagogical university, and they were also both heading to Kunduz. Since we'd be sharing a taxi, we decided that they would pretend to be my younger brothers and that we would tell anybody who inquired that we were traveling as a family. We knew that this would offer us all more protection.

The one problem was that these boys had begun to let their beards grow just a couple of weeks previously so they didn't have beards that were sufficiently long. According to the Taliban, every man's beard should be as long as a clenched fist. Also, they had stylish haircuts and looked too pale and clean to be accepted as local Afghans.

As we drove along the sand-swept road to Kunduz, I was dreading what might happen to us when we crossed into Taliban territory. My younger children were amazed by what they saw before them. They'd been very young when they left Afghanistan and didn't remember the camel caravans and the destroyed mud-brick houses they saw from the car.

I thought about the day my daughter Simin, who was studying in the fourth grade in Tajikistan, came home from school full of excitement. "Mama, you know what our geography teacher told us today? She said that there are windstorms in Afghanistan that fill the air with so much dust that you can't even open your eyes. Is that really true?"

I assured her at the time that it was true. "Soon she'll have a chance to see it with her own eyes," I thought.

✦ ✦ ✦ ✦

The Taliban makeshift border post was located next to a river about half an hour north of Kunduz. After we stopped at the border, our car was quickly surrounded by a group of young Taliban soldiers. One began to open up the trunk, while others opened each of the car doors except mine. "Where are you coming from with all these bags?" one of them barked.

The taxi driver explained that he had picked us up at the border and that he was taking us back to our home in Kunduz.

One guard came to the door where my son was sitting and said gruffly, "Hey you, get out of the car!" When my son hesitated, the Taliban grabbed him by his hair. "What did you do with your hair? Why is it cut like this? Are you a Russian infidel or something?"

My son looked at me with all the anguish of the world in his eyes. His expression seemed to be asking me, "Mama, why did you bring us to this place?"

I couldn't stand it anymore. I decided I had to speak up.

"Can't you see that we are refugees returning from Tajikistan?!" I started screaming from under my burqa. "What do you want from us? Isn't it obvious that we aren't armed people? We are simple civilians. If you're going to treat us like this, I'm going to contact everyone I know abroad and tell them that they shouldn't come back here. The reason we came back is that we want to see how things are. We have many friends who are waiting to hear our reports."

All of the Taliban soldiers froze in place. According to the Taliban, women aren't supposed to speak in public, much less yell at them. I was expecting the worst. But just then, one of the soldiers started tapping on the closed window of my door.

"Teacher! Teacher!" he said. I looked around and saw a young man with a big white turban and a long, matted beard halfway down to his waist. He had pushed his face and cupped hands up against the glass to try to get a good view of me behind the gauze of my burqa.

"Teacher, remember me?" he asked me. "You taught me algebra in eighth grade." He was smiling.

It was only because of his smile and his crystal-clear blue eyes that I was able to place him. I didn't remember his name—maybe Rahim or Karim—but I recognized him.

"You know how I knew it was you, Teacher? Your grating voice gave you away! I remember so many times that you yelled at us for not doing our homework or because we couldn't solve a problem that you said was easy. But you always saved your harshest comments for me. You used to tell me that my head was like a pumpkin and that I had no brains, just seeds. I'll never forget your screaming as long as I live." He was laughing.

Five minutes later he had issued us a special pass that gave us permission to travel to our homes.

Since we no longer owned a house, we were forced to move in with one of Habib's brothers and his family for a week or so. But it wasn't comfortable for any of us to be living in such tight quarters. So my husband decided to rent a house for us that belonged to one of his old friends. No one had lived there for several years, and it needed extensive repairs. Over the course of several months, we upgraded the kitchen, the bathroom, and a couple of the bedrooms. But just when I grew content in our new home, the owner of the house came by and asked us to leave. The lease was only half completed. "I'm very sorry but my daughter and her family are planning to return from Pakistan and they need a place to live," he explained to us. My husband didn't want to create a conflict between him and his friend, so he agreed to accept only half of the value of the repairs we'd undertaken. So once again we were homeless. My husband found a new rental house, but I didn't have the heart to undertake more repairs this time around.

The Taliban were expelled from Kunduz only a few months after we had returned home. Until then, the children and I rarely left the house. But only a few days after we returned from Tajikistan, I decided to go to the bazaar with a few of my daughters to buy them summer slippers. I knew of course about the Taliban rule that all women had to be accompanied by a male relative whenever they left the house, but for some reason I didn't take it very seriously. I figured I had so many young children with me, what difference would it make if they were boys or girls?

There was a particular shop in the bazaar where I always used to buy children's shoes. The shopkeeper remembered me and remarked how much my children had grown. Just as the children had decided on some slippers, and I was about to pay, a Taliban official with a long stick approached me from behind with two of his guards. He stood right behind me as I stood speaking with the shopkeeper. The shopkeeper suddenly cried out, "Don't beat her! Don't beat her! Can't you see that she has little children? She's a good woman—I know her!"

I turned around and saw the Taliban with his long stick staring at me. Without saying a word, he just walked out of the shop.

"What happened? Who was he about to beat?" I asked the shopkeeper.

"You, of course. If you come out of your house again without a man to accompany you, I'm sure you won't be so lucky," he told me.

I was in shock. "Thank you for your help," I told the shopkeeper before handing him the money for the slippers.

The Taliban guy must have felt sorry for me. After all, how could he beat someone with so many young children?

Even after the Taliban were overthrown, it was very difficult to adjust to life back in Afghanistan. My children and I were petrified that they'd catch some sort of terrible disease. Malaria is a big problem in Kunduz as is typhoid and other sicknesses. And my kids weren't at all happy with the education they were receiving in school. The classes were over-crowded, there weren't enough books, and they had trouble studying in their native Dari since they had been studying in Russian-language schools back in Tajikistan.

I would often have long coughing spells when dust storms would whip up the dirt in Kunduz. The doctors told me that it was nothing serious. "You've just gotten used to a different environment," one doctor told me. From then on, when my relatives would hear me cough, they'd just laugh. "Oh the poor city girl can't handle living in her own hometown any-more."

⇀ ⇀ ↽ ↽

In many ways, I've been very fortunate. Sure, my family and I have had to endure a lot of difficulties. But unlike many people in Afghanistan, my husband and children are all still alive and in good health, thank God.

About two years ago I found a job with an international aid organi-zation, and recently my husband started working for a United Nations office here in Kunduz. One of my first assignments was to teach chil-dren in a refugee camp that was located just outside of Kunduz city. The children and their parents would tell me such sad stories. Even though the war was over, they were afraid to go back to their villages. In many cases, their houses had been destroyed, their fields were mined, and they had no idea how they could survive back home. But in the summer of 2002, this camp was closed down, and everyone was forced to find somewhere else to live.

After this, I began to do community mobilization work in different vil-lages around Kunduz province. As part of my job, I speak with women and girls about the problems they continue to face and how they can try to overcome their difficulties. What makes me the saddest is when I hear tales about how our Afghan traditions cause innocent deaths or contribute to additional suffering.

In one isolated village in the hills, a respected, elderly woman, Khanumgul, with whom I used to work on a community-based committee, was almost always in a bad mood. I tried my best to include her in discussions and to do whatever I could to make her feel part of the team I was working with. But she always seemed to be thinking about something else. Some of the people told me that Khanumgul was very religious; she prayed five times a day, and she would always faithfully observe the fast during Ramadan. Sometimes in the middle of our meetings, she'd start muttering to herself, "It doesn't make any difference. God won't forgive me."

One day after a meeting, I asked if I could speak to Khanumgul alone. She had been chosen by her peers to be a member of the community committee, and I wanted to find out how I might be able to help her participate more effectively.

"Khanumgul, I've noticed that you seem very distracted. Is there something that you'd like to talk about?" I asked her.

"I don't know, my daughter," she said as she looked at me skeptically. She paused for a couple of minutes as she looked off into the distance. Then finally she said, "Well, I guess there should be someone in the world I should talk to about this. . . . My conscience has been torturing me for a year now . . ."

She paused for a long time looking down at the ground. Then she continued, "After my brother Sher Agha got married, he and his wife moved to Kunduz. But one day, a stray missile struck their house, and his wife died. She had been baking bread in their kitchen when a piece of shrapnel cut right through her kidney and ended up in the huge sack of flour that had been lying beside her on the floor. My brother was left all alone with three young sons and one daughter. Their oldest child was only eleven years old.

"My brother was so devastated that he decided to come back here to his home village. We wanted him to get remarried, but he always refused. 'Nobody could ever replace my wife,' he told me sadly. He built a small house for himself and his family and would spend almost all the daylight hours working in the fields. Since he didn't have time to look after his children, and there was no older woman in his house to make sure that the kids were behaving morally, many problems began. When his daughter, Sakina, was about twelve, she started spending a lot of time over at her uncle's house where there was a number of older boys around.

"At one point, her stomach began growing, but nobody noticed for a long time. The women here wear such baggy dresses, it's fairly easy to conceal these things for a long time. One evening when my brother came home from his prayers at the mosque, he heard Sakina groaning in pain from the next room. 'What's with her?' my brother asked one his sons. They told him that she had a stomachache. 'We'll have to take her to the village healer to check on her.' His son suggested that they call his aunt next door so that she could take a look at her first. I happened to be visiting my brother's family when my nephew came calling.

"So my sister-in-law, one of my aunts, and I went next door to take a look at Sakina. My aunt and I stopped for a couple of minutes to talk to my brother. When we finally went to see Sakina, I heard my sister-in-law saying, 'I'm going to rip your shameless eyes from their sockets with my fingers! What were you thinking? You're not even married! If anyone finds out about this, you'll probably be stoned to death!'

"My aunt and I didn't have to ask any questions. We understood exactly what had happened. Sakina just looked down at the ground. As we talked among ourselves about how to solve this problem, Sakina started crying more and more from the pain in her stomach. Eventually, we came to the conclusion that we had to induce a miscarriage.

"I told my brother that we'd come back early the next morning to help get her some treatment.

"The next day I took a huge sack full of beans from my house and brought it to Sakina. The bag must have weighed over seventy pounds. All of us women who had gathered the previous evening lifted up the sack and placed it on Sakina's back and told her to carry it across a few fields and up to the mill, which is up on a hill. Once we got to the mill, we told her to continue carrying it all the way to the other side of the mountain, several miles from the village. She was crying from the weight, as well as the pain in her stomach, but we refused to let her put down the sack. Instead, we taunted her with insults, 'This is too easy a punishment for a girl like you! You've brought shame on all of us! It would have been better if you'd died than disgrace yourself like this!'

"After Sakina was nearly completely exhausted, we arrived at a narrow ravine between two high cliffs. We entered a cave near there that is used by shepherds to shelter their animals when it rains or snows out in the mountains. Sakina screamed more and more. But we ordered her to keep quiet. 'What if somebody hears you screaming like an animal up here?' my sister-in-law said sternly. 'What do you think people will say?' Sakina tried to muffle her shouts, but it was clear that she was in tremendous pain.

"As it turned out, she was in labor. The contractions were increasing in frequency, and we knew that she would probably give birth soon. So we found a place for her to rest in the corner and less than an hour later, a baby boy was brought into the world. He was such a beautiful child. He already had some black hair and had a very healthy weight. The baby's cries were so loud that they echoed throughout the cave and down into the ravine. We managed to cut the umbilical cord with a sharp stone. I then put the screaming baby down on the floor of the cave as my sister-in-law retrieved a large rock, which she pushed over toward us. Then my aunt, sister-in-law, and I all picked up the rock with all our strength and crushed the baby to death. The cries ceased immediately. His skull had been smashed in.

"Sakina had begged us not to go through with our scheme. When we ignored her, she just covered her face with her hands and refused to remove them. After carrying out our evil deed, our attention then turned back to Sakina. 'You've brought shame on yourself and your family, you filthy swine!' We started slapping her and beating her with our fists. 'If you had waited until you were married, you never would have had to see this, you wretched fool!' We then put Sakina's clothes back on, placed the sack on her back, and returned home.

"By the time we got back to the village, Sakina was in terrible physical pain. Her back was aching, her eyes were swollen, and she was suffering the agony that all women endure after giving birth. But her emotional pain must have been even greater. When we approached her house, she happened to see one of her two-year-old cousins playing nearby. She swooped the small boy up in her arms and held him very tightly. As she closed her eyes, tears began streaming down her cheeks.

But I grabbed the boy away from her. 'Don't disturb that child,' I told her. 'You're a polluted girl. You've made yourself dirty with your awful sins. You have violated the eternal Sharia laws. . . . We've spilled innocent blood because of you. And you've forced us all to become complicit in this. On the Day of Judgment, we will all have to answer for this crime. I fear that Allah will not forgive us.'

"Every day and every hour for the past year I have been tormented by what I have done. God sees all and he will never forgive me."

Khanumgul died only a month after she told me this story, and I took part in the mourning ceremony. I hope that Allah did, in fact, forgive her. She was truly repentant.

✦ ✦ ✦ ✦

Another horrible story was told to me in a village just outside Kunduz city. A few months after we began working in that community, a middle-aged woman came up to me and asked if I wouldn't mind speaking to her alone. I'd seen her at some of the community-wide meetings, but I didn't know her at all.

"I know that one of the things you're working on here is something related to child protection and child rights," she told me.

I told her that it was.

"Well, I have a terrible story to tell about my one and only child. . . . I don't know who else to talk to about this, and you seem like an understanding person who might be able to give me some advice."

Then she told me the following story:

"A few months ago my husband's close friend came by our house to visit him. When he was about to knock on our front gate, my daughter, Khushkil, who was fourteen years old, happened to open the door. She was on her way to school and had yet to lower her burqa over her face.

"'Is your father home?' the man asked her.

"'No, he went to work,' she said.

"When the man later tracked down my husband, he told him, 'I saw your daughter by chance this morning. She has grown up very beautifully. . . . You know my son has grown into a handsome young man as well. Why don't we arrange a marriage for them?'

"My husband didn't even think of consulting me, much less Khushkil. This man was my husband's close friend, so right then and there—on the side of the road—my husband agreed, and they shook hands on the arrangement. My husband said, 'We are good friends. I have never denied you anything that you wanted in the past. My daughter is yours.'

"In the evening, when my husband returned home, he said to Khushkil, 'My daughter, from now on you shouldn't worry about your school assignments. I've agreed to marry you off to my friend's son.'

"At first, my daughter thought he was joking. But after she realized that he was all too serious, she said, 'But father I'm only in eighth grade, and you know that I've always dreamed about continuing my education and becoming a teacher. . . . Don't you remember how much I suffered when I couldn't go to school when the Taliban were in power? I always wanted to study during those times, but instead I was like a prisoner in the house. Now you don't want me to study because I'm going to get married? I'm not old enough to get married now. Please allow me to complete my education.'

"My husband was very angry. 'Such insolence!' my husband screamed at her. 'I assume that your attempt to disobey me will quickly pass. How dare you speak to me like this?'

"I tried to intervene on my daughter's behalf, but my husband just ordered me to shut up. I learned long ago that it's utterly useless to try to change my husband's mind.

"Khushkil begged my husband to allow her to continue her studies and to reconsider his decision to marry her off. 'Don't be so cruel, father! I don't want to get married now! Please think about my future!' she cried.

"The next day, after my husband left for work, my daughter snuck off to school. Of course in our little village, he easily found out that Khushkil had defied him. So in the evening my husband screamed at her, 'Haven't I ordered you never to go to school again? Haven't I told you that I agreed to marry you off to my friend's son? You no longer have any right to go to school.'

My daughter refused to be intimidated. 'If it's too difficult for you to feed and take care of me, then I will go to my aunt and uncle's house and serve them,' she said. 'They don't have any boys in their family, so you won't have to worry about that. I will be able to go to school every day with my cousins. I will wash their clothes and clean their house in return for their hosting me. That way, I'll be able to earn my bread. One way or another, I will find a way to continue studying!'

"I'd never seen my husband so livid. 'I see that my words are no longer valued in my own house,' he yelled as his temples nearly exploded. 'So you want to run away to your uncle's house? This probably means that you're having some sort of affair. I swear to God that I will burn you alive for your disrespect and depravity.'

"My husband knew that our daughter was not an improper girl. As soon as her lessons were completed, she would always come straight home.

"By this time, Khushkil was in tears. She fell to my husband's feet. 'Please father, I cannot bear to hear these hateful words from you. This just isn't true. Not at all. My girlfriends and I are only interested in our education, and we do everything possible to preserve our honor.'

"But my husband was unmoved by his daughter's pleas. He just continued to heap insults on her and threaten her. Without saying another word, Khushkil ran outside in tears. She found our kerosene tank, which we use to power our small generator, poured the kerosene all over her body, and set herself ablaze. My husband and I rushed outside to try to save her, but on the road to the hospital, she died."

I don't know exactly how many incidents of self-immolation have taken place in Kunduz over the past couple of years. But from anecdotal evidence, I wouldn't be surprised if there were at least a few dozen incidents. Almost all of the stories are similar to Khushkil's—girls who consider suicide a better alternative to getting married or who are living in terribly abusive situations. So now that our country's wars are finally finished, our family members end up killing themselves because of our backward traditions.

My own family still has problems living back here in Afghanistan. But these kinds of stories help me put our difficulties in perspective.

CHAPTER ELEVEN

Abdullah, Son of Hajji Hamidullah Khan and Marwarid, Daughter of Abdul Rahim

ABDULLAH

Marwarid and I became friends when we were seven years old. After school, we used to study Islam together with a mullah in our local mosque. Unlike many parts of Afghanistan, where boys and girls are separated from an early age, here in Taloqan we were allowed to study in the mosque together when we were young.

On our first day of lessons, Marwarid and I were given a prayer book to share. We sat on the floor of the mosque with our book placed on a wooden stand above us. I didn't learn much about Islam in the five years we studied there, but my feelings for Marwarid grew stronger every day. We would talk with one another and giggle about all kinds of funny things. We tried to pay just enough attention so that we could avoid the lashes from the mullah who walked around the room with a long stick to ensure that we were reciting our lessons.

I was almost always late for class, as I was much more interested in playing with my friends on the street than listening to the mullah drone on and on. Sometimes I would come to the mosque and notice that

Marwarid's slippers weren't among the shoes gathered around the door. I would then try to slip out as quietly as I came. When I was unfortunate enough to be stuck in the lessons without her, I was always overwhelmed with boredom. I would stare at the book, and I'd only see her face. While all of my classmates repeated the mullah's words, I would just look at the book and smile. Several times, the mullah's stick on my back would snap me out of my daydreams.

One day, when we were about twelve years old, after all of the other children had filed out of the mosque and we were waiting our turn to exit last, I grabbed Marwarid's hand and pulled her back around the corner. I had watched a lot of romantic Indian movies as a child and that was my main context for love and romance. So I took both of Marwarid's hands in my own and said to her, "You are the love of my life. I can't imagine life without you. When we grow up, why don't we get married? Just promise me that you will always wait for me." She didn't say a word, she just closed her eyes and slowly nodded her head. Then she blushed and ran off. Allah witnessed right there in the holy mosque how we had made a solemn pledge to one another.

But around this same time, one of our classmates must have tattled on us. A few days later, when Marwarid returned home from the mosque, her mother questioned her angrily. "Why are you talking so much with Hajji Hamidullah Khan's son? That Abdullah is probably no good like his old man."

I didn't understand why at the time, but Marwarid's father didn't like my father at all. My father was and is a very wealthy man who had made his name on the battlefield and has four wives and lots of land.

Marwarid tried to deny it. "It's just not true. Abdullah is just the boy I share a prayer book with."

From that day onward, she was banned from taking part in Islamic lessons at the mosque. I was heartbroken when she stopped coming to the mosque. The mullah would beat me again and again because I had lost all interest in learning about Islam.

In a strange way, the Taliban saved me from my mullah. Only a few weeks after Marwarid was withdrawn from our class, the Taliban bombed Takhar for the first time, and I, along with two of my brothers, was forced to flee to Iran. I was very upset to leave Marwarid behind, but my father was convinced that it would be too dangerous for young men to stay in Taloqan. The rest of my family remained behind.

✦ ✦ ✦ ✦

Several years after I left Afghanistan, Marwarid later told me, her father was approached by his friend asking for his daughter's hand in marriage. And can you imagine, her father agreed to marry her off to the first person who had come along? Marwarid was dead-set against the match. At first, she didn't want to concede the true reason for her objection to her parents. But after awhile, she realized that she had no choice but to attempt to win her mother to her side.

"Mother, do you remember the boy, Abdullah, who I used to study with at the mosque? The more that I've thought about him, the more I've realized that he is the only one who's right for me." She hadn't told anybody about our promise in the mosque a few years before. But now that her dreams were about to be shattered, she decided that she had no choice but to inform her mother. "I promise you this: I will only marry Abdullah, no one else."

But Marwarid's mother refused to listen. "There's nothing that can be done about this—it's too late," she responded. "First of all, if this Abdullah of yours is so in love with you, why haven't we seen his parents here asking for your hand in marriage? What makes you think that he's even interested in making an offer? Didn't he flee somewhere a few years ago? Besides, even if his family were interested in you, you know how your father feels about Abdullah's family. Finally, your father has already given his word to his friend that you will marry his son. There's nothing more to discuss. The matter is settled."

Marwarid was desperate to find a way out of the match. So she ran off to visit my oldest sister, Nasiba, who had been married for several years, and was Marwarid's neighbor. Marwarid came inside the house and curled up on the mattress weeping.

"Nasiba, my sister, I need your help. You probably don't know this, but your brother, Abdullah, and I are in love with each other. I've been praying every day for the war to end so that he can return home to marry me. We promised that we would wait for each other. But then today my father announced that he wants my mother to prepare my engagement party. My father's promised me to another man!"

Then she grabbed a knife that had been sitting in front of her and put it up to her neck. "I swear to you that if I can't marry Abdullah, I will cut my own throat. There's no reason to keep on living if I'm sold off to another man."

My sister tried to calm her down. "Please, my little sister, you have to take it easy. I'll tell you what—I promise you that I will go right now to my parents' house so that they can speak with your father. Hopefully, they'll be able to come to some sort of agreement with your parents about you and Abdullah."

When Marwarid returned home, she was enraged with her mother. "You're going to have to help me to solve this problem," Marwarid said. "I'm in love with Abdullah. If you don't agree to discuss this matter with my father, I'll have only two options: either I will be forced to leave the house and move in with Abdullah's family or else I'll kill myself."

Marwarid's mother must have been sufficiently persuaded by the passion behind her words, because the next day Marwarid was informed that the marriage was off. But in order for her father to keep his word to his friend, he decided to offer his younger daughter for marriage instead. Marwarid was very relieved.

After this crisis was settled, she sewed me a beautiful handkerchief and sent it to me in Iran through Nasiba's husband. There was no accompanying note. But I knew that the gift meant that she was waiting for me. As soon as I received the handkerchief, I knew I had to come back to Afghanistan immediately. Luckily, this coincided with the liberation of Taloqan from Taliban rule, so it became safe to return.

Shortly after I got home, my father bought me a new car so that I could work as a taxi driver. But I wasn't thinking about work—I wanted to have fun hanging out with my friends. And of course I wanted to win Marwarid's hand.

I immediately dispatched a couple of my male relatives, including my Uncle Nazir, to Marwarid's house to offer my proposal. My relatives and her father, Abdul Rahim, sat together for many hours discussing the match. At one point, when her father went out to get more tea, Marwarid said to him, "Father, why don't you just agree? I want to marry Abdullah."

Her father flew into a violent rage. He dragged his daughter into another room by her hair and began beating her with his fists. As he swung at her again and again, he said fiercely, "I don't want to ever hear you mention that cursed name again, do you understand me?"

I sent my relatives three or four more times to Marwarid's house to try to persuade her father. But he refused to change his mind. He just said to them, "It's very simple. I will never allow my daughter to marry Abdullah under any circumstance."

My relatives tried to talk me out of marrying Marwarid. "Abdullah," my oldest brother told me after another unsuccessful trip to her house, "I know that you're really in love with this girl. But there are lots of other girls in Afghanistan. I'm sure that you'll forget about Marwarid soon. Just say the word, and we'll negotiate for any other girl in Taloqan. You know, you should be having fun; you don't have to only think about marriage all the time. You're only sixteen years old after all! In any case, Marwarid is from a very simple family. Her father is just a petty businessman. Our father is highly respected here."

I still hadn't had a chance to see Marwarid face-to-face while all this was happening. I wanted desperately to talk with her. I thought I could drop by her house during the Eid Qorbon holidays, when people visit one another's houses throughout the day. This would provide just the cover I needed to speak with my would-be bride. So I stopped by her house, and by luck, her father was away on business in Mazar-i-Sharif and her mother and older brother were out visiting neighbors. She was alone in the house with her young niece when I knocked on their front gate.

We were both very excited to see each other after such a long time. I told her how much I missed her and how happy I was that I'd returned. But I also knew that we had a short time before we'd be discovered. So I came quickly to the point. "We belong together. So why don't we leave together today? Whether or not our parents agree, let's get married! If you really and truly love me, just come with me right now."

She barely hesitated. She grabbed one small bag, and we ran out of the house together and jumped into my taxi. But as we were fleeing from her house, a few of Marwarid's neighbors happened to be walking in the street nearby. They stopped dead in their tracks. "Look," I heard one man call out. "Hamidullah Khan's son is stealing Abdul Rahim's daughter!"

Marwarid was wearing a burqa, but everyone could identify her by her shoes and stockings.

We drove over to my brother's house. I was overjoyed that the girl I had dreamed about for so long was finally mine. For several hours, I was running on adrenaline. But after Marwarid and I had had a chance to catch our breath, the full implications of what we had done began to dawn on me. There is probably a law somewhere in this world that allows boys and girls who love one another to get married and spend their lives together. But in Afghanistan, young people do not have the right to choose their mates. I knew I had to do something to try to make amends for what I had done. I should have gone to my father to ask his advice. But I was too afraid of what he might say or do.

So I left Marwarid at my brother's house with his wife and went to seek counsel from my Uncle Nazir. I was hoping that my uncle could speak to my father about how to resolve this problem. But my uncle was furious with me. He had been involved in some of the earlier negotiations with Marwarid's father and knew about the impasse that had been reached. "How could you do this? This is terrible for our family's reputation and even worse for hers," my uncle told me. "What will happen to her father now? Did you ever stop to think about that before pulling off your hare-brained scheme?"

I couldn't possibly justify my actions. As happy as I was that I was together with the girl of my dreams in spite of her father's objections, I was genuinely upset about what the ramifications would be. "Yes, I know, I did a stupid thing. I wish that I hadn't done it. But it's too late now. So what I'm requesting of you and my father is that you please help me to recover my honor. Can't you both go to Marwarid's father again and try to rectify the situation? Will you help me or won't you?"

My father was terribly disappointed with me when he heard the news. He knew that if he were to go to Abdul Rahim's house himself, it might be very dangerous. As he said to me later, "If someone's son kidnapped my daughter and had the nerve to show his face in my house, I would shoot him before he could even utter a word."

So what he decided to do was gather together four highly respected community leaders and discuss the problem with them. They decided to go to Abdul Rahim's house themselves in order to try to reach some sort of agreement. But when they arrived for the discussions, they discovered that her father was still in Mazar. They raised the issue with Marwarid's older brother, but he declined to get involved. "You'll have to wait for my father's return. I have no authority to address these types of questions," he told them.

After a few days, Abdul Rahim returned from his business trip, and the four community leaders returned to his house. This time, my uncle, who had had a decent relationship with Marwarid's father, went along too. Rahim was enraged. He said a lot of terrible things about me and my father.

Uncle Nazir thought that perhaps the best way to calm Rahim down was to offer him compensation for his daughter. "As you know, my brother is not a poor man. He is prepared to offer you a very fair price for your daughter. He can give you land or, if you'd prefer, money. I'm sure that he would agree to your price. It will go beyond anything that we had discussed regarding a dowry."

But Rahim wasn't willing to accept. "I'm not interested in your brother's money. I'm interested in my family's honor. And you have violated it. The only fair compensation is if one of the girls from your family marries my son."

Uncle Nazir agreed to raise this issue with my father. My uncle's calm diplomacy paid off. By the end of the discussion, Rahim said, "We are not enemies, and we are not friends. Whatever happened has happened. We can't do anything to change it."

When Uncle Nazir informed my father about Rahim's proposal, my father didn't even give it a thought. "I'm not going to give any of my daughters to that simple man's family! If he wants money, I can pay it. Besides, it was his stupid daughter who agreed to leave with my son."

We were hoping that the whole question would somehow just go away. But two months later, I was informed that Abdul Rahim had brought charges against me in court. The formal complaint stated that I had "forcibly removed" his daughter from the house "against her will" and that my father "had used his military authority to carry out this act." In fact, it was his daughter's decision to leave, and she departed of her own free will in broad daylight.

My father was a respected man in the community so they refused to make his new daughter-in-law go down to the police station for questioning. Instead, they carried out the investigation at our house. The judge, the *Qazi*, called each of the principal witnesses together at one time in hopes of resolving the conflict. So one morning Abdul Rahim, my father, my uncle, one of the community representatives my father had chosen to help resolve the conflict, the neighbor who had seen us leave the house together, as well as Marwarid and I all gathered together at our house.

The *Qazi* opened his investigation by asking my wife directly, "On the third day of Eid Qorbon, did you leave your house voluntarily with Abdullah or were you forced to go?"

"Even if a little child were taken away from her mother's lap against her will, she would cry so loudly that everyone would understand that she didn't want to be moved," she responded. "So how could someone grab a person like me—a fifteen-year old-girl—from my house and run off without anyone realizing that I had objections? I told my father that I wanted to get married to this man," she motioned toward me. "But my father wouldn't accept. He wanted to sell me off to someone else. I fell in love with Abdullah, and I never want to be apart from him."

The judge didn't bother asking any further questions. "Everyone who is gathered here now has heard the truth about this alleged abduction," he said conclusively. "If nobody can offer me any proof to refute the principal witness's testimony, I consider this case closed."

The legal wrangling was finished, but the look on Abdul Rahim's face indicated that the situation was far from resolved in his own mind. So as we all sat in the guest room in our house and the *Qazi* packed his bags, my father said, "Now that this case is behind us, let's make peace and try to find a way to live in friendship. After all, we are now relatives."

But Marwarid's father was not in the mood for burying hatchets. "I don't want to be your friend," he practically spat at my father. "I don't want to be your relative. I am and will be your enemy. You humiliated me—you killed me—by shaming me in front of everyone and robbing me of my honor. I want to kill either you or your son."

My father waved his hand. "There's nothing that you can do against us. You're a nobody. You know your place very well."

It's now been about two years since we last saw Marwarid's family.

They don't come to our house and we don't go to theirs. It's too bad that everything turned out the way it did, but it's all in the past now. A few months ago, my wife gave birth to a baby daughter who's a real darling.

→ → ← ←

Recently, I've begun to regret that I went through all that trouble to marry Marwarid. I really was too young to get married. My brother, who had tried to talk me out of marrying her, was right. There are a lot of other girls around. When I drive my taxi around town, I get to see many girls. You might think it's hard to tell them apart because of the burqa, but actually it's quite easy. You can tell if a girl's young or old, beautiful or ugly by the way that she walks, by her shoes, her hands, and her ankles. Actually, everything you want to know about a girl can be seen in her ankles.

Now I'm thinking about getting married a second time. My wife really isn't beautiful anymore. And she's got such an attitude! I often have to slap her around before she'll listen to reason.

MARWARID

There's not an hour that goes by that I don't think about what a fool I was to walk out of my house with Abdullah the third day of Qorbon Eid two years ago.

I miss my parents, brother, and sister a great deal. I haven't seen them in such a long time. Just last week, I was invited to a wedding party where I met a couple of my former neighbors. They told me that everyone in my family is in good health, thank God. But I also heard that my father still appears to be quite upset. He used to be very outgoing and cheerful, but now he rarely smiles, and he walks with his shoulders hunched over. I know it must be because of me. I wish I weren't a source of such pain in his life.

I wish that somehow or other Abdullah's family had reached an agreement with my father and that my departure from home didn't bring such shame on my family. But that probably would have been impossible. My father was always so opposed to our marriage. One time I overheard him saying to one of our cousins, "I would sooner slice open

Marwarid's neck than allow her to marry into that murderous family." My father used to beat me many times when Abdullah was in the process of pursuing me. Maybe that's why I was so eager to escape.

In the beginning of our marriage, things went very well. Abdullah's family all treated me with respect, and we enjoyed a good relationship. But there were too many women in Abdullah's house—his father's four wives and lots of unmarried sisters—and we always found an excuse to pick fights with one another. We've sometimes even gone so far as to have cat-fights over a stupid bar of soap. Abdullah always takes his family's side in arguments, and he'll soundly beat me if I do anything that he finds "disrespectful" to his family.

What's probably hardest for me is that when we have arguments, there's nobody for me to complain to. Since I no longer have relations with my own family, I can't go home from time to time like some of my brother-in-law's wives.

Afghans have a saying: "Marrying out of love is like smearing your face in ashes." Now I understand that it would have been better if I'd just listened to my parents and married the man they wanted me to marry. My sister's husband is a lousy, good-for-nothing, but he's probably better than Abdullah. I really should have obeyed my parents, even if they'd wanted to marry me off to a *kuchi*,* an old man, or even a dog or a monkey. The most important thing was their blessing. If I were married now to someone they had chosen, at least I would have been able to blame them—but now I have only myself to blame.

Recently Abdullah has begun threatening that he will take a second wife. He suffers from this delusion that he'll somehow have a good life with another woman. But I'm sure that he won't be happier with anyone else. Sure, maybe they'd have some good times, but I'm sure that the honeymoon period would wear off soon—as it did for us.

I don't know. It's all so complicated. I just want to cry all the time . . .

---

* Nomad.

Ali Muhammad, Son of Qorbon

I still can't understand why my parents decided to build their house where they did. I'm originally from the village of Ambarku, about two hours by horse from Taloqan. Ambarku is located on the top of a high hill and more than a four-mile hike from the nearest source of running water. You can waste nearly an entire day leading your donkey to and from the river to collect water in large metal jugs for just a couple days' worth of water.

I've been working as a teacher for twenty-eight years. When the Soviets invaded Afghanistan in 1979, I had been the only teacher in Ambarku for the past six years. In fact, children from four neighboring villages would all come to my "school," which was actually little more than a patch of ground located underneath a large oak tree. I was the only person from miles around who had completed the pedagogical university in Kabul and returned home to educate the children of our village. I believed firmly that girls had an equal right to education and encouraged parents to allow their girls to attend my school.

Life was not easy before the Soviets arrived. But at least there was peace. And I was able to support my wife and two young children quite adequately with my salary, which came in the form of wheat from each of the students who attended my lessons. But the Soviet invasion made everything much more complicated. The Russian incursion succeeded in dividing many families as, for example, some brothers would take up arms for the government and other brothers would choose to fight with the mujahedin. My relatives were split by this type of factional squabbling.

My younger and only brother, Niyaz Muhammad, was a champion wrestler. While I was obsessed with books and the Koran, he was interested in sports. Our passions were even reflected in our builds—he was nearly six feet tall and barreled-chested, while I was several inches shorter and always have been something of a weakling. He has always been much more impulsive and hotheaded than me. But he was my younger brother and I loved him dearly.

After the Soviets invaded, Niyaz quickly made the decision to join the government forces. One day, when I came home from school, I found him sitting in the guest room of my small house. He had recently returned from a heated battle against the mujahedin. "You know that there's a war going on all around us. So why are you still wasting your time working in your school?" he demanded to know. "Why don't you take up arms, and we can fight side by side to further the socialist revolutionary movement?"

But I didn't want to give up my teaching job. I thought that I could be of greater service to Afghanistan by educating our children than by carrying a gun. We were a backward country that needed trained people in a variety of professions.

"I'm an educated man, and I have the skills necessary to pass on education to others," I tried to explain to him. "After the war is over, Afghanistan will need educated people to help rebuild. Don't you realize how important it is for me to stay here and continue my teaching?"

But he insisted on taking me to the government's military headquarters. "You're a fairly young man and in good health. At this moment in time, it's your duty to serve the government in the way that is currently the most needed. If you agree to join our cause, I'll provide you with arms and help collect people from our village to fight under your command against the mujahedin. The people here respect you, and I'm sure they would follow your lead.

"What do you think? If the mujahedin win this war, will they allow you to continue teaching? These people are an uneducated mass who don't understand what the word 'education' even means."

My brother had a good point; there was something of an anti-intellectual bent to the battle against the Soviets. But no matter what kind of arguments he tried, I just refused to go along with him. I knew that I would be a poor soldier because I really didn't want to fight for either the government or the rebel forces.

My brother became increasingly frustrated with me. And finally he stood up abruptly. "I'm asking you—as my brother—to fight by my side and to protect me as I would protect you. If you are too much of a coward or are too disloyal to do as I request, that's fine. But you should know that from now on, I no longer consider you my brother. If I die, you shouldn't come to my funeral. If you die, I certainly won't come to yours."

As he towered above, glaring at me, I thought about his words. I felt as though I had no choice. I couldn't imagine losing my one and only brother. So I stood up and hugged him, and off we went to the government-run military base that was located close to Ambarku.

The first day after I arrived at the military base I wasn't able to say my prayers at the village mosque because of some training exercises. But the next evening, I went straight to the mosque. Here in Afghanistan, after the evening prayers are completed, many of us sit around in the mosque, drinking tea and discussing daily events. As usual everyone was seated in the mosque when I arrived that evening. But when I entered, nobody responded to my greetings. I was a respected man in the village because of my education and status as a teacher. I hadn't been at yesterday's prayers so I expected that many people would stand up and say, "Welcome back home. How are you? How is your health?" and so on. But they just ignored me. I know that I should have gone up to my fellow villagers and initiated the greetings myself, but my sense of pride prevented me. I quietly said my prayers and then returned home.

That evening over dinner, I recounted to my brother what had happened to me at the mosque. "You see—what did I tell you?" I asked my brother angrily. "The people from our village are sympathetic to the mujahedin. Now that I've joined you as a combatant with the government forces, they've lost all respect for me."

My brother didn't say anything. But I could tell that he was very upset about what had happened.

A couple of weeks later, I decided to visit my cousin in a neighboring village about an hour away by horse. The road was full of mud, and my *shalwar kameez* was filthy no more than five minutes after I left my house. Along the path, I ran into a couple of other young cousins of mine also riding on horseback who had recently joined the mujahedin movement. When I halted my horse and greeted them, they just kept trotting along without even looking up at me.

When they were already a hundred feet or so beyond me, one of my relatives turned back. "We've been told that you're now serving in the government's army," he said.

"Yes, you've heard correctly," I said without hesitating. I wasn't going to be intimidated.

"Well, I hope then that you have the proper documents," he told me with a sneer.

I was confused. "What do you mean? What kind of documents."

"Don't you know?" he asked angrily. "The documents that certify that you're still a Muslim."

There has always been the latent notion here in Afghanistan that educated people—doctors, teachers, and other professionals who worked for the government—aren't "real Muslims." And I think that the Soviet invasion certainly helped to reinforce some of these ideas.

"My dear brother," I told him. "Muslims don't need to carry documentation to prove their piety. Our Prophet Muhammad said that anyone who says 'La Ilaha Illal Lah Muhamadan Rasulallah' is a Muslim, and the doors of paradise will open before him. I hope that you will never again shame yourself by asking someone for his documents to affirm his Islamic belief. Others will just laugh at you for asking such a stupid question."

I saw their look of disgust as they spat on the ground and rode away. I had defended my decision to join the government forces bravely and honorably, but I was concerned that there might be more repercussions. When I returned home, I once again shared with my brother what had occurred along the road. "It's becoming very dangerous to be labeled as a government sympathizer around here," I said. "I could easily be shot by some of our own ignorant relatives, if not by others."

My brother looked at me very seriously and said, "It's terrible that these things are happening to you. But there's no backing out now. We can't just leave the government forces and go into hiding."

One morning, following the dawn prayers, my brother and I were sitting in my yard looking at the mountains above. And just then I happened to notice that there were about twenty mujahedin soldiers entering our village from the hills above. My brother and I decided to retreat quickly inside the house and pretend that we hadn't seen anything. But a few moments after we had stepped inside, a couple of mujahedin with Kalashnikovs entered our courtyard. The remaining men stood guard outside the house.

The first guy who entered was a very tall man who I'd never seen before, but the second person I recognized. It was Sayid Fakhreddin from the district of Ishkamesh, about eight hours from our village. For several years when we were very young, we had studied together after school with a mullah.

He was very surprised to see me. "What are you doing here?" he asked me.

"This is my house. I live here," I responded. "The real question is what are you doing here, with these types of people?" My Afghan sense of hospitality and graciousness to guests had been temporarily overtaken by the shock of seeing my childhood friend enter my house with mujahedin troops.

Sayid Fakhreddin ignored my question. He shook his head disapprovingly. "So you're the teacher that everyone has been talking about."

It was then that I realized that these soldiers had probably been sent to my village because of me. Since I was the only teacher for miles around, there was no confusing me with anyone else.

I pulled my brother aside. He was already whispering something to me about how we could try to fight off as many of the mujahedin as possible, and if we died, we'd at least die with honor, et cetera, et cetera. But I managed to calm him. Instead I asked him to prepare some chicken and rice for our "guests." "Look, I don't like these people any more than you," I told him, "but we have to treat them as our honored guests. If we don't, who knows what they might end up doing to us?"

After we fed Sayid Fakhreddin and his campanion and I had a chance to catch up with my old friend, they stood up as though to leave. As I began to say my farewells, Sayid Fakhreddin said, "No, teacher, it's too early for good-byes. You're coming with us."

"I'm sorry . . . I can't go with you," I responded, much taken aback.

"Teacher," Sayid Fakhreddin said, his smile vanishing from his face. "This is not a request. It's an order."

"I'm not your soldier. How can you order me to come with you?" I asked.

"What's the problem? We're commanding you to come with us, just like we force other people to join us. Let's go, we're heading off to Ishkamesh right now."

In Ishkamesh, I had a close and highly respected friend named Qazi Islam with whom I had studied at the pedagogical university in the Department of Arabic Languages in Kabul. I had often visited Qazi Islam at his home and had established a very close relationship with his father, who was well known throughout the district. He began to treat me like his own son, and Qazi Islam and I were like brothers.

I actually had recently received a letter from Qazi Islam, inviting me to come to his house to discuss the war and which side I should join. He had already become a mujahedin fighter, and he had probably not yet heard about my recent enlistment in the government's forces.

I showed them the letter from Qazi Islam, knowing that they would be impressed. "As you can see from this letter, I have long had plans to visit my friend in Khwaja Gulgun village in Ishkamesh. I'd actually already set aside a date next week when I would travel there," I explained. "So I'm sorry, but I'm not planning to travel there today. Thank you for the invitation, though. If you'd like to talk to me further, please feel free to drop by Qazi Islam's house next week. I promise to be there."

The mujahedin soldiers just shook their heads at my cavalier attitude. "I don't think you understand," the tall man finally intervened in an exasperated tone. "Whether you think that this fits in with your schedule or not, you're coming with us today. We have orders to take you."

Sayid Fakhreddin interrupted his partner. "My dear teacher," he said with much more respect in his voice, "it'll be all right. Let's just go to a village down the road. There's someone there who wants to speak with you. After that, we'll discuss the next steps, OK?"

I realized I had no alternative but to obey. So I left my guests for a couple of minutes with the excuse that I needed to prepare a few things for the road. When I went to the next room, I grabbed two of my nephews who were probably no more than fourteen at the time. I had some weapons in my house—a Kalashnikov, a 303 Bur, and a Mushkush. I put on a long robe, and hid the Kalashnikov in the back of it. I handed the other arms to the young men and whispered to them, "As soon as I leave the house with these men, I want you to follow me." I saw the puzzled looks on their faces. "If my brother follows me out of the house, I'm afraid that they will suspect something, and a conflict could easily erupt. But if you follow me, they are not likely to be suspicious . . ." They seemed to grasp my train of thought.

"What I want you to do is to make sure that these men don't shoot me in the back as they follow me out of the house. If there are other men who try to shoot me from the front, I will try my best to kill a couple of them with my Kalashnikov before they succeed in killing me." I was terribly frightened, but I was determined to maintain my honor and dignity.

So I left my home under the supervision of twenty heavily armed mujahedin soldiers. We arrived at the village Sayid Fakhreddin had mentioned after nightfall, and we went to the home of a mullah named Hajji Jamal. The mullah slaughtered a sheep for all of us, and we enjoyed a large meal.

When it was time to go to sleep, I told my escorts that my nephews and I would sleep in the neighbor's house as it was too crowded for all of us to cram into one room. I was so happy to be free of the pressure from the mujahedin for at least one night. But of course it was not real freedom. I knew that I would be taken somewhere else come morning. So I asked my nephews to take turns throughout the night standing guard at the door. "If you see anyone coming who looks threatening, don't hesitate. Just shoot him," I instructed.

I couldn't sleep all night. A million questions raced through my mind: "Oh Allah, what did I do to these people? Why did they bring me here? What do they plan to do with me? If they want to kill me, why haven't they done so already? And why would they want to kill me in any case? My blood wouldn't make a small piece of mud brick wet. Maybe these men have been sent by some of my family's enemies?" I remembered a famous Pashtun saying that a university friend would always repeat: "Everyone in Afghanistan has enemies. If you don't have enemies, it means you're just a woman." When I wasn't trying to think through the answers to these impossibly complicated questions, I just cried. I felt so helpless.

As all these thoughts swirled in my head, I did manage to console myself that it would be much better to be killed in this village, where people at least knew me, than to die somewhere out in the mountains. If I were shot in the middle of nowhere, they could throw my body to the wolves, and my family would never see my dead body. "Yes, it's much better to die here," I said out loud, to the shock of one of my nephews who was standing guard nearby.

At two in the morning, the mujahedin soldiers woke us up. It was time to get on with our trip. When I entered the room where the mujahedin were assembling their things, I saw that they had been joined by Commander Mu'allim Wahab. He was a famous mujahedin commander—and he had also been a teacher! I was surprised to see such an educated man in the company of such simple illiterates. I greeted Commander Wahab, and after some obligatory pleasantries, I asked him, "I respect you a great deal because you are a teacher. But please answer just one thing: Do you really believe in jihad or are you just taking advantage of your status to help people settle scores with their personal enemies?"

He, of course, told me that he was a real mujahedin who was devoted to cleansing our homeland from infidels.

"So in that case," I said, "I would respectfully suggest that you limit yourself to fighting the invaders rather than getting involved in internal disputes in our communities. We are neighbors, and we are perfectly capable of resolving our personal conflicts ourselves."

"In order to carry out a successful jihad," he told me, "there's really no alternative but to get involved in these local disputes. In any case, this is none of your business. So I would respectfully suggest that you butt out!" he said mockingly.

I was certain that I had a death sentence hanging over me. So I decided to roll the dice and take a big gamble.

"Oh, it's none of my business? Well then, you listen to me," I said with my voice full of false confidence. "Everyone in this village has known and respected me for many years. Last night, while you were sleeping here, I went to the mosque and assembled men from the village. I told them how your troops had, without cause, taken me from my house and led me here against my will. 'Allah as my witness,' I said, 'I am an innocent man and I have been kidnapped.' I convinced them that if they allowed me to be taken from their village, it would be like allowing their own wives to be taken from their houses.

"You should know that this house is surrounded by people who are only waiting for my signal to come to my defense. If you think that you'll be able to remove the gun from even one of my men in this village, you can . . . you can treat me like your own wife."

The commander appeared to buy my story. After all, I hadn't slept in the same room with them at night, and nobody had considered guarding me. "What kind of trouble could a teacher cause us?" they probably thought. The commander's face turned an ashen gray. He didn't know that there wasn't even a dog in the village that was ready to wag his tail in my defense.

The commander's tone changed 180 degrees. "What are you talking about, my respected teacher?" he said with a broad smile. "We just wanted you to help us get across a river that is in control of the government. We knew that the honor and respect with which you are held in these parts would help guarantee us safe passage. That's all that we wanted from you."

My strategy was actually working! With even greater confidence, I said, "If this was, in fact, your aim in taking me with you, why didn't you just tell me from the very beginning?" I asked. "I would have willingly helped you. I am always a gracious host to my out-of-town guests."

I then instructed one of my nephews to ride down to the river that the mujahedin soldiers were interested in crossing and to check for government tanks. A boy riding alone in the dark would be unlikely to attract any attention, I thought. I told him to shoot a gun toward the West if there were no government forces that could impede their safe passage. But if there were troops barring their way, he should quietly return to the village. After we heard a single shot ring out, the mujahedin fighters hurriedly went on their way.

"Thank you for your service to the mujahedin cause," Commander Wahab called out to me as his fighters pulled out of the village. "I hope that this will be your first act of many in the battle against the communist infidels."

After that terrible night with those simpletons, I knew the time had come for me to leave my home village. My fellow villagers hadn't bothered to come to my defense when I needed them most, and I saw that they had lost all respect for me. Almost all of them had by then withdrawn their children from my courses.

➔   ➔   ❖   ❖

It was years later, in 1997, that the Taliban captured Kunduz. By that time, I had six children—three daughters and three sons. My two oldest girls had already been married off, and one of them had moved to Tajikistan with her husband. We decided to send off one of my sons to accompany her so that she wouldn't be too homesick. So I had two sons at home, Fawad, fifteen, and Karim, twelve, and one daughter, Farzona, who was eleven.

I was working in a girls' school in Kunduz city at the time. The day after the Taliban took control of the city, my school was closed, and I became unemployed. The school was converted into military headquarters for the Taliban, and the school's yard was filled with tanks and other military equipment. My measly salary was taken away from me, and the only property of value I could fall back on was a few small farm animals, such as sheep and goats. I hold the Taliban responsible for the current state of my nerves. From the time they overran my school, I started to lose my temper and get worked up over all kinds of little things.

For a few weeks, we managed to survive on our animals. But when we had consumed or sold off almost all of them, I knew that we'd run out of decent alternatives. So with my wife and three children, I left the city for the small village of Dahanai Shurob in western Kunduz province, where some of my relatives lived. Since I knew Arabic, I was able to get a job as a local mullah in the village mosque. I led the daily prayers and taught children the Koran. To compensate me for my work, the villagers provided me with about 50 pounds of wheat per month.

After a few months, the Taliban captured Dahanai Shurob as well. The local commander heroically tried to defend the village, but after he was wounded, the villagers lost hope and most of us fled. None of us had motorized vehicles, so we loaded up our most precious items into a few bags and left on foot with our donkeys, horses, and other livestock.

My relatives and I were forced to leave in such a hurry that we hardly brought anything to eat or drink. I had one horse and one donkey to carry many of our things so my hands were more or less free. As we walked hour after hour, day after day, our children started crying, "Please, Daddy, give us some water." It was the middle of summer, and their throats were parched. But we had only one large thermos of water, which we needed to ration until we reached the next fresh-water stream. I hid the thermos under my robe because we knew that if any armed men saw us with a supply of drinking water, they would undoubtedly guzzle all of it.

We were forced to travel from one small settlement to another, living off the good graces of others for a night or two before traveling further. We lived like vagabonds for several weeks. There was war, displacement, and suffering everywhere, and we were stuck in between the front lines controlled by the Taliban and those controlled by the Northern Alliance commander Ahmad Shah Mas'ud. On several different occasions, each side would fire above us as we looked for a place to settle.

One day, some of my relatives and I were walking along a narrow path in a single file line at the foot of a large hill. I was at the head of the line, and I happened to notice that there were some Taliban gathered at the top of the hill towering above us. I couldn't imagine that they would open fire on us. After all, we had so many women and children in our group. Our possessions ought to have made it obvious that we were fleeing refugees, not enemy combatants. Nevertheless, I kept one eye on the Taliban above, and with the other, I looked around for scattered boulders that might provide some cover if they were to begin shooting.

Then, suddenly, there was a huge explosion. I thought the Taliban were attacking us. I turned toward the hill where they were positioned and, with my hands in the air, started yelling, "Don't shoot, don't shoot! We're refugees—look at all the women and children!" As I looked back to see if anybody had been hit, several of my family members screamed out in fright, and I saw that my cousin Farough, who was only fourteen, had been injured. His leg had been blown off, and it was lying a few feet away from the rest of his body. Farough let out a blood-curdling shriek.

As others nearby ripped apart their clothes to stem the bleeding with a homemade tourniquet, I heard a Taliban soldier yell out, "We didn't fire on you. The place where you're walking is full of mines. You see that wheat field over there," he said pointing in a different direction. "If you want to prevent further accidents, you should go over there." But in order to get to the field that the Taliban advised us to use, we had to continue walking through this minefield for another couple of hundred yards.

We managed to lift Farough up onto my donkey and were ready to lead my poor injured cousin onward, when one of the Taliban cried out, "Send your wounded man up here!"

I was hesitant to comply with this command, given my feelings toward the Taliban, but I realized that we had no alternative. The hill where the Taliban were positioned was too steep for a donkey to climb. So Farough's friend, who was traveling with us, and I took him off the animal and put the poor boy on our own backs. Every time we moved Farough, he trembled with pain. We then slowly carried him up the hill to the place where the Taliban were entrenched. To this day, I still don't know how I mustered the strength to carry my cousin up that treacherous hill. But Farough's friend and I were the only able-bodied males in our contingent, so we really had no choice.

By the time we arrived at the top of the hill, the commander had radioed others, asking them to send a car to assist my injured cousin. The soldiers took my cousin and asked, or perhaps more precisely, ordered us to continue on our way. I was panting for breath and my shirt was covered in Farough's blood. But I had become fearful about the path ahead. "I'm sorry, but we can't continue along this path," I said. "How am I supposed to know how many more mines we'll face before we reach that field over there? Then I would be responsible for killing or maiming more of my family!" I knew that it was probably unwise to be speaking in this tone of voice to a group of armed Taliban, but I was overcome with emotion. The Taliban commander in charge told me, "Why don't you just go back the way you came? There's no safe road forward. . . . But before you leave, I want you to go back down the hill and get some mattresses for this poor boy."

I scurried down the hill, leaving behind my cousin's friend, who was holding Farough's hand and trying to comfort him. I tried to make it back up again as quickly as I could with our mattresses, but I was too late. By the time I got to the top of the hill, they'd put my cousin in a pick-up truck and taken off. All I could see was a cloud of dust rising from the back of the truck. "Where have they taken the injured boy?" I asked a Taliban soldier as I panted heavily. "They took him to some clinic. But I have no idea which one. The names of all these places around here confuse me."

That evening, while I prayed for Farough at the mosque, I reflected on what the Taliban forces had done for us. Maybe these fundamentalists weren't as terrible as I had once thought. They received nothing in return for helping my cousin. But I still didn't know where they had taken my poor Farough.

In the morning, my cousin's friend appeared. "How is my cousin?" I asked. "Will he survive? Where is he?"

"They took him to the clinic in Khanabad city," he told me slowly. Without waiting for the answers to my remaining questions, I jumped on my horse and headed off to the Khanabad clinic, which was at that time in the hands of the Taliban.

In the clinic, I met the doctor who had examined Farough. "Yes, I saw your cousin when he arrived here yesterday," the middle-aged doctor told me sadly. "But after I saw his condition, I knew that we couldn't do anything for him here. I don't have the right medications or a sufficient supply of blood. The Taliban just dropped him off and drove away as quickly as they had come, so I didn't have the means to get him to the Kunduz city hospital. . . . I'm sorry to inform you that your cousin died at two o'clock this morning."

While I broke down and cried, the doctor put his arm around me. "The Taliban grabbed me from my home in Parwan a few months ago and forced me to come work here," he told me. "I haven't heard from my family since." The doctor was just as distraught by the Taliban as the rest of us. "I want to get out of here somehow. Do you know of a good escape route?" he asked me. Of course we'd also been looking for the same thing for several weeks, so I couldn't give him any useful advice.

→   →   ←   ←

A few days later, I found work as a farmhand on a large farm in a small village in Khanabad district. It was a disgrace for me to take such a lowly job, but I had no choice—my family's survival depended on it. But it was not safe for my family to remain with me in such an unstable area. So out of desperation, I sent them off to live with some friends in Kunduz city, while I stayed behind waiting for the end of the harvest.

When the local villagers heard about my background as a mullah, my status in the community increased dramatically—even though I was one of the only ethnic Uzbeks in this Tajik village. Then one day a man in the village who was a relative of a Taliban official invited some of his neighbors, including me, as well as some Taliban to his house. The food was excellent, but the atmosphere over dinner was decidedly gloomy. Everybody sat in silence—nobody laughed or talked, not even in hushed tones. One would never have guessed that thirty people were gathered in a room in which you probably could have heard a mouse scurrying past. There were five young Taliban and one older mullah dressed in white turbans, and they had placed their Kalashnikovs at their sides. We all just sat on the host's mattresses and stuffed our faces.

I found the whole scene uproariously funny for some reason. The silence went on for so long that I couldn't control myself any longer. I just burst out laughing. Everyone stared at me. I had to say something. So I looked at the Taliban mullah and said, "I'm very lucky—you're a mullah and I'm a mullah, too. So why are we sitting here in silence? We should talk."

The old Taliban mullah smiled and said graciously, "All right. Why don't you start?"

"No problem," I responded with a grin. "But I know that you are local people, and I'm afraid that if I say something inappropriate, you'll beat me on the street with your whips made from donkey's tails."

The Taliban and other guests looked at one another and started laughing. Finally the mullah spoke up. "I've heard that you're a respected man here. Don't worry. You should feel free to say whatever you want."

I knew that almost all the Taliban were our Pashtun brothers, and yet here I was at a Tajik house with Tajik Taliban in our midst. So I asked, "I know that most of the people who are Taliban are Pashtuns from a different part of the country and that many of them have lived in Pakistan all their lives. For them, it's relatively easy to come up north and kill people. It's like they are murdering foreigners. So what about you?" I looked at the younger Taliban. "Why do you young men—who are Tajik after all—take orders from Pashtuns and participate in killing your brother Tajiks and Uzbeks and Hazaras?"

A dark expression came over the faces of all the Taliban. The mullah in particular grew very serious. He was obviously not happy that I had so brazenly opened such a delicate subject.

"I'm sorry, I was afraid you might find the questions I wanted to ask inappropriate. I hope you're not offended," I offered humbly.

The Taliban mullah sat for a minute and then said gravely, "Why are you, a mullah, attempting to divide Afghanistan into separate nationalities?"

"Very good answer, very good answer," I interrupted him with a big smile. "Now I understand that you're very good people. I just wanted to know your perspective on this question."

The tension instantly lifted, and the guests all went back to reclining on their soft mattresses, sipping their tea, and nibbling on dried fruits and nuts from the plates in front of them.

"I have another question for you, if you don't mind. . . . According to the Koran, our Prophet Muhammad said that anyone who says 'La Ilaha Illal Lah Muhamadan Rasulallah' is a Muslim, and the doors of paradise will open before him. Isn't that right?"

Everyone, including the mullah, nodded in agreement.

"These words are recited by our Shi'a Muslims and our Sunni Muslims—and they equally are devoted to this central tenet of Islam. So how can you possibly justify your actions when you murder so many innocent Shi'a Muslims, like Hazaras?"

Everyone bolted upright again, wondering where this conversation might lead. The Taliban mullah calmly responded, "We've collected various Islamic documents from a variety of sources that have confirmed the propriety of our actions. We believe that our leaders have been graced by Allah, and it is our obligation to follow their orders and the words of the Koran."

I persisted with my questioning. "What will happen after you capture all of Afghanistan? What are your plans for the future? What do you want from the population? How will you rebuild our poor, war-ravaged country? For example, if a democratic government came to power, they would have certain plans about creating a constitution and building an elected system of government. Communists have their own ideas of what to do. Even the mujahedin movement, which is fighting against you, has its own cursed plans. So what about you? What are your plans? Can you give us something to read that can help us answer some of our most basic questions about you?"

"There's a very simple answer to your questions, my brother. Our constitution and all of our plans for the future can be found in the Koran. Our goal is to implement the strictures of the Koran and cleanse our land from infidels."

"I completely agree with you," I said. "But everyone here is a Muslim, and we all respect the Koran. I don't think there is a single person here who would stand up and say that he is an infidel. But nevertheless, you know that there are many people, many who are even now fighting on your side, that used to believe in different movements—mujahedin, communist, democratic. What do you think about this?"

"Our technique is to use the hands of our former enemies to kill our present-day enemies. When the jihad is complete, we will then cleanse our own ranks," the mullah replied calmly.

I had asked more than enough questions for the day, and I'd seen how my poor host was sweating heavily in the corner. For several minutes, he'd actually been trying to send me hand signals that I should cease and desist. When this didn't work, he said to me, "Why don't you eat more, or maybe you'd like more tea? . . ." So I thanked the mullah for all his "wise answers" and didn't say another word for the remainder of the dinner party. My host released an audible sigh when he realized that I had said my piece.

On my way back home, I began wondering about the future of our poor country. What kind of life could my family and I expect if men like this mullah would be ruling the entire land?

I also thought about the past. Unlike so many of my relatives and friends, I had never left Afghanistan in spite of all the fighting. I was too committed to my work as a teacher. I genuinely believed that if I left, Afghanistan's children would suffer a small but important loss. In order to supplement my small income, I had even sent my young sons to work in the bazaar after their lessons. I remember how they would sometimes come home in tears because they'd been beaten up or pushed out of the way by armed men. But I was determined not to leave my homeland in spite of all these indignities. Bravely, we had stayed put.

But that evening, as I walked home, I had given up all hope. I made up my mind then and there to leave. So that autumn, after the harvest was completed and I had enough money, my family and I headed off for Iran. But before I left, I managed to finagle a letter of permission for my travels from the Taliban authorities. The letter said that I was traveling to Iran in order to retrieve my son who was scheduled to have a wedding party back in Kunduz.

↷   ↷   ↶   ↶

My family and I traveled by bus clear across the country to the southwestern province of Nimruz, which was home to a bazaar where many Iranians and Afghans gathered. I was told that I could find smugglers in this bazaar to help shepherd us across the border. But before I could even get to this famed marketplace, I was grabbed by some Taliban policemen. They told me that I needed to get a new permission letter from the provincial office of the Department of Defense before I went any further. I arrived at the Defense Department at two in the afternoon, but I was told that everyone who had a position of authority had already left for the day. So I was forced to spend one more night in my homeland.

The next morning I went back to the Defense Department and found one middle-aged mullah sitting behind a large desk uncluttered by a single sheet of paper. He was a good man who agreed to help me right away. He issued me a new letter and also offered me a useful warning. "You have to be very careful. This letter will allow you safe passage to the Iranian border, but once you get to the other side, the Iranian police will create many problems for you if they catch you with it. The Iranian authorities are not friends of our political system. . . . So I would suggest that you destroy this letter as soon as you get to the border." I thanked him warmly. But then as I walked out, I thought to myself, "Actually, I'm not at all afraid of the Iranian authorities. I'm much more afraid of your crazy Taliban."

We found smugglers in the market who agreed to take us over the Helmand River by boat. The passage across the border was very easy. But as soon as we crossed, we had to race off to a patch of trees nearby where there was a Baluchi smuggler waiting for us. For an extra fee, he agreed to escort us all the way to the city of Zahedan. As soon as we got on the road, we knew we were in a completely different land. It wasn't since the Soviets had invaded Afghanistan that I had ridden on such a smooth road. And my children, who had known only war and destruction their whole lives, had never seen such road construction, even out there in the middle of a desert.

But just a few minutes after we took off in the Baluchi's car, our driver spotted a policeman along the road. The smuggler sped up, and when we reached a village, he veered the car off the main road, and we wound our way through narrow back alleys. Then he stopped abruptly in front of a house and told us all to get out quickly. We grabbed all our things and ran inside as our driver sped off.

We all became very nervous as a result of this strange turn of events. "So what are we supposed to do now?" I asked the elderly man who had become our unexpected host. "Don't worry about it," he reassured me. "This happens all the time. After it gets dark, another car will pick you up and take you the rest of the way to Zahedan." As promised, another car showed up after dinner and drove us to our planned destination. I already liked Iran—people kept their word.

It was very difficult for us in the beginning to live in this foreign land. Everything was new, and it took us a long time to understand how we could make the system work for us. We stayed in Zahedan for twelve days while we sought a way to travel to Tehran. We were told that there were many opportunities for work in the capital. Besides, both my wife and I had relatives who had settled in Tehran. But we'd also been informed that it was very difficult to travel all the way to Tehran because there were dozens of checkpoints along the way. The police would require proper documents from all who passed, even Iranians. Eventually, I found a man who told me that he could issue us false documents that indicated that we were official refugees. These documents, he claimed, were issued ten years earlier during the Ayatollah Khomeini regime but were still recognized by the authorities. For 30,000 tuman, or about $170, he agreed to provide my whole family with these "foolproof" documents. But I was skeptical. Maybe these documents would serve precisely the opposite purpose, identifying us as illegal immigrants when we showed them to the police.

A few days later I met another man who said that he knew of a German-made bus that could take us to Tehran. He told me that this luxury bus usually received scant inspection at the checkpoints because the police generally assumed that anyone who could afford the seats on this bus were not likely to be illegal immigrants. But the cost of traveling in this way was steep. The agent said that it would cost us 10,000 tuman per person to get to Tehran. In fact, we heard that Iranians paid only 2,500 tuman for a ticket, but us poor—and illegal—Afghans were forced to pay a huge sum. This man had a great business. He could have sent the bus off empty except for eight Afghans and still made a healthy profit! We didn't have any better options, so we boarded the German-made bus to Tehran.

As we got on the bus, the driver pulled me aside and said, "There is one very strict checkpoint about half way to Tehran. It is very difficult to get past this post. But if you make it, you can consider yourselves in Tehran. However, if you don't manage to get through, you might as well consider yourselves back in Nimruz." I took a big gulp and hoped for the best.

We had given the agent the last of our money. What would I do if my family and I were sent back home penniless? I prayed to Allah to ensure our safe passage to the capital. Several hours after we had set out, our bus was stopped in a long line leading up to this dreaded checkpoint. I noticed that the driver nodded his head to me through the rearview mirror, indicating that this was the place he had mentioned. We immediately understood that what the driver had warned us about was true. As we waited more than half an hour for our turn, we saw several Afghan families, including little children and women, being grabbed from cars and other buses and forced into the police station. We saw how the inspectors boarded buses and checked everybody aboard for proper documents. Almost all of the detained Afghans were crying along the side of the road, shivering in the November chill, before they were marched into holding cells. Young men were gazing vacantly into the distance, no doubt wondering what the future held for them back in Afghanistan.

When I saw our poor countrymen suffering this terrible fate, I couldn't control my tears. I cried for them and also for us, because I feared we would soon be joining them.

But by the time our bus crept forward, the most vigilant inspectors had left for their lunch break. I saw them instruct some young soldiers to continue their work, but as soon as the inspectors disappeared, the young men just waved our bus through the checkpoint. I thanked Allah for his divine intervention. "Thank you God! Thank you a thousand times!" I nearly screamed.

✦ ✦ ✦ ✦

On the way from Afghanistan to Iran, I met an Afghan guy, Nazir, who had spent many years shuttling back and forth between the two countries. He knew all the tricks of the trade and had lots of contacts inside Iran. Nazir had given us a lot of invaluable advice about who to contact and where we might stay in different cities in Iran. He knew of a couple of apartments where many Afghans lived in Tehran, but the only problem was that they were used almost exclusively by single men. So it wasn't a good option for us. We needed a temporary place to stay while I tracked down my relatives. So he gave us the name of his friend, Hossein, who Nazir assured us would gladly host our family for a little while and, if necessary, help us to find a place of our own.

Hossein and his wife, Fatona, lived in a part of the capital called Tehran Pars. It turned out that he was an ethnic Turk while his wife was Persian. I don't know of any words to describe how kind our hosts were. We lived in their house for fifteen days, and the whole time, they made us feel as welcome as you might feel at the house of your own closest relatives. One of our first days there, they took us on a tour of the vast city. All of us were completely overwhelmed by the tall buildings, the historical places, and the orderly design of the city. My children—Fawad, Karim and Farzona—were spellbound. They couldn't even say a word all day— they just gaped. It was in such sharp contrast to anything they'd ever seen in Afghanistan.

During our time in Tehran, my wife would often cry about our two daughters and one son who were living far away from us. My wife had never lived so far from her children, much less in a foreign land, and she missed them terribly.

Fatona always found the right words to comfort my poor wife. "I understand exactly how you feel. Your situation actually is very similar to my own. After the Islamic Revolution in our country, many of my relatives scattered around the world. They lived as poor refugees for a long time before they were able to make their way in a new land. The problem of loved ones being separated is something that affects all of us everywhere. For me, it was very difficult at first to get used to living so far away from those I care so deeply about. But you must have faith that they are being looked after by Allah and that they will be all right. " This is how my wife was cheered up by this kind Iranian woman, who quickly grew to become her close confidante.

I also grew close to Hossein. In the evening, we'd spend hour after hour talking about Iran, Afghanistan, the Taliban, and the world.

One time Hossein asked me, "Tell me, my brother, after all the years that I've lived so close to Afghanistan, I never could understand why these wars just never seem to end. Why can't people understand that they are being used like puppets by power-hungry politicians? What's the reason for this?"

"Ignorance and anger are the main reasons people have continued killing each other for so many years," I told him. "Millions of young people have been killed in these wars. But what most people don't understand is that most of them died as a result of personal vendettas. Everything else—being a communist or a Taliban or a mujahedin or whatever—that was just a pretext. Those who had power used their authority to murder their enemies, their family's enemies, their friends' enemies, and their neighbors' enemies. And then when the survivors got power, they would in turn seek retribution. This is how the cycle of violence perpetuates itself. You look at me and see that I'm alive. But I'm alive only by pure luck." Then I would tell him some stories from my own life.

A few days after we arrived, several of my wife's relatives who were living and working in Tehran came to visit us. These relatives were almost all single men who had left their families back in Afghanistan and were sending money home periodically to support their loved ones. They offered to provide us with whatever help we needed, especially in terms of locating a place to live. "We understand what you are going through right now," one of them told me with his arm around my shoulder. "It wasn't so long ago that we ourselves were new immigrants in this country, and those who had been here longer assisted us. Now it's our turn to return the favor."

I thanked them earnestly for their generosity. But I told them that I also had some relatives in the area who would no doubt help us. "But if they prove unable to assist us, we will very gratefully take you up on your kind offer." I didn't mean any disrespect to my wife's relatives, but I didn't want to take my family—especially my twelve-year-old daughter—into an environment dominated by young, single men.

I wanted to live in a setting that was more family friendly. That's why I was so eager to track down my relatives. I knew that several of them had come over with their children or had started families in Iran. Eventually, by asking this person, who knew that person, who knew that person . . . I was able to find some of my family in the district of Varamin, which was located about forty miles from Tehran Pars. The day after I finally was reunited with my relatives, we rented a small house near theirs.

The evening before we moved out of Hossein's house, I offered my most sincere thanks to Hossein and his wife for their wonderful hospitality. "You opened up your heart and your home to me and my family, and we will forever be indebted to you. Your kindness came at such a crucial time for us—when we really needed a place to get accustomed to this new land, to gather our thoughts, and to make plans for the next stage. And you . . . you provided us with just the respite we needed." I couldn't go on any further. I have never been at a loss for words, but at that moment I was totally choked up. I couldn't believe how kindly they had treated us, especially since we were complete strangers to them. Hossein, ever the gracious host, said, "We would be happy to host you here in our house for as long as you'd like. We've very much enjoyed the time that you've spent with us and hope that you will grace us with your presence often in the future!" He gave me a big warm hug.

When we left their house, Hossein and Fatona gave us a kerosene lamp, a carpet, a tea set, mattresses, and pillows. They knew that we had none of these essentials, necessary to starting a new life. They had now gone far beyond realm of generous hospitality. As the children and I gathered together our supplies, Fatona and my wife cried for a long time before we headed off. "I've gotten so used to living with you in these short fifteen days that I feel as though our family is being broken apart," Fatona blurted out as she said her good-byes. "Whenever you possibly can, please come back to visit us!" We left them our address so that they might stop by, too. I don't know how to convey how immensely grateful we are to Hossein and Fatona.

We thought that moving into our own house near my relatives would signify a new and better stage in our lives. But none of us—neither I, nor my wife, nor our three children—could find any work for ourselves. I told my sons to go out to the bazaar and other places around town to scout for work. I also asked around for jobs for myself. But to be honest, I really couldn't imagine doing anything other than teaching. My experience as a farmhand succeeded in earning me money, but my tired old body was not cut out for that kind of exertion.

I had been teaching for more than twenty years at that time, and I didn't know any other way to live. Unfortunately for me, there were plenty of literate people and teachers in Iran, and they certainly did not need a refugee fresh from Afghanistan to help them out. For the first several months in Iran, we depended on the assistance of our relatives, who would often leave us food and money when they came by to visit.

What we feared most was the Iranian police, and we tried not to leave the house except when it was absolutely necessary. As a result, we ended up spending long stretches of time sitting around the house picking fights over just about anything. This person was at fault for not finding a job . . . that person didn't clean the house or cook well . . . this person shouldn't have brought us to Iran in the first place . . . that person shouldn't have ever become a teacher because that wasn't a good source of income . . . and so on and so on. We began to wonder why we had bothered to come to Iran. At that time, I really thought that it would have been best to have stayed in Afghanistan—even if we died at the hands of the Taliban. At least we would have died in our motherland.

Then one evening one of my relatives, Khalil Khan, who had lived in Iran since the 1960s invited us over for dinner. When we were speaking with him in his house, we happened to notice that a couple of his children were preoccupied with something in the next room. They were assembling chandeliers from pieces of scrap metal and discarded plastic. Khalil Khan told me that some company was paying them one tuman per chandelier. I looked at my wife and whispered, "I'm sure we could do this kind of work as well." She quickly nodded her agreement.

So I turned to our host and asked, "Would it be possible for you to help us find a job doing this kind of work? We don't have any money, and we really need to find a way to make a living."

"I'll see what I can do," he said. "But in the meantime, why don't you help my kids with the current load they're responsible for?" For the rest of the evening my boys sat in the room with our host's children, observing and assisting them as the chandeliers were assembled. In this way, by the time we were ready to return home, my children were ready to undertake this work themselves. When we were leaving, our host sent us home with a big bag full of the scrap metal and plastic parts necessary to make the chandeliers.

We were thrilled with this new opportunity. Our familial relations improved suddenly and dramatically after this work began, and we realized that all of our conflicts had been a result of our economic situation. Two days later, when Fawad and Karim had finished assembling the chandeliers, we returned the completed work to Khalil Khan. He was obviously impressed by the quality and speed of our work. Through his connections, Khalil Khan managed to organize full-time work for my sons assembling chandeliers.

My sons continued with this enterprise, working very hard. One day several months later, my children told me that their boss had asked them to take all of the chandelier parts home and find other Afghans to join us in our work. The next day a huge truckload of plastic and spare metal parts arrived at our house. We put them everywhere we could until there was hardly room for us to move about. The work was far more than we could handle. So we decided to advertise the position among Afghans.

Two days later, dozens of Afghan refugees—especially women and children—came to our door begging for work. We decided that we would play the role of supervisors and distributors, while others would do the work. For each chandelier that was assembled we were paid 1.15 tumans by the company. In turn, we paid our twelve new employees one tuman for each chandelier they produced. In this way, we were able to make a very handsome profit for ourselves.

A couple of months after our modest family-run business was launched, Khalil Khan came to our house to ask me a favor. "I believe that Allah has brought you here to our land. We've now been living in Iran for twenty-two years. And throughout all of the Ramadans we've celebrated here, we've never had anyone to lead the *tarobeh* prayers for us every evening before we break the fast." The *tarobeh* are the additional twenty prayers that are recited after the five regular prayers during Ramadan. "So I'd like to request that you lead us in the recitation of the *tarobeh* for me, my friends, and neighbors."

"It would of course be a great honor for me to serve you in any way I can," I willingly agreed. I would have happily done anything for my relative, who had already helped us so invaluably. So throughout Ramadan, every evening, dozens of men would come visit me in the guest room that had been set aside for me in my relative's house. And as they streamed out of the room every evening, each of the worshipers would leave me some money. When Ramadan was finished, I had managed to accumulate about 30,000 tumans—more than $170—for my work! When I reached into any pocket of my clothes—my vest pocket, my pants pocket, anywhere—I found money. There was money everywhere. This was my first paid work in Iran. For every Ramadan I spent in Iran, I made good money this way.

Our lives became comfortable, and we managed to return the money that our relatives had given us. My older son found an additional job selling shoes from a cart that he would wheel around the bazaar. We completely forgot the days when we had cursed the misfortune of our coming to Iran. Almost every day we'd now say to one another, "Thank goodness we decided to come here! Think about how badly we would be living if we had stayed in Afghanistan."

→ → ← ←

Our success in Iran contrasted sharply with conditions back home. Every day we would hear stories about the suffering of people who had stayed behind in Afghanistan. And in the evening, the Iranian-run television stations were filled with news reports about how the war and drought were affecting the Afghan people. I was very upset. After all, this was our homeland. I think that if your homeland is torn apart by war, even if you're living safe and sound in a foreign land, you can never be content. You're always thinking about your friends and relatives who are less fortunate.

As the thirteenth-century Persian poet Sa'adi Shirazi wrote:

Bani odam a'zoi yak paikarand,
Ki dar ofarinish zi yak gawharand.
Chu uzve ba dard ovarad ruzgor,
Digar uzvhoro namonad qaror.
Tu, k-az mehnati digaron beghami,
Nashoyad, ki nomat nihand odami.

(*Human beings are all members of one body.*
They are created from the same essence.
When one member is in pain,
The others cannot rest.
If you do not care about the pain of others,
You do not deserve to be called a human being.)

When I hear news about fighting in other lands, I am deeply saddened. So when I saw my own homeland exploding on television before my very eyes, I was completely devastated. Now that my family's economic situation had grown secure, I became obsessed with the fate of Afghanistan. I could never manage to eat in the evening after listening to the news. The food just refused to go down. My nerves became so shaky and my blood pressure rose so high that I had to go to the doctor for drugs to calm me. I learned at this time that I was diabetic.

There were many Afghans in Iran who were more or less indifferent to the fate of their homeland. In many ways, I envied them. They worried about things in their lives that they actually had some control over. I had no power to change the political situation in my country. So I just quietly suffered in this foreign land.

There were a few—really very few—Iranians who were openly prejudiced against us Afghans. Sometimes, out on the streets, we'd hear young men call out, mockingly, "One kilogram of Afghans for five tumans. All right, one kilogram of Afghans for four tumans." There were poor Afghan refugees everywhere, and it was true that many of us were willing to work for very low wages in order to survive. When we'd hear these chants, we'd just duck our heads and scurry off as quickly as we could.

The world had forgotten about Afghanistan until that dark day, September 11, 2001. It's tragic that they paid attention to us again only because they themselves suffered as a result of our chaos. We all saw the images on television of the two airplanes crashing into those beautiful tall buildings in America. And we were all very saddened for the innocent people who had lost their lives. In the days that followed, there wasn't a single Iranian or Afghan with whom I spoke who wasn't heartbroken for the American people.

But, of course, it was America—in alliance with several other countries—that had laid the groundwork for the Taliban movement. Afghans have a saying: "The child that once clung to the hem of my skirt in the end grabs me tightly by the collar." I am ultimately very grateful that the result of this tragedy was that the American people remembered us and our sad plight. But it is such a sad irony that so many people had to die in the West in order to save so many lives back here.

When the interim Afghan government came to power in December 2001, I immediately wanted to return home. Most of my friends and relatives thought that I was out of my mind to rush back to Afghanistan while the security situation continued to be so uncertain. My oldest son, Fawad, especially was adamantly opposed to my plans to return. "Father, what are you rushing off to? Tell me, we all know that the Taliban has left, but who has come to power? It's the same mujahedin who kidnapped you and then put a gun to your head and forced you to feed fifteen men. It's those same people. Do you remember when I was young and I sold some chocolate, chewing gum, and cigarettes in the bazaar, and they would come and push me in the ditch with all my goods? And then they'd beat me if I raised even a murmur of objection? It's those same people. You shouldn't have a romanticized view of the new government!

"Now when I work in the bazaar and my cart filled with shoes is blocking the small alleyway, policemen sometimes stop me and say, 'Son, please don't take up the entire road with your cart—how will the other creatures of Allah be able to pass?' See, the authorities here even call me 'son.' What a contrast!

"In the name of Allah, where do you want to run off to? We've just begun to build normal lives for ourselves in a normal country. We've just begun to understand what it is like to live a peaceful life. . . . As long as I live, I don't ever want to return to Afghanistan. I would be perfectly happy if I never even pronounced the word 'Afghanistan' again. Why are you so eager to leave for this God-forsaken place? If you leave, I'm sure that you will regret it."

My son was exactly right. But my mind was made up—I missed my homeland too much.

I left Iran—alone—the next day. I planned to move close to my nephew who'd been living here in this village, Hajji Husain, for many years. I really didn't consider going back to my native village of Ambarku. It had been utterly destroyed by the Taliban five years ago. Almost five hundred houses were burned down by the invading forces, and most of the population scattered to the seven winds. I've heard that some brave souls have recently returned there to rebuild, but there are too many ghosts for me in Ambarku.

No sooner had I arrived in Afghanistan than I realized I had made a big mistake. I knew that my wife was probably worried to death about me because of my illness. And some people here began to say, "What kind of a wife allows her sick husband to travel home alone?" If I died, I was sure that my relatives would have never forgiven her. The doctors were not able to help me as much as those I'd met back in Iran. Nevertheless, I refused to leave the land of my birth ever again.

Six months after I'd returned, my wife and younger children came back here, too. But Fawad, who had so vehemently opposed my decision to return to Afghanistan, refused to accompany the rest of our family. He told his mother, "You can go yourselves, but you should know that you are leaving over my strong objections. There's no life for you back in Afghanistan. Every evening when you gather together for dinner, I promise that you'll remember my words."

And sure enough, once again, he was absolutely right. Every night when our family gathered to eat, we thought of Fawad. My teacher's salary hasn't been sufficient for the medication to calm my nerves as well as to provide proper food for my family. Actually, Fawad sends money back home from time to time to help support us. Here in this village we have no running water, and the only electricity we have is produced by a small generator that requires a lot of expensive fuel.

I used to teach in the school that's just a couple of miles up the road. It was recently reconstructed by an international aid organization. But as soon as the work was completed and I no longer had to teach in a hot, sweaty tent, my neighbors asked me to begin teaching here in this village. I'm grateful that I no longer have to hike such a distance to the school. And I'm happy that I'm able to offer my last strength to help start a small filial school in this village and provide an education for the boys and girls who live here.

A couple of months ago, my son, who had been living in Tajikistan with my daughter, was granted asylum in Canada and left. I'm very happy that so many of my children have been able to find a way for themselves in this complicated world. However, nothing would thrill me more than to have all my children nearby for at least a little while before I die. But rather than coming closer together, our family has spread farther apart. Now I have one son in Iran, one in Canada, one daughter in Tajikistan, one daughter living with her husband's family, and two children with me here at home. I suppose I could join one of my children in another land. But I'm a sick man, and I'm sure that one day in the not-too-distant future, I will die. And whatever happens to me, I don't want to die as a refugee in a foreign land. I want my bones to lie here in my homeland, alongside those of my ancestors and among the people I've worked so hard to educate, for all eternity.

Timeline of Recent Afghan History

1919   Afghanistan declares independence from Great Britain after third and final Anglo-Afghan war.

      Lenin calls Amanullah Khan leader of the only independent Islamic state and encourages him to rally enslaved Muslims around the world to the cause of independence.

1921   Afghan-Soviet Treaty of Friendship signed.

1924   Soviets aid Amanullah with warplanes to eliminate opposition to the Afghan leader's modernization policies.

1925   First invasion by the USSR: the Soviet annexation of Utra Tangi Island on the Amu Darya.

1926   USSR returns the island to Afghanistan, a gesture followed by a treaty of neutrality and nonaggression with Afghanistan.

1927   Amanullah visits Europe and the Middle East.

1928   Photographs of Queen Soraya reach Afghanistan showing her in Western clothes and without veil.

1929   Rebellion against King Amanullah and his Western ways forces him out of the capital Kabul. He flees to Kandahar in his Rolls Royce.

      Habibullah Kalakani (Bachai Saqaw), an illiterate, proclaims himself king and surrounds himself with bandits and peasants.

Ghulam Nabi invades Afghanistan, seeking to help overthrow Bachai Saqaw and reinstate Amanullah.

Nabi captures Mazar-i Sharif and marches toward Kabul with an army of 6,000 supporters.

Word spreads that Amanullah has fled the country. Nabi's rebellion loses drive and eventually fails.

General Nadir Khan marches from Kandahar to reclaim Kabul from Bachai Saqaw.

Kabul falls and Bachai Saqaw is captured and hanged. Nadir Shah is proclaimed king of Afghanistan.

King Nadir Shah reverses all of Amanullah's reforms and reinstates traditional values.

1930   Soviet army invades Afghanistan in a campaign to capture Ibrahim Beg, a Uzbek rebel fighting against the Soviets in Uzbekistan.

1931   Afghan army forces Ibrahim Beg out of Afghanistan. He is captured by the Soviets and killed.

1933   Nadir Shah is assassinated and immediately replaced by his son Zahir Khan. Power, however, remains in the hands of Nadir's brothers.

1947   British forces withdraw from south Asia. India declares independence, and Indian Muslims proclaim their own nation of Pakistan.

1948   Pashtuns of Pakistan also declare independence and accept neither Afghanistan nor Pakistan as their legitimate government. The hundred-year contract of Pashtunistan ends, and, in a scenario similar to Hong Kong's return to China in 1997, land is transfered from Britain to Afghanistan.

1954   Afghan Prime Minister Daud sends his brother Prince Naim to the United States to appeal for military assistance.

U.S. Secretary of State John Foster Dulles rejects the request for aid, stating that Afghanistan is of no interest to the United States.

1955   Prime Minister Daud asks the USSR for military assistance.

First Soviet Secretary Nikita Khrushchev and Prime Minister Nikolay Bulganin visit Kabul and grant $100 million in credit for the development of Afghanistan.

1963   Prime Minister Daud resigns over disagreement with Zahir Shah. Troops patrol the streets of Kabul for several days watching for a possible coup attempt by ex-Prime Minister Daud.

1964   Zahir Shah introduces the New Democracy program, calling for a constitution, a parliament, free elections, a free press, and the freedom to form political parties—all measures inspired by Prince Daud.

1965   Peoples Democratic Party of Afghanistan (PDPA), a communist party headed by Noor Mohammad Taraki, is formed.

        Hafizullah Amin, a member of the faculty at Kabul University, recruits students for the PDPA.

        Elections are held in Afghanistan for the first time with the participation of 10 percent of the population.

1966   Khalq newspaper, headed by Taraki, begins printing communist propaganda and is shut down by Zahir Shah.

1967   PDPA splits into two factions: Khalq, headed by Taraki, and Parcham, headed by Babrak Karmal, a communist leader with strong ties to the Soviet embassy in Kabul.

1969   Elections are held in Afghanistan. PDPA members make inflammatory statements that derail plans for a constitutional monarchy.

1970   Zahir Shah increases his hold on power, naming those loyal to him to key government positions.

1972   Prince Daud makes plans with political parties, military leaders, and both Parchamis and Khalqis to oust Zahir Shah.

1973   Zahir Shah leaves for Italy for medical reasons. While Zahir Shah is taking a mud bath in Ischia, he learns that Prince Daud has organized a successful coup against the monarchy.

        Prince Daud makes a radio announcement proclaiming Afghanistan a republic and himself as the first President of the Republic of Afghanistan.

1974   President Daud reduces the number of leftist cabinet members. Other members of the government are dismissed or sent abroad as ambassadors.

1975   Pakistan accuses President Daud of training fifteen thousand Pashtuns to carry out a rebellion against its government.

1977   President Daud visits Leonid Brezhnev in Moscow, where the Soviet leader presents Daud with a list of complaints about his policies. President Daud responds, "I want to remind you that you are speaking to the president of an independent country, not one of your Eastern European satellites. You are trying to interfere in the internal affairs of Afghanistan, and this I will not permit!" and storms out of Brezhnev's office.

1978   With the aid of the USSR, Parcham and Khalq are reunited as the PDPA. Determined to oust President Daud, the party plans during the day and trains in deserts and forests at night.

        President Daud makes visits to India, Pakistan, Egypt, Libya, Turkey, Yugoslavia, Saudi Arabia, and Kuwait, seeking to build ties.

President Daud signs trade agreements with China and plans to visit President Jimmy Carter in Washington, D.C.

Mohammad Reza Shah Pahlavi of Iran visits Kabul to build closer trade relations between the two nations.

Mir Akbar Khyber, a communist ideologue, is murdered and fifteen thousand supporters of the PDPA march in military order on the day of his funeral.

President Daud sees the PDPA as a real threat and arrests Amin, Taraki, and Karmal.

Amin communicates orders for a coup through his teenage son while in detention. Military leaders General Aslan Watanjar and Colonel Dagarwal Abdul Qader begin to organize the coup among the ranks of the military.

The coup begins on April 27 when tanks protecting the presidential palace, Dar ul-Aman, turn against President Daud and the air force bombs the palace by order of Colonel Qader.

Colonel Qader declares the "end of the Mohammadzai rule in Afghanistan and the transfer of power to the people of Afghanistan," without identifying transitional leaders.

On April 28, President Daud and all members of his family, including grandchildren and close family aids, are killed.

A radio announcement is made on April 30 that the "revolutionary council has gained power in Afghanistan, headed by Noor Mohammad Taraki."

People of Afghanistan rebel against the PDPA government, branding them as atheists leading a country of devout Muslims.

PDPA puts restrictions on the practice of dowry, bans arranged marriages, and declares land reforms without aid to farmers.

1979 U.S. Ambassador Adolph Dubs is killed in a botched rescue attempt in Kabul.

Shah of Iran falls and is replaced by the anti-American Ayatollah Khomeini. The ensuing hostage crisis diverts American attention away from Afghanistan and the Soviet Union's military buildup.

Afghan soldiers join forces with rebels in Herat in confrontations with the government, resulting in thousands of casualties.

Balah-i sar rebellion against the government fails. Forty-five hundred Soviet advisors are sent to Afghanistan to maintain order.

USSR plans the assassination of Amin, who is considered in control even though Taraki is head of state.

Amin is informed of this plot by Taroon and Shah Wali.

Amin fires Watanjar, Sheijan Mazdooryar, Sayyid Muhammad Gulabzoi, and Assadullah Sarwari from government posts to strengthen his position against a possible coup.

Taraki invites Amin to the presidential palace with the reassurance of Soviet ambassador Alexandre Puzanov. Upon Amin's arrival, a shoot-out erupts, and Taroon saves Amin's life by standing in front of him during the shooting. Amin escapes.

Returning at night with his supporters, Amin kills Taraki in his sleep by suffocating him with a pillow .

On September 9 a radio announcement of Taraki's death is made, attributing it to illness, and announces Amin as the new leader of Afghanistan. Gulabzoy, Watanjar, Mazdooryar, and Sarwary seek refuge in the Soviet embassy.

Time magazine reports that 30,000 have been imprisoned and 2,000 executed by Khalq regime.

Amin declares Afghanistan an independent state and vows to defend its sovereignty even against the USSR. The Afghan leader begins to buildup Afghan-American relations.

USSR begins military buildup in central Asia. Amin, fearing an attack on him, calls in vain for a meeting with Pakistan president Muhammad Zia ul-Haq for a possible amnesty deal.

USSR sends General Ivan Pavlovski, the mastermind of previous Soviet invasions in Eastern Europe, to Afghanistan.

Soviet soldiers move into Afghanistan on December 24. They secure airports, and launch an attack on Dar ul-Aman, the presidential palace.

Amin is killed.

In a radio announcement, Babrak Karmal declares himself the new leader of the PDPA and asks the Soviet army to help him subdue the uprising against the government.

1980 Karmal begins to sovietize Afghanistan, while the Red Army battles fiercely with the mujahedin.

1981 The Afghan army, initially numbering 100,000 strong, drops to 30,000 after defections to the mujahedin.

1982 The United States tries to create a coalition of resistance fighters under Zahir Shah in order to supply them with weapons, but resistance leaders, with encouragement from Pakistan, reject this approach.

Seven groups launch the resistance from Pakistan, including those headed by Burhanuddin Rabbani, Gulbuddin Hekmatyar, and Sebghatullah Mojadedi alongside other smaller groups.

1983 CIA assumes an active role, funding the leaders of resistance groups through Pakistan.

1984 With the help of the CIA, new foreign sources of aid to the cause of the Afghan people emerge, in particular, religious students, charities, and wealthy Arabs, among them Osama Bin Laden.

1985 Ronald Reagan calls Afghans "heroes of freedom," and "champions of the free world" and proclaims March 21 National Afghanistan Day in the United States.

1986 Stinger missiles are introduced. Karmal is replaced with the notorious Mohammad Najibullah (former head of Afghan secret police) by the USSR.

1987 Afghans gain the upper hand in the battle against the USSR.

1988 USSR begins to pull out of Afghanistan. Najibullah remains in power as president of Afghanistan.

1989 Major cities slowly fall to the mujahedin, and the communist regime weakens.

1990 Abdul Rashid Dostum, a communist general under Najibullah foresees the fall of the communist government, switches sides and establishes the city of Mazar-i-Sharif as his stronghold.

1991 Communist government falls as the mujahedin begin to advance from different sides of Kabul.

1992 To replace Najibullah, an interim government, headed by Mojadedi, is established in Pakistan. Najibullah seeks refuge in the United Nations building.

1993 Elections are held and Rabbani is proclaimed president. The Afghans await U.S. assistance in rebuilding their country. Civil war erupts in Kabul as Dostum, Ahmad Shah Mas'ud, and Gulbuddin Hekmatyar fight for power.

1994 Warlords and renegade generals rule in the areas they control.

1995 Mullah Mohammed Omar and a few others begin to disarm the warlords and to march toward Kabul. Hekmatyar falls to the Taliban. Rabbani government falls as the Taliban capture Kabul and hang Najibullah.

1996 Osama Bin Laden helps the Taliban financially and establishes his own group consisting largely of Arabs based in Afghanistan. Pakistan also aids the Taliban and uses Bin Laden to further its causes in Kashmir.

1997 The Taliban displace Dostum from Mazar-i-Sharif and gains control of 95 percent of Afghanistan.

1998 Dostum, Mas'ud, Hekmatyar, and Rabbani establish the Northern Alliance with the help of Russia.

1999 Bin Laden sends his men to fight in Kashmir, Chechnya, and several other countries, and establishes his base in a lawless Afghanistan.

2000 Pakistan begins training Taliban soldiers and provides Bin Laden with intelligence to fight in Kashmir and other nations.

2001 Mas'ud, leader of the Northern Alliance, is killed on September 9 by men posing as journalists with a bomb planted in a video camera.

On September 11 the World Trade Center in New York City and the Pentagon in Washington, D.C., are attacked by members of al-Qa'eda using hijacked planes.

U.S. launches airstrikes in Afghanistan in retaliation, targeting military bases and Taliban and al-Qa'eda soldiers.

U.S. ground forces begin their attack on Afghanistan after air strikes leave thousands dead.

Kabul falls without violence on November 13.

Taliban stronghold in the southern city of Kandahar falls on December 7.

After a UN-sponsored meeting of Afghan power brokers, Hamid Karzai is sworn in as chairman of a six-month interim government on December 22.

2002 Former king Mohammad Zaher Shah returns to Afghanistan on April 18 after twenty-seven years in exile.

On June 11 the Loya Jirga, or grand tribal council, convenes to discuss a new 18-month government charged with drafting a new constitution.

On June 13 Karzai is elected head of state of the new government of Afghanistan by the Loya Jirga.

2003 New currency is issued by Da Afghanistan Bank.

Draft constitution is presented.

Loya Jirga to ratify the constitution started Sunday, December 14. Mojadedi elected Jirga President.

2004 On January 4 the council adopts a charter creating an Islamic state under the presidential system sought by Karzai, opening the way for elections but also exposing enduring ethnic divisions.

About 10.6 million Afghans are registered to vote by August 20, after a nearly year-long process during which twelve election workers are slain.

A thirty-days campaign period starts for presidential election on September 7.

The election is held on October 9.

Hamid Karzai wins in a landslide victory, taking 55 percent of the vote, while Yunus Qanooni, his closest rival takes 16 percent.

(Timeline reprinted by permission of Afghanland.com)

Acknowledgments

There are many people who have played critical roles in bringing this book into reality. First and foremost, we would like to thank all of the brave women and men around Kunduz and Takhar provinces who recounted their personal stories to us. We cannot begin to express our deepest appreciation to all of the generous Afghans who have opened up their hearts and their homes to us at various points over the last four years, and particularly during the month of April 2004 when we conducted the research for this book. As we were writing and editing, we would often recall several women who cried and hugged Gulchin after interviews, saying something along the lines of: "Please tell the rest of the world about what has happened to us Afghans. We don't want to be forgotten again." These words and emotions inspired us—and continue to inspire us.

We would also like to thank our many friends who work, or have worked, for Child Fund Afghanistan in providing all the support necessary for us to undertake this project. In particular, we would like to thank Nasrullah, Fawzia, Dur Muhammad, Yaqub, Mirweis, Aziza, Takhir Khan, Feda Muhammad, Farina and Lloyd McCormick for their invaluable assistance. If they had not introduced and vouched for us to friends, neighbors, colleagues and people in villages in which they worked, this book would not have been possible. We would like to express our particular appreciation to Nasrullah and Feda Muhammad who provided background on particular cultural traditions and historical information about which we had not heard or read.

We want to also convey our gratitude to George Mürer at Seven Stories Press whose encouragement, patience, and close attention to detail helped to improve this book in a variety of ways.

Finally, we would like to thank our families for their love and continuous support—even when we decide to do slightly unorthodox things, like go to Afghanistan for our honeymoon. Our parents, as well as Ibrohim, Farzon, Aziz, Andaleb, Manzura, Fred, Laura and even little Adam, Nathan and Khudodod were always in our thoughts as we undertook this project. They all provided us with invaluable support throughout the work on the book, as they always do. For this we are very grateful.

ABOUT THE AUTHORS

ALEX KLAITS has worked for several international aid organizations in Afghanistan, Tajikistan, Uzbekistan, Kyrgyzstan and Washington, D.C. He was a Peace Corps volunteer in Kyrgyzstan from 1995-1997. Between January 2002 and September 2003, Alex undertook relief and reconstruction work in Afghanistan with Christian Children's Fund/Child Fund Afghanistan. Most recently, he worked for the United States Agency for International Development (USAID) in Badakhshan, Afghanistan, focusing on the Alternative Livelihoods program, which is a part of Afghanistan's counter-narcotics campaign. Currently Alex works for the United Nations Development Program in Tajikistan. Alex has a B.A. from Vassar College and a M.A. from Stanford University.

GULCHIN GULMAMADOVA-KLAITS has worked for a variety of international aid organizations in her native Tajikistan, including Care International, the Central Asian American Enterprise Fund, and the Asian Development Bank. She holds a B.A. in economics from a university in Dushanbe, Tajikistan, although her studies were interrupted when she fled her hometown to escape the country's civil war. In addition to her native Pamiri, Gulchin speaks Russian, English, Tajik/Dari. Gulchin and Alex live with their one-year-old son in Dushanbe, Tajikistan.